Spy Wars

ESPIONAGE
AND CANADA
FROM GOUZENKO
TO GLASNOST

J. L. GRANATSTEIN
DAVID STAFFORD

KEY PORTER BOOKS

Canadian Cataloguing in Publication Data

Granatstein, J. L., 1939-
   Secret wars: espionage in Canada from Gouzenko to glasnost

Includes bibliographical references.
ISBN 1-55013-258-X

1. Espionage — Canada — History — 20th century.
2. Espionage, Canadian.   I. Stafford, David,
1942- .   II. Title.

FC609.G73 1990   327.12'0971   C90-094370-X
F1034.2.G73 1990

Key Porter Books Limited
70 The Esplanade
Toronto, Ontario
Canada M5E 1R2

Typesetting: Southam Business Information and Communications Group Inc.

∞ Printed on acid-free paper
Printed and bound in Canada by
T. H. Best Printing Company Limited

90 91 92 93 94 6 5 4 3 2 1

CONTENTS

PREFACE

The world of espionage may seem remote to most of us, a game played on hidden stages in distant, sometimes exotic places. It may seem all the more remote in a country like Canada, a minor player on the international scene, with no active foreign-intelligence agency of its own or "Eyes Only" military secrets to be stolen. And yet, even here, espionage has had an effect on the nation's history and, every now and then, on our lives as "private citizens."

The authors of this book have been fascinated by the subject of espionage for many years, mainly because it played a part in our studies of history and international affairs, but also because we have both had minor personal encounters with spyhunters. Apparently trivial, these encounters nonetheless indicate how seriously members of Canadian security forces have taken their jobs over the last few decades.

Granatstein's Story

In May 1961, at the age of twenty-two, I graduated from the Royal Military College of Canada and went to Camp Borden, Ontario, as a lieutenant in the army. In September, I took up an MA history fellowship at the University of Toronto, where I began a course in Canadian political history with John Saywell, one of the rising stars in the field. I had some trouble finding a subject for my research paper, and Saywell suggested that the Communist party during the Second

World War would make a good one because of the way the party had repeatedly changed its position in response both to directives from Moscow and to the events of the war. I agreed, duly contacted the party headquarters on Cecil Street in Toronto, and with no particular difficulty arranged access to the headquarters' archive of party records for the prewar and war years.

Only at this point did it dawn on me that making repeated visits to party headquarters might not be very sensible for a brand-new soldier. To cover myself, I decided to call the Intelligence officer at Central Command HQ in Oakville, then the nearest seat of military power. He promptly referred me to a Sergeant X at RCMP headquarters in Toronto. I dutifully telephoned the sergeant, who, in what stands out in my memory as a paranoiac tone, first asked me where I had got his name, and then promised to get back to me.

A few days later the sergeant called. He had had Saywell checked out, he said, and he was okay, "not a pinko like so many of those professors at the U. of T." He also wanted me to know that the Communists had run their own security check on me. (How did he know? Was I okay to the Communists? If so, what would this do to my career in the army? I wondered.) Then he got to the meat of his message. I could do the paper on the Communist party, but I had to agree to undergo a lengthy debriefing after each and every visit to Cecil Street — Who and what had I seen? What had people said to me?

That was too much. Very simply, I didn't have the time to be debriefed every day. I was trying to get my MA, carrying four heavy courses with enormous reading requirements, and also settling into marriage. I told the sergeant that I thought it might be better if I changed my subject, which I did. First, I had to apologize to Saywell for getting him investigated ("It's not the first time," he said) and then to decide on another topic with him. My new subject was the Progressive Conservative party during the Second World War, one for which no security clearance was necessary, but one in which the exposure to paranoia provided by my barely dipping a foot in the murky waters of espionage proved not entirely unhelpful.

Stafford's Story

My first contact with counter-espionage, at least the first that came to my notice, was in 1977.

It arrived by way of a telephone call to my office at the University of Victoria, British Columbia, where I was then teaching. A voice at the other end of the line introduced the caller as Corporal X of the RCMP. He would appreciate a few words with me in private, he said, and would be happy to save me a trip downtown by coming to my office. After I had determined that he wanted to ask a few questions "concerning a motor vehicle," I arranged for him to drop by the next day, between classes. And because our automobile was registered in my wife's name, she came along for the meeting, as mystified as I was by the sudden summons.

Corporal X, who arrived with a punctuality disturbing to one grown used to academic time, turned out to be a bushy-tailed and bright-eyed young man whose all-too-correct civilian uniform immediately gave him away as a Mountie in disguise. The shoes hard and bright, the trouser creases like knives, the back ramrod straight, and the hair cropped like a cornfield could be the product only of the Regina academy. He handed me his card. "RCMP Security Service" it read, redundantly.

Ill at ease in professorial surroundings, Corporal X galloped briskly to the point. From a check on licence-plate numbers, the RCMP had discovered that an automobile spotted at the Montreal docks had been rented in my name. It was, he noted, "adjacent to a Soviet ship." Had I indeed been the person involved, and, if so, could I help him discover why?

Intrigued rather than offended by the intrusion, I searched hard to activate my memory of the affair. It had happened four years — or was it even five years? — earlier. I had been about to embark on a year's leave in England and, because my wife and I both enjoyed the transatlantic boat trip and had had a considerable amount of luggage that travelled free, we had arranged to sail to Southampton from Montreal. By then, Canadian Pacific had abandoned the route, and only the Russians and Poles had regular sailings. To get to Montreal, we had rented a series of cars across the country. That explained the car in the vicinity of the *Alexander Pushkin*, I told Corporal X. He nodded deferentially as I confirmed what, undoubtedly, he already knew from comparing the passenger lists with rental car records.

Of course, what he really wanted to know was what had happened on board during the six-day crossing. The gallop slowed to a sideways trot as he manoeuvred away from embarrassment, and shifted to avoid my wife's gaze. The Soviets, he solemnly explained, were constantly attempting to recruit people. Certain groups and professions were more likely to be targeted than others. Professors were high on the list. Of course, they were as loyal as anyone else. But sometimes — here he took a firmer seat in the saddle — individuals did foolish things and laid themselves open to blackmail. Shipboard fun-and-games could have serious results, and the ship's entertainment officer was trained to exploit any opportunity.

Then, as brusquely as he had begun, Corporal X stopped and looked hard ahead as though searching for the distant prairie horizon. I felt sorry for him. He was doing his job the best he knew how and had probably never even seen an ocean liner, let alone a Russian.

Still, the game had to be played out.

"You didn't have an affair with the entertainment officer?" I asked my wife.

"No — did you?" she replied, and we all laughed, Corporal X obviously relieved that the most difficult part of the interview was over. The reins of conversation slackened. We told him that the most exciting event either of us recalled on the voyage was when the largely geriatric dance band had made a bid for freedom by once daring to play some Western rock 'n' roll. Otherwise it had been borscht and boredom, and if there had been any orgies with two-way mirrors and hidden cameras, they had not included us. Corporal X listened politely, made a note in his book, and then left as quickly as he decently could, disappointed perhaps that he had failed to corral a couple of Soviet spies.

These stories are fun to tell over dinner and a bottle of wine (and we have both dined out on them for years). The bungling approaches have both dined out on them for years). The bungling approaches of the security officers, their paranoia about domestic Communists and the Soviets, and the absurdity of their suspicions are more than slightly ridiculous. Nonetheless, they raise interesting and difficult questions about Canadian security and intelligence operations.

We can laugh at the Cold War now, in the 1990s, but even a year or two ago it was very real, and it involved a deadly international game that had been played for more than forty years. In recent times, though, the game has become even more elaborate: while fears of "Godless Communism" and the "Red Menace" have subsided, the threats of techno-espionage and terrorism from other countries have come to the forefront. Canada has been a player from the very beginning.

What we set out to explore in this book was the role Canadians have played in the world of security and intelligence, who we have acted with and against, and how well we have carried out our duties. We also wanted to study the other players and how their roles have affected Canada and our allies. We had no desire to write an encyclopedic history; instead, our object was to identify the key people and events that shaped Canadian intelligence activities. What we found was sometimes startling, sometimes frightening, and sometimes unintentionally funny.

How well has Canada reacted to crises such as the defection of Igor Gouzenko? Was the notorious "Munsinger Affair" about a serious breach of security, or simply part and parcel of a nasty political war between John Diefenbaker and Lester Pearson? And what does the revelation that terrorists have been allowed into Canada say about our ability to respond to the threat of imported terror tactics?

We found some unexpected answers to these and other questions. We were troubled, for example, by France's involvement in Canadian affairs during the violent separatist activities in Quebec in the late 1960s. With friends like those in Paris, who needs enemies? And the creation of the myth of Sir William Stephenson, "the man called Intrepid" and a crowned Canadian hero, now seems a sad, if largely harmless, case of self-glorification.

Time and again, we found the same themes emerging in the cases we explored, and they helped shape our approach to the subject. The first and most important is that Canada is not now and has never been an independent player in the secret wars of espionage. We have little free-standing status in the intelligence sphere; we have few military or technological secrets of our own that are worth protecting. Instead, Canada's importance lies in being a part of the Western alliance and having access to some of the secrets of our friends and neighbours. Moreover, we are part of the alliance's intelligence community and have been since the Second World War. Under a series of agreements, we collect data for our friends, and in return they provide us with information — when they believe we should have it. In other words, in this area, as in so many others, Canada is a branch plant. As Ron Atkey, the first chair of the Security Intelligence Review Committee, put it before the House of Commons Justice Committee on May 30, 1989: "I think one has to locate [CSIS] in the global context, in terms of a middle-sized country, next to the giant United States with a large and powerful CIA and the FBI." That honest, blunt assessment seems exactly right to us.

Second, as befits a minor player in what Rudyard Kipling long ago, in *Kim*, called "the great game," the Canadian government's reactions to espionage on our soil have always been acutely attuned to the international and domestic political contexts of the day. If the Cold War atmosphere was bad, Soviet diplomats were likely to be expelled with maximum publicity for their information-gathering sins, often in co-ordination with our allies' own expulsions. If the RCMP's Security Service was under attack for its inefficiency or its excesses, a spy could always be sent packing to demonstrate the ever-present watchfulness being exercised on the Canadian people's behalf. Or, if detente was in the air, Ottawa might well be prepared to tolerate the activities of a foreign power that, during tenser periods, it could not. Very simply, international and domestic politics play their parts in everything that follows.

Finally, as these two key points should suggest, Canada is essentially a reactive player in the Spy Wars. We have no Secret Intelligence Service, no Central Intelligence Agency to carry the espionage struggle abroad against the enemy, whoever that might be. Instead, our role has always been one of counter-espionage, and that, by definition, is passive, not aggressive.

Some subjects were beyond the scope of this book. Spying on Canadians by their own government is itself an issue worthy of extensive study; we have dealt with this subject only when it is connected to the international aspects of espionage. Such domestic catastrophes as the FLQ Crisis of 1970 have been dealt with exhaustively elsewhere.

One final caution to readers: this book was completed in the midst of the most extraordinary period of change in world politics since the end of the Second World War. We have tried to bring the story up to date, but there is no doubt that events will outpace us.

We are grateful to many people who have assisted us in a variety of ways in the research for this book, not all of whom can be named publicly. Of those who can, we especially wish to thank James Barros; Robert Bothwell, who, with Granatstein, did research for a book on Pierre Trudeau, some of which is used here; David Kahn; William Kaplan, who permitted us to consult his papers relating to John Watkins at the University of Toronto; Jim Littleton; and Reg Whitaker, who shared his research on Igor Gouzenko with us. David Kilgour as editor offered constructive suggestions that made the manuscript more readable, and Jasper Malcomson helped with some early research.

JLG & DS,
Toronto,
May 1990

ABBREVIATIONS

BRUSA   Britain-United States 1943 Agreement on Signals Intelligence
BSC   British Security Co-ordination
CBNRC   Communications Branch, National Research Council
CIA   Central Intelligence Agency (U.S.)
COCOM   Co-ordinating Committee for Multilateral Export Controls
CSE   Communications Security Establishment
CSIS   Canadian Security Intelligence Service
DEA   Department of External Affairs
DND   Department of National Defence
DST   Direction de la Surveillance du Territoire (France)
FBI   Federal Bureau of Investigation (U.S.)
GCHQ   Government Communications Headquarters (U.K.)
GRU   Glávnoe Razvédyvatel'noe Upravlénie —
           Chief Intelligence Directorate of the Soviet General Staff (USSR)
HUMINT   Human Intelligence
KGB   Komitét Gosudárstvennoi Bezopásnosti — Committee for State Security (USSR)
MfS   Ministerium für Staats-Sicherheit (East Germany)
MI5   Security Service (U.K.)
NADGE   NATO's Air Defence Ground Environment System
NATO   North Atlantic Treaty Organization
NKVD   Navódnyi Komissariát Vnútrennikh Del —
           People's Commissariat of Internal Affairs (USSR):
           precursor to the KGB
NSA   National Security Agency (U.S.)
NSIS   National Security Investigation Service
OSS   Office of Strategic Services (U.S.)
RCMP   Royal Canadian Mounted Police
SDECE   Service de Documentation Extérieure et de Contre-Espionnage
           (France) until April 1982
SIGINT   Signals Intelligence
SIRC   Security Intelligence Review Committee
SIS   Secret Intelligence Service (U.K.)
SOE   Special Operations Executive (U.K.)
SOSUS   Sound Surveillance System (U.S.)
STB   Statni Tajua Bezpecnost (Czechoslovakia)
UKUSA   United Kingdom–United States 1948 Agreement on Signals
               Intelligence

1.
THE STATE OF THE ART

I n early 1990, Canadians, along with millions of other North Americans, flocked to see the movie *The Hunt for Red October*. Starring Sean Connery, who rose to stardom as British spy James Bond during the 1960s, the film, like the Tom Clancy thriller on which it was based, was a block-buster. Its soundtrack echoing the spectacular and sinister effects of underwater conflict, it told the story of a defecting Lithuanian-born commander of a Soviet nuclear submarine taking his vessel and crew with him across the North Atlantic to the United States. Hunted by the Soviet navy, pursued by U.S. ships and submarines unaware of his mission, and constantly tracked by sophisticated underwater monitors, the Soviet commander finally makes it to safety and freedom, on the coast of Maine.

Even though by the time the movie was released the Cold War was conspicuously ending, communism in Eastern Europe had collapsed, and Lithuania had defiantly declared its independence from Moscow, *The Hunt for Red October* had one major achievement to its credit, quite apart from that of providing a good night's entertainment. Like many a piece of fiction before it, Clancy's thriller dramatically highlighted for the general public an issue that had previously been of concern only to specialists. Some ninety years earlier, Erskine Childers's novel *The Riddle of the Sands* had catalyzed concern in Britain about the Kaiser's navy. *The Hunt for Red October* provided its readers and audience with an introduction to the reality of the underwater nuclear-power game that had been

1

played for years by Moscow and Washington. Here, thousands of feet below the surface of the water, huge nuclear arsenals cruised unheard and unseen, carrying deadly missiles targeted at the enemy's heartland. Simply, tracking Soviet submarines was vital to the West. Two years before Sean Connery's appearance as the Soviet commander, Canada's part in this silent struggle was dramatically brought home by a real-life case of espionage.

At about four o'clock in the afternoon of May 17, 1987, outside the Hotel Newfoundland in St. John's, a man in his mid-twenties approached a woman waiting for him on the sidewalk. He identified himself as "Michael" and said he had been sent by "Peter." The two moved to the hotel parking lot. Inside the woman's parked car, the man gave her some instructions, discussed suitable places for future meetings, and handed over $2,000 (U.S.) in $100 bills.

As he left St. John's by plane for Montreal, the man, Stephen Ratkai, must have felt pleased. The woman he had just been talking to was Donna Geiger, a thirty-year-old U.S. Navy lieutenant working at the nearby U.S. naval base at Argentia. The deal they had struck was that, in exchange for more money, she would hand over secret material about a highly classified American underwater sound-surveillance system known as SOSUS, which the Pentagon saw as the technological edge in the balance of power between East and West. Ratkai was working for the Soviets.

On any day of the year, somewhere close to the shore of North America, a Soviet submarine will be on regular patrol. It may be a Yankee-class SSBN, a ballistic missile-firing submarine that forms part of the Soviet Union's nuclear strategic arsenal. Armed with SS-N-6 missiles with a range of 1,600 nautical miles, the ageing Yankees (most of which date from the 1960s) are less-frequent visitors than they used to be. Still, it would take only one to wreak catastrophic damage on North American command, control, and retaliation capability. And the Yankees are only one among several varieties of nuclear-attack submarines. The Akula, for example, is reputed to have a top dive speed of forty-two knots, and incorporates the very latest technology, including SS-N-21 submarine-launched cruise missiles (SLCMs). These missiles fly at subsonic speed, have a range of about 1,865 miles, carry 300-kiloton nuclear warheads, and launched offshore can strike deep, at targets well inland. This strike capability makes them of particular concern to Canada's defence experts: Winnipeg, for example, can be hit from a submarine operating in the Davis Strait.

Whatever the Soviet craft, North American defences will certainly detect it, identify it, and proceed to track its movements. This monitoring is done mainly through systems deployed off the Pacific and Atlantic coasts. SOSUS is the backbone of this defensive shield, a fixed installation system made up of hydrophonic arrays strategically located along the Continental Shelf. It can determine the position of a submarine to within a radius of fifty nautical miles or less. Data are then automatically fed into the Fleet Satellite Communications System (FLTSATCOM), a satellite network that combines SOSUS-acquired intelligence with other information and links it with powerful shore-based computers that can produce highly accurate assessments of the location of Soviet vessels. Along the Atlantic coastline, SOSUS facilities stretch from Trinidad in the south to Newfoundland in the north.

Ratkai's misson was to discover the secrets of SOSUS. His target, Argentia, is on the west coast of Newfoundland's Avalon Peninsula, overlooking Placentia Bay. Here, on board the USS *Augusta*, Churchill and Roosevelt had signed the Atlantic Charter in 1941. The previous year the British had leased to the Americans the land around the town for a naval base, part of a wider deal in exchange for which the Americans granted Britain fifty urgently needed destroyers. By 1943 the base had more than 12,000 personnel serving the largest U.S. task force in the Atlantic. Although the base at Argentia has since diminished in size (it currently is staffed by about 500 U.S. and Canadian personnel), it remains highly significant. It is the northernmost end of the U.S. surveillance and command system in the North Atlantic — a key component of the SOSUS chain.

Ratkai had a troubled past. The heavy-set young man with dark brown hair and moustache, who spoke with a sometimes incomprehensible accent, had been born in Antigonish, Nova Scotia, in 1962. His father was a Hungarian and had fled his country after the 1956 uprising, his mother a Cape Breton Islander with a daughter from a previous marriage. On Christmas eve 1967, tragedy struck. Stephen's mother shot his half-sister, went next door to phone the police, and on her way back turned the gun on herself in front of her five-year-old son. After this traumatic murder-suicide, his father sent Stephen to live with his grandparents in Hungary. After eight years he returned to Nova Scotia, where he lived in Antigonish until his father died of cancer in 1983. At age twenty, living off unemployment insurance, Ratkai sold his father's possessions and returned to Hungary.

He carried with him some painful and bitter memories of life in Canada; he had been rejected by his mother's family after her suicide, mocked at school for his Hungarian accent, and — the bitterest pill of all — rejected for service at age eighteen by the Canadian Armed Forces because he was overweight. Settling in Budapest, he worked as a labourer and then enrolled in college as an engineering student. To make ends meet, he dabbled in the currency black market. The best place to do this was a local whirlpool spa where, in 1986, a man Ratkai knew only as "John" made him an offer that he could not refuse. John, a bald man of about fifty, who wore a big gold-and-gemstone ring on every finger, told Ratkai that if he travelled to St. John's and picked up a package, he would be paid "lots of money" — $11,000 (U.S.), to be exact.

To Ratkai — to anyone in Budapest — that amount in hard currency was a small fortune, and he readily agreed to John's proposal. For the next few months, in a two-roomed apartment in Budapest, he was trained by John in basic agent tradecraft, learning how to use secret inks and how to avoid surveillance. Then he made his first rendezvous with Donna Geiger outside the Hotel Newfoundland and flew back to Hungary to collect his reward. To the young man who delighted in being able to return from Canada with a Polaroid camera because "it makes you a pretty popular guy if you can take pictures of girls and give them to people right away," the road seemed wide open to a future filled with material delights and the good life. In reality, it was a quick route to a Canadian prison.

For what neither Ratkai nor his Soviet controllers knew was that Donna Geiger was the "dangle" — the bait — in a carefully planned sting operation that had involved more than forty American

4

and Canadian agents since 1986. To understand the case, we have to see it in a broader picture of KGB Cold War operations against North America.

Beginning in the 1960s, the Soviet Union set out to build up its navy to match that of its superpower rival. As a result, the U.S. Navy became a special target of Soviet intelligence and subsequently, in the 1980s, the victim of several highly publicized spy cases that embarrassed the United States. Most dramatic and serious of these was the Walker case of 1985. John Walker, a former U.S. Navy communications officer, his son Michael, his brother Arthur, and a friend called Jerry Whitworth were arrested on espionage charges dating back to 1968. For seventeen years, the Walker ring had traded cryptographic information for money. Their spying had given the Soviets access to thousands of classified U.S. naval secrets. To demonstrate the severity of the offence, John Walker was tried and sentenced to life imprisonment.

The Walker case spurred the U.S. Naval Investigative Service to launch a renewed counter-offensive against Soviet intelligence activities. SOSUS was known to be a Soviet target, and there had long been strong suspicions about Soviet ships docking at St. John's. One such visit in 1984 had involved the 6,000-tonne research vessel *Vityaz*. Heavily equipped and carrying a crew of sixty-six, and fifty researchers, this ship contained twenty laboratories and "special dive" facilities. Three years later, Italy denied it entry to a Naples-based Sea Fair because its researchers showed excessive interest in the U.S. Fleet moored in Naples harbour.

In 1986, the Americans approached Ottawa with a proposal. Would the Canadians help out in a sting operation to identify suspected Soviet spies? Ottawa said yes, and the Canadian Security Intelligence Service (CSIS) joined forces with the Americans.

The opening gambit would be a simple "walk-in," where the dangle openly approached the Soviets with a direct offer. The approach had worked before in other cases involving the U.S. Navy. In a 1977 FBI sting operation, Lieutenant-Commander Arthur Lindberg, a Navy supply officer, had been used successfully as a dangle to entrap three Soviet intelligence officers who were arrested in New

Jersey the following year. And Walker had enrolled with the Soviets by simply walking into their Washington embassy and offering his services. Chosen from among the U.S. employees at the Argentia base for the 1986 operation — codenamed "Beacon" by the RCMP and "Night Watch" by CSIS — was Lieutenant Geiger.

The dark-haired thirty-year-old mother, who would give birth to a second child before the sting operation was over, made her initial approach in December 1986 when the Soviet research ship *Akademic Boris Petrov* docked in St. John's. The *Boris Petrov* and its crew of sixty-nine were homeward bound after a sensitive mission in the Atlantic, where they helped to maintain a Soviet surface presence at a point about 600 miles east of Bermuda known as "Yankee Datum" — the site where a Soviet Yankee-class submarine with sixteen missiles on board had sunk earlier that year. Ever since, the Soviets had kept watch to see that the Americans did not reach the vessel.

On boarding the ship, Lieutenant Geiger met the captain and the first mate and, to show them she was serious, told them she had already rented a post-office box for receiving clandestine correspondence.

The captain, Rein Kasak, took her name, rank, and serial number; asked where she was based and what information she had access to; and said he would radio her offer to Moscow. Someone, he told her, would soon be in touch through the postal-box number she had provided. Before she left he presented her with a small jar of caviar.

Seven weeks later, Geiger received the first of several letters. All were postmarked either Montreal or Ottawa, the letters in one handwriting and the envelopes in another. The first read as though written by a fan of bad spy novels. "Dear Donna," it said. "Thank you for your letter and I will be glad to get such warm letters in future and hope to see you in March or April after I have been to sea. Love, Peter." But it was no fiction, and soon after, in spring 1987, Lieutenant Geiger made the crucial first rendezvous with Ratkai. "Are you Donna?" he asked. "We are really glad you have come. We have some business to discuss."

The three meetings that followed over the next thirteen months were classics of the spy trade. All took place under heavy surveillance and were photographed or videotaped in and around St. John's.

During the first, Geiger handed over a supposedly secret U.S. Navy document on the acoustic characteristics of submarines and was paid $2,000. She also confessed to Ratkai that she was afraid of being caught. To reassure her, he gave her a name and address in East Berlin to which she could write if she felt she was in danger. In any case, he told her, if she did get caught she'd be swapped in an East-West spy exchange and comfortably set up in a Russian villa.

At the second rendezvous, an unidentified man with a camera arrived two hours before the scheduled meeting time, checked out the lobby of the hotel where contact was to be made, and then, after going outside and walking down a dead-end alleyway, suddenly turned back as if to see whether he was being followed. He then took several photographs of a plaque on a memorial that was completely covered with snow. This procedure mystified the surveillance team and was never satisfactorily explained. When Ratkai and Lieutenant Geiger met up, she handed over two U.S. defence manuals in a large Labatt's beer case carefully wrapped in Christmas paper and tied with a bow so that it would be easier for the surveillance team to tail Ratkai. This time he gave her $1,000, a camera to photograph documents she said she could not remove from the base, and a pad of specially treated writing paper for secret messages.

At the third meeting, on June 11, 1988, the spycatchers, now led by the RCMP, decided to make their move. Secretly videotaping a meeting between Ratkai and Geiger in a room in the Hotel Newfoundland, the RCMP obtained conclusive evidence that would hold up in court. Geiger handed Ratkai eight pages of what the U.S. Navy called "the bible of anti-submarine warfare," a top-secret manual that described exactly how the Americans track Soviet submarines and surface vessels. In response, Ratkai offered Geiger $40,000 (U.S.) if she could give him all the information the U.S. Navy had on the acoustic characteristics of Soviet submarines. "We want all secret and classified information," he said. As the two left the hotel, Ratkai with the document in his possession, the Mounties swooped and made their arrest.

Hidden in a moneybelt around Ratkai's waist was $2,500, and another $6,500 was stuffed in his pockets. He was carrying a portable photo laboratory (the chemicals were in a Diet 7-Up bottle) and wearing a digital watch programmed with coded information.

At first, Ratkai pleaded not guilty. But, at the trial in Newfoundland's Supreme Court, in February 1989, he suddenly and unexpectedly changed his plea. The defence argued that Ratkai was essentially small potatoes, a novice and a sad case who had been blackmailed and exploited into service by the Soviets for the Argentia case alone. The Crown argued otherwise. Corporal Gary Bass, head of RCMP intelligence in St. John's, testified that Ratkai had shown all the skills of a highly trained intelligence officer. He had demonstrated some careful tradecraft while under surveillance, and under interrogation had revealed little that was not already known to the spycatchers. "He made very few mistakes," said Bass. "Had Lieutenant Geiger not been working for us, it was doubtful he would have been caught." Describing the scene before Ratkai's final meeting with Geiger, Bass said that the defendant had spent two and a half hours checking out the hotel and its environs to see if he was being watched. In all of his seventeen years of police work, Bass told the court, "I have never seen such a procedure where a person spent two and a half hours drycleaning himself."

Investigators were convinced, moreover, that Ratkai knew more about Soviet espionage activities in Canada than he was admitting. To bolster their case, the Crown brought in as an expert witness the American author of several works about the KGB, John Barron, whose latest book was about the Walker case. "The type of knowledge given to him [by the Soviets] was of the type given to a case officer," Barron argued. "This is not a crime against one person," said the prosecutor in his summing up, "it is a crime against millions of people . . . the damage from the documents passed would be extensive." The judge agreed and handed down a nine-year sentence, the heaviest meted out under the Official Secrets Act in almost forty years.

The Ratkai case is doubly interesting. First, it was a joint U.S.–Canadian operation. Its focus on military secrets from an American naval base on Canadian soil illustrates how closely woven together is Canada's secret service with that of its major ally. Canada's interest in defending the secrets of SOSUS is as great as that of the United States, or indeed of any of its other NATO allies.

Second, the timing of the "kill" was clearly not an accident. The affair revealed little that was not already known or suspected about Soviet espionage against allied maritime targets. The purpose of Operation Beacon was to use the case for broader political ends. Those controlling the operation were the Canadians and Americans. Ratkai's arrest served a triple purpose. It sent a clear signal to the Soviets that their intelligence attacks on U.S. and allied naval secrets had gone too far. It told Canada's friends that Ottawa was a loyal ally in the wider Western intelligence community. And it demonstrated to the Canadian public, at a time when confidence in the CSIS, established only four years earlier, was still low, that Ottawa's spycatchers had "real" targets to pursue and were not just concerned — as a flurry of press reports had been suggesting — with peace groups and other imagined domestic subversives.

On June 14, 1988, three days after Ratkai's arrest, Solicitor General James Kelleher, the minister responsible for CSIS and the RCMP, phoned the Prime Minister's Office to request an urgent meeting with the prime minister. That afternoon he and Brian Mulroney were joined in the latter's Parliament Hill office by External Affairs minister Joe Clark; his under-secretary of state, James Taylor; the director of CSIS, Reid Morden; and the prime minister's chief of staff, Derek Burney. The reason for the high-level urgency was Soviet spying by Moscow's diplomats. CSIS, Kelleher revealed, had assembled an impressive catalogue of Soviet espionage attempts. While some of the operations dated back to the 1970s, others were still current. And while none had been successful, they provided dramatic proof of the continuing Soviet threat to national security. The time to act decisively had come, Kelleher said. He wanted those involved to be expelled immediately.

Clark pointed out the dangers. The Soviet intelligence officers identified by CSIS were operating under diplomatic cover, some from the Soviet embassy in Ottawa, others from the consulate in Montreal.

9

Expulsions could cause a major row with Moscow. There might be Soviet retaliation that could set back relations that had only recently begun to thaw with Gorbachev's arrival in the Kremlin. There was already talk about the prime minister going to Moscow. A lot of patient diplomatic fence-mending by Clark's officials could be quickly unravelled by hasty and radical action.

In the end, after considerable discussion, the prime minister came down on Kelleher's side. But to contain the damage and assuage Clark, it was agreed that the expulsions would be done quietly and without fuss. The next day, Soviet ambassador Alexei Rodionov was privately informed of the decision by the head of External Affairs's division of Soviet and East European affairs. Eight Soviet diplomats would have to leave, and nine others who had very recently left would be banned from re-entry. By the end of the week those ordered out were back in Moscow. It seemed that all had gone according to plan.

Within days, however, the strategy so carefully worked out in Mulroney's office had come undone, and Ottawa was embroiled in a dispute with Moscow that rapidly escalated out of control. News of the expulsions quickly leaked to the media, and CSIS was flooded with phone calls. One week after Kelleher's first phone call to Mulroney, the prime minister confirmed the story at a press conference. The next day, June 22, Joe Clark informed the House of Commons that those expelled had engaged in "unacceptable activities which were a threat to the security of the country."

The publicity provoked immediate Soviet retaliation. Moscow expelled two Canadian diplomats and banned three others from re-entry. Tit-for-tat, Ottawa responded by expelling another Soviet diplomat and reducing the official Soviet diplomatic quota in Canada from sixty-three to sixty. Moscow then dramatically raised the stakes. It expelled the Canadian military attaché, banned the return to Moscow of seven other diplomats, and withdrew twenty-five of thirty-seven Soviet members of the Moscow embassy staff.

The severity of this move firmly put Ottawa in its place. Abruptly, almost as quickly as they had begun, the spy wars came to an end. Moscow had severely damaged Canada's ability to conduct any diplomacy at all with the Soviet Union. Vernon Turner, the ambassador in Moscow, was left virtually helpless. Some of the most experienced External Affairs officials with Soviet expertise were now banned from ever returning to the Soviet Union. Further escalation by Ottawa could lead to Soviet retaliation that would be fatal to diplomatic relations. Besides, the Soviets had a vulnerability of their own. In Montreal, Soviet workers were rebuilding the Soviet consulate general that had burned down the previous year. Clark reminded the Soviet ambassador that they were on visas that would have to be renewed at some point. After a meeting between the two men, a truce was called, and the affair quickly dropped from the headlines. Behind the scenes, patching up began. That September, Clark and Soviet foreign minister Eduard Shevardnadze met at the opening fall session of the United Nations in New York. Afterwards it was announced that the Soviet support personnel at the Moscow embassy would soon return to their posts. "We have decided," announced Clark, "that relations between Canada and the Soviet Union are sufficiently important that we should put the events of June behind us." Barely a year later Prime Minister Mulroney was in Moscow on an official visit. Moscow and Ottawa were back on track.

Behind the apparently simple drama of spy expulsions that got out of hand lay a more complex affair that revealed a considerable amount about the politics of espionage.

It was clear from the beginning that Solicitor General Kelleher's determination to blow the whistle on Soviet spying was driven by the urgent need for CSIS to prove it was an effective security intelligence agency. There was grave public doubt about its value at the time, and officials in Ottawa were worried. Ted Finn, the first CSIS director, had resigned the previous September at the height of the Atwal warrant scandal (see Chapter 11). There had followed a special review that had revealed several serious internal problems at CSIS that were still being repaired. In February, the "Triple M" affair had again thrown CSIS under the spotlight of hostile press comment (see Chapter 11). The fledgling agency badly needed a victory, some good news that would re-establish its credibility in Ottawa. Most of the Soviet activity at issue was not new, and there was more than one operation involved. The decision to "package" them as one and seek the simultaneous expulsion of all those involved was deliberate. It would be a major coup by CSIS counter-intelligence that would amply demonstrate the agency's effectiveness and importance. Ratkai's arrest had clearly helped the cause. Although the two affairs were operationally unrelated, they nonetheless fused very nicely — and almost certainly not coincidentally — in the minds of those who ran CSIS. Kelleher, in particular, was known to be in a hawkish mood.

If bureaucratic politics played their part in the story, calculation of political advantage was scarcely absent in Brian Mulroney's office. Exactly how news of the expulsions leaked to the media is not clear, although the sudden and unexpected departure of several Soviet diplomats could have been guaranteed not to pass unremarked in Ottawa and Montreal. Once the story broke, however, it was quickly turned to advantage by the prime minister. The moment was no ordinary one, after all. In Toronto he was hosting fellow Western prime ministers at the annual G-7 economic summit. With the international spotlight focused on his final summit press conference, Mulroney was able to confirm Canada's expulsion of the Soviet spies. With this, Ottawa sent yet another clear signal to its allies, and to the Western public in general, that they could count on Canada to stand on guard with them for Western security interests. This was important for NATO, and for Washington. Gorbachev's popularity in the West, and rising public hopes for an end to the Cold War and for disarmament, were running well ahead of official opinion. From several capitals over the previous few months, especially London and Washington, had come warnings about continuing or even increasing Soviet espionage. Kelleher himself had spoken publicly in April of the Soviet espionage threat and had repeated standard Western estimates that some two-thirds of Soviet diplomatic personnel were intelligence officers. Such statements were timed and presented carefully to make it clear that *glasnost* and *perestroika* weren't all they were supposed to be, as well as to send signals to the Soviet Union to cease and desist. Ottawa's summer spy wars were part of a larger campaign. As well as helping CSIS internally, they filled some useful international needs. The CIA was quick to send its congratulations to Morden the day the expulsions were announced.

There was a price to be paid, however, and there were miscalculations in Ottawa. Those who pressed for the expulsions forgot some recent history and overlooked the domestic pressures on Gorbachev to make a strong response. Just eight years earlier there had been a similar case involving Ottawa and Moscow. Canada had expelled three Soviets for spying, and, after some quid pro quo retaliation, Moscow had suddenly and unexpectedly withdrawn some twenty members of the local staff employed as maids, drivers, telephone operators, translators, etc. "They played an essential role in the embassy," wrote Canadian ambassador Robert Ford in his memoirs, "and the withdrawal . . . caused us enormous trouble." The Soviets applied similar massive retaliation against the Americans in 1986, so Ottawa should have been well warned. A strong response was particularly likely, given Gorbachev's domestic agenda. Just as Mulroney was on centre-stage at the Toronto summit, so the Soviet leader was playing to a vast crowd in Moscow. Pushing hard for his reforms, he had convened an extraordinary congress of party members that, at that very moment, was meeting in full public gaze in the Soviet Union. He, too, had a domestic and international audience to please. Already under fire from hardliners for going too far too fast, Gorbachev had little choice but to react forcibly once the expulsion became public. So the road was opened up for the tit-for-tat war. All round, politics of one kind or another had played a major role in the story.

The Ratkai case and the summer 1988 expulsions revealed more about Ottawa's political needs than about the reality of Soviet spying. Spy cases are barometers, measuring pressure in the heady atmosphere where intelligence and politics mix. When the pressure builds too much, the barometer issues a warning. Such was the case in 1988. At issue was the rapidly warming climate of East-West relations.

Since Mikhail Gorbachev single-handedly opened the door in the mid-1980s to a future beyond the Cold War, public pressure had been mounting for the West to respond. In Ottawa, Washington, and London, conservative governments were being urged to move faster.

When *perestroika* and *glasnost* finally reached the KGB, and Western TV showed pictures of smiling intelligence chiefs in Moscow publicly fielding criticism; talking of democratic accountability; appearing on talk shows to chat about sex, James Bond, and the secret lives of secret agents; and suggesting that the CIA and KGB collaborate to fight terrorism, the inevitable question arose in many people's minds. If the Cold War was over and the KGB now had a human face, what was the future of the spies and the spycatchers, East *and* West? Unemployment insurance? Transfers to the Ministries of Fisheries and Pensions? Perhaps the day had finally come to implement a "proposal" made by spy novelist Eric Ambler in the 1950s, for the creation of the E. Phillips Oppenheim Memorial Park, an international spy reserve named after the popular writer who had intrigued millions of readers on both sides of the Atlantic between the two world wars with his tales of international derring-do. Here, as in a game park, a dying breed would be preserved in the old fortress on Île du Levant, off the south coast of France, spending their time spying on the old fortifications and organizing breathtaking escapes to the mainland. It was another spy novelist, however, who pointed out that the age of *perestroika* did not mean the end of the spy. "Do not imagine for one second," John le Carré warned after the Berlin Wall opened, "that because the Cold War is over the spooks are not having a ball. In times of such uncertainty as this the world's intelligence industries will be beavering away like never before."

Spy chiefs in the West rushed to prove his point and dispel any notions of an end to spy wars. The Ratkai arrest and Ottawa's expulsion of Soviet diplomats for spying were forceful reminders, CIA chief William Webster told an audience of lawyers in Toronto in August 1988, that the KGB and GRU still represented the most significant threat to U.S. interests at home and abroad. Noting that since Gorbachev had come to power three years earlier, there had been more penetration of the American defence and intelligence community than at any time in U.S. history, Webster went on: "The methods employed by the Soviets are becoming more aggressive and more sophisticated. We expect to see greater Soviet efforts to recruit U.S. personnel abroad; increasing use of third countries for clandes-

14

tine meetings with American agents . . . greater efforts to penetrate allied governments that might be privy to U.S. secrets; and greater emphasis on exploiting the intelligence-collective capabilities of Warsaw Pact allies."

Strong echoes of Webster's view were to be heard in Ottawa. In June 1989, CSIS director Reid Morden appeared before the Justice Committee to defend his $157 million budget. The largely unspoken question in the minds of MPs, of course, was why all this was necessary with the Cold War so visibly melting. Not surprisingly, Morden, whose own affable manner concealed his feisty tough-mindedness, quickly moved to throw cold water on any notions that the Russian bear had suddenly been transformed into a cuddly toy.

He accepted that *glasnost* and *perestroika* were sweeping Soviet society. But, he warned, Soviet military and intelligence capability had not diminished. *Perestroika* merely redefined the Soviet threat; it did not remove it. "The efforts made in the Soviet Union to implement [*perestroika*] will define the threat that the East will hang over the West in matters of intelligence in the 1990s," the CSIS director warned. "Eastern European countries will have to make serious changes in order to face up to the political and economic difficulties that confront them, and this will entail a more, not less, intensive need for intelligence." East-bloc intelligence services would need, under the impulses of *perestroika*, "to control restive minorities and populations anxious for real improvement and greater independence, influence foreign policy and government opinion, and acquire more advanced technology. Minority problems especially," he concluded, "can be expected to lead to attempts to penetrate and manipulate ethnic communities in Canada."

Morden declined to go beyond generalities or to reveal operational secrets in his statements to the Justice Committee. He had been more explicit about the Soviet threat a couple of weeks earlier. To a meeting of security and intelligence specialists in Quebec City on May 31, he said that CSIS and its allied intelligence services had already detected a "more aggressive direct approach and appeal for support" by Soviet-bloc services, and that "efforts to accelerate covert activities and acquire advanced technology should persist and even accelerate" under the demands of *perestroika*. As evidence, he pointed to the summer 1988 expulsions, Ratkai's conviction, and a barely completed British expulsion of Soviet and Czech diplomats. "There is without a doubt intense pressure on the Soviet intelligence services to achieve results," he told the group. "Covert attempts to influence policy through groups have become more subtle, in keeping with *glasnost*. There are already signs of less emphasis on controlling popular movements and more on deceptively influencing legitimate advocates in the West. This," he concluded, "is likely to be a more effective tactic."

Even after the tide of *perestroika* had swept into Eastern Europe, and Poland's first non-communist government in forty years had been installed in Warsaw, Morden's views remained unchanged. Only a week before the opening of the Berlin Wall in November 1989, he stated bluntly to the special parliamentary committee examining the CSIS Act that it was too early to conclude that there is any "fundamental re-alignment of Soviet strategic objectives going on." In the following four weeks, the Iron Curtain dissolved, popular revolutions swept away old leaders in East Germany and Czechoslovakia, and the world saw a continent transformed. But, as dire in his warnings as Morden had been, CIA chief William Webster was there to tell the West that the Soviet intelligence threat remained. "Let us not assume that because we are getting friendly [with the Soviets] and seeing freedom come up from the streets," he told an audience at Washington's National Press Club, "that freedom has been endorsed by some of these aggressive [Soviet-bloc] intelligence services."

Webster was right to be sceptical about overnight changes inside East-bloc intelligence. The people of Eastern Europe were suspicious too, as demonstrated early in 1990 when crowds in East Berlin ransacked the Stasi headquarters and rejected attempts to preserve the secret police, while mobs in Romania set out in lynching parties to hunt down the feared Securitate. Eventually, of course, the democratic tide swept away KGB allies in Eastern Europe. By the time the East Germans elected their first democratic government in almost sixty years, for example, one Stasi building in Potsdam had been transformed into a popular café, while in Czechoslovakia

President Vaclav Havel, the former dissident dramatist, had announced that all links to the KGB were to be broken.

Still, even in the new world of 1990, it seemed unlikely that the spies would be redundant. Spying is the second-oldest profession, and the ending of the Cold War, as le Carré pointed out, only added to uncertainty. States have no friends, only interests, and this means that even allies are considered legitimate targets of espionage.

Nevertheless, a mirror would have been helpful to the CIA director and his allies in Ottawa. Resistance to change was deeply entrenched at CIA headquarters in Langley, Virginia, and elsewhere. Vested interests were desperately attempting to deny that their very existence might be challenged by the revolution sweeping the Soviet Empire. For forty years Western counter-intelligence experts had defined their lives by the Soviet threat. Their emotions, their careers, their futures, were intimately bound up with it. As the adversary visibly changed before their eyes, many found it simply impossible to accept that *any* change was real. The KGB, warned Webster in February 1990, had not slackened its spying against the West. Indeed, CIA counter-intelligence experts saw "robust intelligence activity by the KGB throughout the world," even as East-West tensions relaxed.

Yet, while the chorus sang its old refrains about the Soviet menace with more gusto than ever, a new tune could be heard emerging from intelligence sources. To many, it struck a more relevant chord. Terrorism, it sang, not the old Red Menace, was now the real threat to national security. Here, to protect Canadians against the militant fanatic with a grievance and a cassette player stuffed with Semtex at 35,000 feet, the spycatchers of old would find a new mission and a new life.

Since at least June 23, 1985, when Air India flight 182 from Toronto and Montreal to New Delhi and Bombay plunged into the Atlantic Ocean off the coast of Ireland, killing the crew and all 307 passengers (nearly all Canadians), the top priority of CSIS had, indeed, been counter-terrorism. The disaster, most experts believed, was the result of a bomb placed aboard the plane in Vancouver. "The most heinous act of violence in Canadian history" is how former Tory minister and chairman of the Security Intelligence Review Committee, Ron Atkey, described it to the Justice Committee in spring 1988. Most Canadians shared Atkey's feelings, and the 1987 report of the Senate Special Committee on Terrorism and the Public Safety hammered the point home. The major threat to Canada came not from domestic issues, it concluded, but from "international terrorism" — terrorism motivated by events, history, old hatreds and issues in other countries, using Canada as a base or venue for getting at these other countries, their representatives, or their symbols.

Morden himself had made the same point. "I think in terms of the threats," he told the Justice Committee two weeks after Atkey, "I would put at the top the protection of public safety through the efforts of our counter-terrorism programme." Canada's vulnerability to international terrorism most clearly sprang, he argued, from extremists in immigrant communities. Canada was still attracting thousands of people each year seeking to escape poverty, violence, and repression. Inevitably, a small minority would seek to pursue "homeland issues" through violence. "Terrorist threats," the CSIS chief said, "will in our view largely be a function of extremists in various committees who will use Canada as a base to organize support, conduct operations against other countries, and shelter or try to shelter persons wanted for acts of terrorism elsewhere." And this meant — although Morden was careful not to point the finger at any particular group — that Canada was not immune from further attempts of the kind that other countries were suffering.

Counter-terrorism had shot to the top of the national-security agenda after the Air India crash. CSIS work and resources had been diverted to counter-terrorism, and the RCMP had established the National Security Investigation Service (NSIS), employing more than 130 people. To a Justice Committee hearing on June 1, 1989, Solicitor General Pierre Blais unveiled a new federal government initiative — the setting up of a national security co-ordination centre for counter-terrorism and planning. That fall, Blais made explicit what had been clear for some time. The top priority for CSIS, he announced, was public safety — "the safety of air transportation and of the travelling public against terrorism threats."

Counter-terrorism will remain high on the national-security agenda for the foreseeable future. Terrorism is here to stay for a considerable while. Yet one does not have to be a cynic to believe that counter-terrorism will remain a priority for other reasons, too. To put it bluntly, counter-terrorism sells well to the public. Anyone who flies on an aircraft is glad to know that CSIS and the RCMP are standing on guard for their personal safety. And there is the appeal — and the danger — of a strong counter-terrorism mandate. The public's fear of terrorism can easily be exaggerated and manipulated to make people more readily accept that the nation's spycatchers should have extensive investigative powers to pry and snoop into the private lives of its citizens. Hence, the cure can become worse than the disease, and intelligence agencies may retain and expand their intensive powers at the expense of civil liberties. CSIS, it might be noted, has not suffered from recent federal belt-tightening, nor have the dramatic changes in the Soviet bloc cut into its resources. On the contrary: in 1990–91, its budget will increase by 20 percent, taking it close to $180 million.

Blais announced the counter-terrorism priority for CSIS at a public conference of intelligence experts in Ottawa. This in itself was a watershed. Never before had the subject of national security been discussed in such a format in public. Moreover, a major parliamentary review by a special committee of the workings of the 1984 CSIS Act was about to begin. In spring 1990, this review was in full swing, and what amendments would be made to the act were still unclear. What was apparent, however, was that, with the passing of the Cold War and a new security service finding its feet, Canada's Spy Wars were entering on a uncharted course.

No one quite knows what to expect, but it seems obvious that the future will be more than the past in replay. It is a good time to pause and look back on the path that has brought us to the present.

2.
JOINING THE RANKS

What has been described as the strongest arm of Canada's intelligence network operates from a 1950s five-storey brick structure known as the Sir Leonard Tilley Building on Heron Road in Ottawa's Confederation Heights. Almost everything about it is considered secret, including its annual budget and number of employees. Although administratively part of the Department of National Defence, it receives its mandate not from the federal Defence minister but directly from the Cabinet committee on security and intelligence through the intelligence and security co-ordinator in the Privy Council Office. "It was my responsibility," former co-ordinator Blair Seaborn told a parliamentary committee in February 1990, "to provide policy and to some extent operational guidance." Seaborn also stressed that the agency was "ultra secret." That was an understatement. Its director never speaks to the press, and its employees never publicly identify themselves as working for the Communications Security Establishment (CSE). The existence of CSE was not acknowledged by the government until 1983, and even some ministers were unaware of its work. Neither Allan Lawrence, the solicitor general, nor Allan McKinnon, the minister of Defence, both members of the Clark government of 1979-80, seems to have been told by his officials at his swearing-in about the agency that is undoubtedly the most important and potentially the most intrusive of Canada's intelligence agencies.

Lawrence revealed in 1984 that he learned about CSE only when he questioned his officials about the source for some information he received in his weekly intelligence report. He then discovered that McKinnon had not heard of it either. So, said Lawrence, "We decided to find out together and went down there to see what they were doing." In 1983, during parliamentary debates over the creation of CSIS, Solicitor General Robert Kaplan refused to reveal CSE's mandate. Unlike CSIS, CSE operates with no watchdog committee and is subject to no parliamentary scrutiny.

Yet enough is known to establish that CSE is the agency that ties Canada most firmly to the Western intelligence community. The price is high. Some sources estimate that the CSE annual budget is in the $150-million range, and since 1984 more than $100 million has been spent to upgrade its facilities and equipment, including the purchase of a Cray supercomputer. Its employees are estimated to number between 600 and 800, and include computer technicians, cryptographers, and intelligence analysts. They have some of the highest security classifications in Ottawa. The most senior are forbidden to take commercial flights in case hijackers force them to reveal secrets. For years, most of them were also under standing instructions not to enter East-bloc countries.

The secret CSE mandate is twofold. The agency's first task — as its title suggests — is to protect government communications. This means employing cryptographers to develop codes and ciphers for the federal government and also participating in a NATO-wide program codenamed "Tempest," which protects particularly sensitive Allied secrets from Soviet eavesdropping. This side of CSE's work has received little attention. Yet, in most respects, it has been the single most important weapon in Canada's security-intelligence armoury. Despite the inevitable focus on stories of human espionage (HUMINT), during the Cold War signals intelligence (SIGINT) was the principal battlefield. Here, Soviet capacities were, and have remained, formidable, probably the largest ever in the history of intelligence. For example, the GRU, Soviet military intelligence, alone operates some forty signals regiments in the Red Army and runs SIGINT operations from more than fifty surface ships and half as many aircraft. There are more than 500 Soviet SIGINT ground stations, and SIGINT operations are carried out from all Soviet posts in foreign countries. In Canada, this means the Ottawa embassy and the consulate in Montreal. The biggest Soviet SIGINT base in the Western Hemisphere, at Lourdes in Cuba, occupies 20 square miles and employs some 2,000 people. World-wide, Soviet SIGINT employs over 300,000 specialists — five times as many as the U.S. codebreaking outfit, the National Security Agency.

CSE's work in helping to counter the Soviet SIGINT offensive is complemented by its other mandate to acquire intelligence by attacking the communications secrets of other powers. The Signals Intelligence Programme, according to an internal CSE document, "involves the collection and processing of foreign radio, radar and other electromagnetic transmissions." This means that CSE listens in to radio and telephone communications between embassies in Ottawa and their home countries, or between embassies and their consulates; monitors all national and international telephone calls; listens in to many foreign radio communications; and reads the electromagnetic transmissions from embassy typewriters, word processors, etc. Although government officials have frequently denied that CSE intercepts private phone calls, it was revealed in 1984 — an appropriately Orwellian date — that the agency keeps a personal-information databank on people, both Canadian and foreign, who are considered potential security risks. The databank also includes, in the words of a federal index of personal-information databanks, "personal information relating to sensitive aspects of Canada's international relations and defence. This information," continues the document, "is used to advise the Government with respect to international affairs, security, and defence." It should be of no surprise to anyone that the CSE databank is classified as an "exempt" bank under the federal Privacy Act. This makes it impossible for individuals to review whatever material about themselves it may contain.

Legitimately, many people worry about CSE's potential to target Canadians, and the complete lack of public accountability for its breathtaking power. Here, indeed, is Big Brother. The crucial point about this Big Brother, of course, is that his parents and siblings live overseas, beyond the full control of his nominal masters in Ottawa.

CSE priorities and procedures spring from agreements signed with the National Security Agency in Washington, GCHQ in London, or other signals-intelligence agencies in Australia or New Zealand.

As they have done since they set up shop in 1941, Canada's codebreakers work as members of a multinational operation. Inevitably they are a subordinate, if important, part.

CSE's listening posts are operated in conjunction with the Canadian Forces Supplementary Radio System. Most are located in Canada. There is one in the Arctic, at Alert on the northern tip of Ellesmere Island. Another is to be found on the west coast, on the Queen Charlotte Islands, and another operates from Leitrim, close to Ottawa.

But the codebreakers also work jointly within the Americas. CSE has a stake in the U.S. naval base at Argentia, Newfoundland, the target of Stephen Ratkai's mission. And the linkage with the Americans also involves at least one overseas CSE post. This, curiously enough, is on the British Crown colony of Bermuda, thus providing perhaps the only example of Canada's occupying the territory of its former imperial ruler.

While Bermuda is well known to Canadians as a winter holiday spot, it is not generally appreciated that it is also the spot from which, quite literally, the world could be destroyed in a nuclear war. Tourists flying into Bermuda land at Kindley Field airport, which is also a U.S. Naval airbase. From here Lockheed P-3 Orion surveillance aircraft shadow Soviet submarines lurking off the North American seaboard, complementing and reinforcing the SOSUS underwater defences. More ominous is that Kindley Field also houses two specially converted U.S. Lockheed C-130 Hercules transports. Known as TACAMO aircraft, the acronym for "Take Charge and Move Out," these are the planes that carry the go-codes for launching U.S. nuclear missiles, such as the Trident, the Polaris, and the Poseidon, carried aboard submarines. Spending twelve hours each day patrolling the North Atlantic, they remain in constant contact with the submarines below. Should war between the United States and the Soviet Union ever break out, or should Washington decide that it is imminent, the controllers on these planes have the power to launch the missiles and destroy the future.

So Bermuda is more than a holiday spot in the sun. From here CSE operates jointly with the Americans in their surveillance activities, and there is a strong suspicion that it also co-operates in a world-wide network known as Autovon, which relays scrambled telephone messages between allied governments. The airfield at Bermuda, along with Argentia several thousand miles to the north in Newfoundland, was leased to the Americans by the British during the desperate year of 1940. That fifty years later CSE runs joint operations with the Americans on the soil of one former and one present British colony is a forceful reminder that in the Spy Wars of intelligence Canada is still no more than a partner — and a junior partner at that — in a wider transatlantic community.

Historically, Canadian intelligence has always been largely an ad hoc affair, and dependence on the imperial power — Britain or the United States — has never really disappeared. In the 1860s, Sir John A. Macdonald established a network of undercover agents directed by Gilbert McMicken to counter the menace of Fenians intent on invading Canada from the United States to help the cause of Irish independence. Many of the agents operated in U.S. border cities, sending back regular reports to McMicken. Some became "moles," or penetration agents, working within the Fenian movement. The most successful was Thomas Miller Beach, better known as Major Henri le Caron, the name he adopted to join and penetrate the Fenians in 1867. Working from a Fenian cell in Illinois, the "Prince of Spies," as he became known, rose in their ranks to become inspector general of the Fenian forces while continuously providing detailed military information to McMicken in Canada.

Le Caron was a British intelligence officer, and his ultimate loyalty was to Britain. So was that of another veteran of Canadian intelligence before the First World War, William Hopkinson. In the decade before 1914, an extensive intelligence campaign was waged in British Columbia against Indian nationalists at work in the Sikh immigrant community in and around Vancouver. By the time war broke out, there existed a recognizable and effective faction of informers within the Sikh community reporting on nationalist attempts to acquire arms, their links with left-wing movements, and their extensive contacts with Sikhs in the United States. Hopkinson ran this network, sometimes personally infiltrating nationalist cells, where "he used to dress in a turban with a fake beard and moustache and old clothes and go to the temple."

Officially, Hopkinson worked for the Canadian Immigration department — and later for the Dominion Police — in Vancouver and he owed his appointment in large part to a recommendation by future prime minister Mackenzie King, who had been sent to India by Sir Wilfrid Laurier to report on the impact of events there on the situation in British Columbia. But Hopkinson was there because of British and Indian concerns about nationalist agitation on the west coast of North America, and he arrived in Vancouver from India where he had worked for the police in the Punjab and Calcutta since the age of sixteen. His cover as a Canadian proved particularly valuable in establishing contacts with U.S. officials in Seattle and San Francisco who would otherwise have balked at working with the British and especially "imperial" authorities. Hopkinson's reports went to the Colonial Office in London via the governor general, he kept in touch with the Indian police, and in 1913 he began to report directly to the Government of India.

Hopkinson's Canadian intelligence work in the service of Empire came to an abrupt end in 1914. Following the *Komagata Maru* affair, in which a boat carrying 376 Punjabis, most of them Sikhs, was refused permission to land in Vancouver, Hopkinson's role as a spy on the Sikh community was fully exposed. Violence broke out, and two of his informants were murdered. A third shot his way out of trouble and was sent for trial in Victoria. Hopkinson went to testify for him, and there, on October 21, 1914, the Englishman whose father had died in the service of Empire at Kabul in 1879 himself was killed outside the courtroom when a Sikh militant shot him at point-blank range in the chest.

The First World War only served to emphasize the reality of, and the need for, close intelligence linkages with Britain and the United States. Canada's military contribution to the war resulted in a valuable flow of military intelligence from London that continued beyond 1918, while the entry of the United States into the conflict as an ally opened up new intelligence channels to Washington. Both Britain and the United States assisted with counter-intelligence against German threats closer to home. Most of these emanated from the fertile mind of Berlin's military attaché in Washington, Captain Franz von Papen, who later made a more significant mark in history by paving the way to Hitler's dictatorship in the 1930s. Von Papen launched a campaign to disrupt Canadian communications by smuggling saboteurs across the border into Canada and mobilizing the German-American community in support of the Kaiser. The plot failed after a botched attempt to destroy a bridge on the Canadian Pacific line near the Maine border and the capture of a German agent. Here again, the Canadians had depended heavily on British intelligence in following events. The entire sabotage campaign had been initiated in 1916 by a telegram from Arthur Zimmermann, the German foreign secretary in Berlin, to the embassy in Washington. This telegram, like the later and more infamous Zimmermann Telegram that brought the Americans into the War in 1917, was intercepted and decoded by British codebreakers who then passed it on to others, in this case the Canadian authorities.

Between the two world wars Canadian intelligence efforts were directed mainly against real or imagined internal subversion from the left, with the secret service being lodged in the Criminal Investigation Branch of the RCMP. The Winnipeg General Strike of 1919 convinced the Canadian government that counter-subversion should be the top priority of its intelligence efforts. As many accounts of the RCMP have shown, this remained the focus of Mountie intelligence work throughout the 1920s and 1930s.

Still, the efforts were on a small scale, and the resources for counter-intelligence as distinct from counter-subversion work were almost nonexistent at the outbreak of the Second World War. The RCMP's entire Intelligence Branch across the country consisted of just over twenty men, and in its headquarters in Ottawa there were only two commissioned officers.

Inexperience and inept handling by the RCMP ruined the one wartime case that held out the promise of reaping a useful counter-intelligence harvest. The Watchdog case began with an *Abwehr* (German military intelligence) spy landing by submarine off the Gaspé peninsula in November 1942. Having clumsily given himself away on his first day in Quebec by using outdated dollar bills to pay for his lunch, the man was arrested and interrogated by the RCMP. After confessing to be an enemy spy, he agreed to become a double agent and was set up with a transmitter that began to send messages back to Hamburg. The officer in charge of the operation, Cliff Harvison, later became a postwar head of the Force. In his memoirs, *The Horseman*, he painted a glowing account of a successful operation with himself as the controlling hand. "The handling of a double agent is a tricky and complicated business," he noted. Indeed it is, but what he failed to tell his readers was that the reality of the affair was strikingly different from the one he painted.

The German agent, a man called Janowski, had lived in Canada for three years prior to the start of the war and spoke English well. He so impressed Harvison with the information he gave that Harvison immediately rushed the transcripts of his interrogation to London in the belief that they had revealed vital information about the *Abwehr*. Here the small team of experienced MI5 (British Security Service) experts running German double agents in the elaborate "Double Cross" campaign of deception immediately realized that Janowski had completely fooled Harvison. "The papers from Montreal gave us more laughs than a comic paper," one of them recently recalled to one of the authors. "They had made a monkey of Harvison." Eventually RCMP commissioner Stuart Wood asked the director general of MI5 in London to lend him an experienced officer to see if Janowski could, indeed, be run as a double agent. The officer was one of MI5's most experienced in this field, Cyril Mills, who had been the first case officer assigned to the most famous German double agent of the Second World War, Garbo. In December 1942 Mills flew to Montreal. After interrogating Janowski, he decided to run him as a double agent under the codename "Watchdog." This he did until August 1943, when he had to return temporarily to Britain on other business. Back in Canada a few weeks later, he discovered that Watchdog had informed his German masters that he was under control but that the

RCMP officers running him, Harvison included, had failed to spot this. This meant the end of the operation. With Commissioner Wood's approval, Janowski was shipped back to Britain and imprisoned for the duration of the war. Accompanying Janowski to London was a subdued Harvison. After he had handed the German over he was sent for several months' instruction on tradecraft from MI5.

The Watchdog affair exposed how badly equipped the RCMP was to handle serious counter-intelligence cases on its own, and how dependent for success it remained on the British. Reliance on wider allied intelligence resources and expertise, indeed, is a major theme of Canadian intelligence history.

As with the contemporary Western intelligence community as a whole, the Second World War was the catalyst for the founding of what would become CSE and for the establishment of Canada's role in international SIGINT (Signals Intelligence). From the beginning, it was starkly clear that there would be costs as well as benefits to Canada from membership in the international espionage network. In 1941, Herbert Osborn Yardley was the world's most famous cryptologist. Chief of the U.S. military intelligence code and cipher work in the First World War, he had gone on to direct its peacetime Cipher Bureau, the "Black Chamber" (a literal translation of *le cabinet noir*, the name given the French Cipher Bureau). Its triumphant achievement, and the basis of Yardley's personal fame, was the breaking of Japanese diplomatic codes, which had permitted the United States to outwit Japan's delegation at the 1921–22 Washington Naval Conference and establish a favourable ratio for U.S. battleships in the Pacific. The public knew about this because Yardley's book, *The American Black Chamber*, had been a bestseller when it appeared in 1931. It was, wrote one critic at the time, "the most sensational contribution to the secret history of the war . . . which has yet been written by an American. . . . Its deliberate indiscretions exceed any to be found in the recent memoirs of European secret agents."

Yardley was instantly notorious for having revealed some of America's most closely guarded secrets. He had written the book to decry the closing down of his operation in 1929 by American secretary of state Henry Stimson, the man reputed to have protested that "gentlemen do not read each other's mail." Out of a job, Yardley toured the lecture circuit, publicizing his past successes and bemoaning America's future without a cipher bureau. Throughout the 1930s he lived off his wits. Always something of a buccaneer and maverick, as well as a witty and entertaining raconteur, he even wrote a couple of novels. One, *The Blonde Countess*, was adapted by MGM into the movie *Rendezvous*, starring William Powell, Rosalind Russell, and Cesar Romero. Then, in 1938, Generalissimo Chiang Kai-shek hired Yardley to break the codes of the Japanese forces that had invaded mainland China the previous year. For almost two years he lived in the bomb-damaged capital of Chungking, solving low-level tactical communications systems of the Japanese army. Then, in late 1940, he returned to Washington. He expected to get work codebreaking again, but found himself thwarted at every turn. His old nemesis, Stimson, was now secretary of war, so Yardley found himself killing time by writing up an account of his Chinese experience for the Signal Corps.

It was undoubtedly with relief and gratitude, therefore, that in the first week of May 1941 he received a telephone call asking if he would come to the Canadian legation in the U.S. capital to discuss a possible job for the Canadian government. On arrival, he found that one of his hosts was a University of Toronto mathematician, Gilbert de B. Robinson. Robinson was well aware, as he later wrote, that "Yardley was a man who had blazed a flaming trail across the cryptographic sky." He revealed to Yardley that he had been sent to Washington to explore the possibility of setting up a Canadian cryptographic bureau. For that he needed advice on how to organize and staff an office. Major-General Mauborgne, chief of the U.S. Signal Corps, had strongly recommended Yardley as the man who could establish it for the Canadians. Was he interested? Robinson asked.

Yardley definitely was. Within days he travelled to Ottawa for a preliminary meeting with officials at which he told them what he thought was needed. The next day, May 13, 1941, at 10:00 a.m., in Room 123 of the East Block of the Parliament Buildings, members of the interdepartmental committee on cryptography, a group of highly placed officials who had been pursuing for several months the idea of an independent Canadian operation, met to consider his appointment. All were to play a major role in Canada's wartime intelligence activities, and many continued as players into the postwar years.

Chairman of the committee was Dr. Hugh Keenleyside, who had been an officer of the Department of External Affairs since 1928. Keenleyside was horrified to learn that an earlier attempt to establish a Canadian operation had been rejected on grounds of cost by the chiefs of staff of the armed forces, and he had become the principal driving force behind the initiative to send Robinson to Washington. He pushed hard and successfully for Yardley's appointment.

Also present at the meeting to appoint Yardley was Norman Robertson, the acting under-secretary of state for External Affairs and the man who really ran Canadian foreign policy for Mackenzie King. On security and intelligence matters, Robertson played his cards close to the chest, committing little to paper and informing King only of the bare essentials of what he needed to know. Accompanying him from External Affairs was Thomas Stone, who eventually ended a distinguished diplomatic career as Canadian ambassador to The Hague in the 1960s. A short, heavy-set man with long, thick hair, Stone was a convivial and dynamic figure who had joined Exernal Affairs in 1939. At the time of the meeting about Yardley, he was establishing himself as a key figure in the department, having responsibility for intelligence and security matters such as censorship reports and prisoner-of-war intelligence material.

Joining the diplomats were two military men from the Department of National Defence (DND). Brigadier Maurice Pope represented the Army General Staff. The son of Sir Joseph Pope, the man who had created the Department of External Affairs in 1908, Pope was soon to become vice-chief of the General Staff and then head of Canada's military staff mission in Washington. His colleague from the DND, Lieutenant-Colonel W.W. Murray, represented the Army Intelligence Branch. The final person at the meeting, represented but not personally present, was C.J. Mackenzie. President of the National Research Council and the government's chief scientific adviser, Mackenzie was a powerful and influential figure and had personally suggested Robinson as one of the people to go down to Washington and explore the ground for cryptographic experts.

The five men quickly agreed with Keenleyside that Yardley should be appointed as head of a Canadian cryptographic unit for a six-month experimental period. If, at the end of six months, the enterprise was not considered worthwhile, it would be abandoned. However, if it seemed promising, there would be a good case for getting government support. In the meantime, the project would be secretly funded out of the National Research Council's appropriation.

Foremost in everyone's mind was the need for as few people as possible to know about it. "The project should be one of absolute secrecy," Robertson said. Keenleyside thought that not even the Chiefs of Staff Committee should be told. "Would it be possible to have Major [sic] Yardley employed for six months without anyone knowing he was here?" Robertson asked finally. Murray suggested that Yardley assume a false name, and the others agreed. With that, the meeting closed, and Yardley accepted the job immediately. To disguise the operation, the harmless title of "Examination Unit" was chosen. Mackenzie donated two rooms for the Unit's operations at a new aeronautical laboratory that had recently been built on the outskirts of Ottawa, thus providing it with the necessary cover. It was, one of those who worked there later recalled, "a secret building with no street and no place to go to lunch." The unit operated on the second floor. Beneath it was a wind tunnel, and on the way out a radio station where the messages for decoding were collected. With a small staff of nine, Yardley, assisted by his secretary (and later wife) Edna Ramsaier, quietly got down to work. On Monday, June 9, 1941, the Examination Unit began operations as Canada's first independent codebreaking centre.

Within weeks it became apparent that the Unit's independence was an illusion. The issue that made this clear was Yardley himself. In writing *The American Black Chamber* he had marked himself as an intelligence officer who had betrayed the secrets of the service. One immediate result had been that Japan — where Yardley's book sold even better than in the United States — changed its codes. For this, neither the American nor British professional codebreakers, both concerned about Japan's ambitions in the Pacific and each busily reading its ciphers, could ever forgive Yardley. Nor were they prepared to trust him ever again with their secrets. The British were as determined as the Americans on this score because Yardley had revealed secrets passed on to the United States by British Intelligence in the First World War.

Yardley's notoriety was known to the Canadians involved. But they had mistakenly taken Mauborgne's personal recommendation as a signal that there would be no official objection by Washington to his employment in Ottawa, and were ignorant of the deep hostility to Yardley among leading American codebreakers. The desire to have Yardley enter Canada posing as a simple tourist called Herbert Osborn was to throw the press off the scent, not to conceal his appointment from Canada's friends and allies. Certainly, the device failed to hide Yardley from the notice of British Intelligence. Almost as soon as Yardley arrived in Ottawa, the RCMP was informed by British sources in New York that he was working there under the alias "Osborn."

The first real inklings of trouble came from London in a message from Canadian High Commissioner Vincent Massey to Norman Robertson less than a month after Yardley's appointment. Even before the Examination Unit officially began work, Robertson had asked if Britain could advise on its organization and whether the decrypters at Bletchley Park, the British codebreaking centre, would assist it. They had already been helping to decipher some messages picked up by Canadian intercept stations. The question now was whether this co-operation would continue with Canada's own separate agency. In particular, the Unit needed a regular supply of raw material in the form of intercepts of enemy communications that Canada itself at the time could not provide. There was a Canadian army station at Rockcliffe providing intercepts of *Abwehr* messages between Hamburg and Nazi agents in South America, but coverage was spotty and limited. Navy stations on the west coast were picking up Japanese radio traffic, but the Navy's priorities came first and those of the Unit second. So perhaps Bletchley Park could help fill the gap? "We should also be glad to know," Robertson told Massey, "whether there is any particular field in which our cryptographers could co-operate with those of the United Kingdom or in which these latter could give us any assistance or leads."

London must already have received word of Yardley's move to Ottawa. Although an error in coding Robertson's Most Secret telegram to Massey had transformed his name to "Emeley," the British response was to seek a reassurance that this was not "one Colonel Yardley." On learning that it was, they made it clear that they would not co-operate until he was removed.

What had seemed a triumph in acquiring Yardley was rapidly turning into a disaster. Brought in to solve it and reassure Canada's allies was Lester B. Pearson, for whom this was to be an early exercise in the intricacies of Anglo-Canadian-American diplomacy.

Pearson had just returned from a diplomatic posting at the Canadian High Commission in London, and was now second-in-command to Norman Robertson at External Affairs. Robertson delegated Canada's future prime minister to deal with the crisis. It took several weeks to clear up, but Pearson did a superb job in the circumstances. "I am very much impressed with Pearson's sanity and competence," noted Mackenzie in his diary as the Yardley affair reached its sorry and inevitable conclusion. Neither London nor Washington would co-operate with the Examination Unit until Yardley went, a message reinforced by the drying up of sources that they had previously made available. Soon the writing was on the wall. Thomas Stone told Vincent Massey in September that Yardley would soon be gone. "Co-operation between cryptographic and intelligence officers in Ottawa, Washington, and London is of the highest importance," Stone said. "We propose not to renew arrangements with Yardley." In a painful interview with a bewildered and angry Yardley on November 22, 1941, two days after the British promised to supply a replacement, Pearson gave the famous cryptographer the news. "We had a most unpleasant half-hour," noted Stone, who accompanied Pearson. "Yardley accused us of bringing him up here and picking his brain dry and turning into other hands various new methods of cryptographic problems which he had developed." It was a messy and embarrassing situation all round. So Pearson decided to travel down to Washington to see what more could be learned about American hostility to Yardley, and to consult further with American and British experts in the U.S. capital. On November 27, 1941, just ten days before the Japanese attacked Pearl Harbor, Pearson met with Admiral Noyes, the chief of U.S. Naval Signals. "Noyes was emphatic and categorical," reported Pearson, "that the Navy Department would, as he put it, 'not touch Osborn [Yardley] with a ten-foot pole.' They considered him to be most untrustworthy, most unreliable, and only ordinarily competent. The Admiral said that if he had his way he would put Osborn in jail." Similar opinions were expressed by others.

Pearson's Washington visit merely confirmed Yardley's fate. His continued protests were to no avail. In desperation, he even appealed to Eleanor Roosevelt, but Pearl Harbor intervened. An appeal to New York governor Thomas Dewey mobilized some support, but Dewey ran into a stone wall in his efforts on Yardley's behalf. The author of *The American Black Chamber* and his wife packed their bags and returned to Washington. "It reminded me of Napoleon in Russia," Mrs. Yardley later recalled, "winter, snow, cold defeat. When we went up [to Ottawa] flags were flying and it was warm. We left the External Affairs building in cold depression."

Back in Washington, Yardley did a variety of business and war work, but nothing involving ciphers. In 1956, after he retired, he wrote yet another bestseller, this time on how to win at poker. When he died shortly afterwards of a stroke, he was buried with military honours in Arlington National Cemetery.

Yardley's successor was Oliver Strachey, the English codebreaker promised by Bletchley Park. His arrival in Ottawa symbolized both Britain's commitment to the Canadian effort and Canada's willing surrender of its independence as the price of joining the global signals-intelligence war. Strachey was no mean figure in the cryptographic world. Brother of the famous essayist Lytton Strachey (author of the iconoclastic *Eminent Victorians*), he had worked during the First World War in the British Admiralty's famous codebreaking unit "Room 40," under the legendary Admiral Sir Reginald ("Blinker") Hall. Room 40 was responsible for, among other codebreaking triumphs, the Zimmermann Telegram affair that, in revealing Germany's intentions to launch unrestricted submarine warfare, played such an important part in influencing the United States to join the war against the Germans in 1917. Armed with this experience, Strachey fought the Second World War as a member of the codebreaking team at Bletchley Park. Here he was one of the small group of pioneers who paved the way for the massive and successful onslaught on German codes.

A tall, stooped, bespectacled man with greying hair whose favourite pastime was playing duets with Benjamin Britten on the grand piano in his London flat, Strachey had made his own special contribution to breaking German ciphers. Working closely with Dillwyn ("Dilly") Knox, the mastermind behind the cracking of the German codes encyphered by their Enigma machine, Strachey concentrated on the ciphers used by the *Abwehr* in communicating with its agents in the field, of whom a number were operating in North and South America. These were hand, not machine, ciphers (unlike Enigma ciphers), and the deciphered messages uncovered by Strachey's work became known generally as ISOS (Intelligence Services Oliver Strachey). These *Abwehr* messages were usually highly specific, referring to particular espionage operations and individuals. ISOS, therefore, was super-sensitive, the raw material for the capture and turning of *Abwehr* agents and the linchpin of the so-called Double Cross system in which the Allies recruited double agents and deceived the Germans into thinking they were running a successful network of agents in Britain. As a result, the Allies possessed the crucial weapon in mounting a succession of strategic deception campaigns against Hitler.

Strachey embodied the genius of Bletchley Park and decades of British experience in cryptography. Although he stayed in Canada only a short while, his arrival signified a new start for the Examination Unit. From early 1942 until the end of the war, first under Strachey and then under his successor, F.A. (Tony) Kendrick, another Englishman from Bletchley Park, the Unit emerged as an important and vital member of the allied signals-intelligence family. The links with Bletchley Park grew and strengthened. Promising new arrivals at the Unit, many of them graduates or professors from the universities, were sent to Britain for training in cryptographic methodology. The British codebreakers provided the Unit with considerable raw material to complement the products of Canada's own intercept facilities. Bletchley Park also provided Canadians on occasion with high-grade diplomatic ciphers for their own use.

Settlement of the Yardley débâcle also cleared the way for the War Committee to approve special funds for the Examination Unit on January 28, 1942 — the first time it had officially learned of its existence. For the rest of the war Robertson kept Mackenzie King informed of major developments. He often saw that intercepts of special interest reached King's desk. The prime minister was fascinated by the material, commenting frequently to Robertson on the unique perspectives the reports offered amid the confusion of war. Such was the case with the message Japanese prime minister General Tojo sent to Adolf Hitler at the time of the Normandy landing. Intercepted and deciphered by the Examination Unit, the message conveyed Tojo's best wishes to the Führer and his confidence that he would seize the opportunity to win a brilliant victory.

At the same time, King was desperately concerned that Canada's codebreaking efforts should be kept as secret as possible. In April 1943, for example, Robertson provided him with reports covering the interception of Japanese-Portuguese communications and implicating Spanish officials in espionage work for the Japanese. King's reaction was one of immediate alarm that leaks might reveal Canada's eavesdropping on two neutral states. He instructed Robertson to tighten security surrounding the Examination Unit operations by obtaining a written list of all those who regularly or even occasionally read such reports. In addition, he told Robertson, the departments that received the material should be reminded of the possible consequences of any actions based on such special intelligence. These were so sensitive and involved so many other powers, King said, that the initiative for any reaction should be the monopoly of the Department of External Affairs — of which King himself was the minister.

Later, in 1944, again for reasons of security, King threw his weight fully behind a reorganization of all Canadian intercept operations. The changes grew out of a plan to have Canada establish and operate a special Meteorological Intercept Unit to supply the Allies with Japanese military weather reports that revealed areas of Japanese interest and were thus of major operational value. Tommy Stone of External Affairs, to whom Sir Edward Travis, the director of Bletchley Park, had personally floated the idea at his headquarters the previous September, seized on the idea to further place Canada on the international SIGINT map. It quickly became clear once again that Canada would have to meet stringent Allied security requests. "While Canada is only engaged in certain aspects of the work in highly secret intelligence in a small way, we have nevertheless reached the point at which security considerations are equally as strong as in the United Kingdom and the United States," Stone told Robertson and King in March 1944. "One leak in Canada," he added, "could undo the work of literally hundreds of people in both London and Washington and could actually prolong the war." In the end, work on Japanese meteorological ciphers was taken over by the U.S. Navy, and Stone's plans for greater centralization were put on hold until after the war, when overall authority for SIGINT operations was placed in the hands of Prime Minister King, Defence Minister Claxton, and NRC head C.J. Mackenzie.

The intent of these changes was clear. Canada was becoming more and more involved in the greater Allied intelligence community. To play anything like an equal role in Allied meetings, a national intelligence organization had to speak with one voice and make commitments that would bind all the players at home. Credibility with its allies also meant accountability at the highest level — to the prime minister and the Department of National Defence. "The United Kingdom authorities," noted Stone, "have indicated that they would feel much freer to consult with us at a higher level in matters of such secrecy." Last but not least, reorganization meant that the "need to know" principle operated even within the government. The more senior the directing committee, Stone recommended, the greater would be the authority to request the co-operation of other branches of the services and other agencies of the government without revealing the exact nature of the work being done. "This aspect of security," Stone pointed out, "is becoming more and more important."

By the end of the war, therefore, Canada possessed a centralized signals-intelligence system that was closely linked with those of its allies. So, when most of the staff of the Examination Unit dispersed in summer 1945, it did not mean the end of SIGINT. On the contrary, in some respects it was just the beginning. It was for Gilbert Robinson, the mathematician who had recruited Yardley and who had then been one of the mainstays of the Unit throughout the war, to put the case for peacetime work most clearly. "The world will be a troubled place for a long time to come," he advised Norman Robertson in November 1944, "and there will undoubtedly be countries in whose activities we shall be particularly interested. . . . Canada has been led to a window on world diplomacy which, otherwise, she might never have looked through. Whatever is decided concerning this office, most countries of the world will continue doing cryptographic work after the war is over and I cannot agree that Canada will improve her position in world affairs by renouncing all activity in this work."

The original intent in setting up the Examination Unit had been to crack the ciphers of the Vichy French legation in Ottawa, which had been allowed to continue operating although the Vichy regime in France was pro-German and hostile to Britain. Once operational, the Unit also worked on messages from the French embassy in Washington, work done mostly by Robinson. The reason for Canada's interest was that Mackenzie King and his officials feared attempts by the Vichy French to promote anti-war sentiment in Quebec. Interception of their communications (whether radio, cable, or regular mail) seemed the only way of finding out what was happening. In addition, Vichy messages could reveal important information about events in the French colonies in the Western Hemisphere still under Vichy control, such as St. Pierre and Miquelon and the Caribbean islands of Martinique and Guadeloupe. This was particularly important. The attitudes and behaviour of the French could be crucial in the intensive struggle against German U-boats throughout the western Atlantic in 1942.

For this reason, and because Canada had also sent diplomat Pierre Dupuy to France on several occasions to gather information, the Department of External Affairs insisted on permitting the Vichy legation in Ottawa to function despite intense public pressure to expel the Vichy minister from Canada. "Vichy is a listening post," Norman Robertson told Prime Minister Mackenzie King in May 1942, "where military as well as political information can be obtained on France and the whole of Europe." Although referring to Dupuy's missions to Vichy, Robertson might equally well have had in mind the eavesdropping operations being carried on by the Ottawa codebreakers.

A case in point arose that same month. Off the coast of Martinique, Vichy Admiral Robert commanded a French fleet that had lain at anchor since the fall of France in summer 1940. If it joined with the Germans, it could wreak considerable damage on Allied interests. To prevent this, the U.S. government demanded that all weapons be removed from the ships. In addition, it insisted that all French merchant ships and gold that had been transferred to Martinique should be turned over to the Allies. To block the Americans, the Germans persuaded French prime minister Pierre Laval to instruct Admiral Robert to scuttle the ships. Laval's message was intercepted by the Canadian station at Rockcliffe and deciphered by the Examination Unit. Norman Robertson immediately gave it to the Americans, the first news they had of Laval's orders. In the event, no U.S. measures were needed, as Admiral Robert refused Laval's orders. But the incident illustrated the contribution the Examination Unit could make to the war against Vichy codes.

Another target for Canadian codebreakers was the German *Abwehr* network in South America. Because of favourable atmospheric conditions, the Rockcliffe intercept station could frequently pick up messages between *Abwehr* agents in South America and their headquarters in Hamburg. On special occasions it even intercepted messages from Hamburg to German agents behind Soviet lines on the Eastern Front. Before the Examination Unit was established, Edward Drake, a captain in the Royal Canadian Corps of Signals, had been reading such signals, and his success had made him an active member of the small group that urged the need for a proper Canadian cryptographic bureau. Work on *Abwehr* ciphers continued during the Yardley period. With the arrival of Strachey, an expert on the subject, early in 1942, it was put on a more organized and effective footing.

Canadian interest in *Abwehr* messages related both to national security — the fear that *Abwehr* agents might penetrate Canada — and to a more generalized concern about security in the Western Hemisphere. Nazi agents in South America were particularly interested in Allied supplies and shipping convoys across the Atlantic and between South American ports and the United States. The Examination Unit thus learned a lot from the *Abwehr* traffic about the extent of German knowledge in this area, helping Allied counter-measures and the protection of Allied shipping. Ninety-five percent of early intercepts were concerned with naval information, and were sent on to Washington. The intercepted messages also revealed considerable detail about *Abwehr* networks in South America. They frequently instructed agents on the measures they should take to protect their security. "Destroy all compromising material and abandon broadcasting for your safety's sake," read one typical message from the *Abwehr* to an agent in Argentina.

Throughout 1942 German-agent activity in the Western Hemisphere remained a live concern. Following the North African landings and the German surrender at Stalingrad, however, the codebreakers shifted their gaze to the Pacific and the war against Japan. The Examination Unit finally dropped work on *Abwehr* traffic in January 1943. It was "deficient in interest to Canada," they declared. German spies, in short, were no longer feared.

Japan and the Pacific now consumed most of the codebreakers' efforts until the end of the war. Not surprisingly, given his background, Yardley had established Japanese diplomatic traffic as a major target as soon as he arrived in Ottawa. After Pearl Harbor, the attack on Japanese material intensified. In response to a British request, the Examination Unit added to its list of target messages between Tokyo and undercover Japanese agents, communications that could be easily intercepted from a station that opened in Victoria, British Columbia, in January 1942. Most of it concerned Japanese agents working undercover in South and Central America. To help the codebreakers in

Ottawa, London sent out another of its top experts, Lieutenant-Colonel Stratton of the Radio Security Service (the Radio Security Service, MI8, concentrated on the messages of enemy agents, and was a division within the Government Code and Cypher School [Bletchley Park] working closely with Section V [Counter-Intelligence] of the Secret Intelligence Service), to arrange full-time co-operation. To the Japanese diplomatic and agent traffic, the codebreakers then added Vichy French messages from Indo-China as part of their campaign to open an intelligence window on the Pacific campaign.

The volume and variety of messages relating to the Pacific now became so great that, before the end of 1942, the codebreakers set up a special division within the Examination Unit to deal with it. The job of the Special Intelligence Section was to assess all the incoming intelligence about the Japanese and deliver fully analysed reports to the government for action. Conceived by Tommy Stone as a way of making a unique Canadian contribution to the Allied signals-intelligence war, the Section was headed by the controversial diplomat Herbert Norman.

Norman's career as an alleged Soviet agent will be dealt with later (see Chapter 5). Suffice it to say here that Norman was Canada's leading academic expert on Japan and that he was highly thought of at this time by the Americans and the British. A member of the Canadian legation in Tokyo, he had been interned at the time of Pearl Harbor and was not repatriated to Canada until several months later. In October 1942, shortly after his section was established, he made a secret visit to the United States to establish liaison with William Stephenson, the head of British Security Co-ordination (BSC) in New York, and Allen Dulles, then working for the OSS and later to be director of U.S. Central Intelligence. Stephenson was so impressed that he tried unsuccessfully to lure Norman away from Ottawa to work for him in New York.

Under Norman's leadership, the Special Intelligence Section became the flagship of Canada's codebreaking efforts. Its analyses were useful to the military, as well as to those directing Canadian thinking on postwar Japan. And although small, with a staff of only two officers (one of whom was Arthur Menzies, later Canadian ambassador to China) and three assistants, the Section also undertook special research projects for both the Department of External Affairs and Stephenson's outfit in New York. "During 1943 particularly," records the recently declassified but still censored history of the Examination Unit in commenting on the work of Norman's section, "the reports of Japanese diplomats from Europe and South America were of the greatest value in forming a picture of the progress of the war."

From New York, the BSC kept Ottawa supplied with intelligence material of all kinds. Since speed and security in its handling were paramount, Lester Pearson reached an agreement with Stephenson early in 1942 to establish a direct telekrypton link between the BSC and the Examination Unit. The telekrypton, or TK, was a machine for enciphering and sending telex messages. The first material to be transmitted to Ottawa was the traffic of *Abwehr* agents.

The TK link with BSC New York led to an increase in the exchange of intercept material between Canada and its allies. With exchange came a division of labour.

Britain's request after Pearl Harbor that the Canadian codebreakers switch their concentration to the codes of Japanese agents worried Ottawa. What about the German *Abwehr* material they were being asked to relinquish, they asked London, particularly as some of it might have a direct impact on Canadian national security? The British reassured them by providing a full exchange of the relevant material that was being intercepted elsewhere by British or American operations. Gradually, this became a pattern for all signals intelligence.

Even before Pearl Harbor, the Americans and British had been pooling intelligence data. In spring 1942 the British sent a special mission to North America, under Captain H.R. Sandwith, to rationalize and co-ordinate Allied efforts in signals intelligence. At a special Radio Intelligence Conference in Washington, D.C., that April, American, British, and Canadian experts agreed on distributing radio frequencies for special targeting and the exchange of intercepts from military, naval, air, diplomatic, and commercial sources — a global division of labour. One result was that the United States was given the leading role in breaking codes in the Pacific theatre of war. For Canada, an immediate result was that intercept stations on the west coast became enmeshed in the American network operating out of Seattle. This later provided a minor but graphic example of what joining the Allied community meant for fully independent Canadian actions. When Ottawa tried to lend some of its officers from the west-coast network to the Australians, the Americans refused permission on the grounds that it would be disruptive to the North American operation.

However, Canada was not a completely subordinate partner of its allies or, for that matter, merely a passive consumer of other people's intelligence. Important intelligence achievements of its own provided a bargaining counter that helped it benefit from inter-Allied arrangements. If the codebreaking of the Examination Unit was one example, the work of naval intelligence was another.

Daily battles against U-boats and other German ships in the North Atlantic preserved Allied lifelines and guaranteed ultimate victory. To track the positions and movements of enemy shipping, the monitoring of their wireless communications was vital. Known as "Y" work, it became, along with enemy escort duty, the Canadian navy's greatest contribution to the war. A U-boat tracking room was established in the Operational Intelligence Centre at Naval Headquarters in Ottawa, and by mid-1942 Canadian "Y" experts were in sole charge of covering the western Atlantic. Commander "Jock" de Marbois, the naval reserve officer who more than anyone else deserved credit for creating the Canadian naval "Y" service, noted proudly that "we have now become the best organized Y and DF [direction-finding] Operations Division among our great allies, even far ahead of our grandmother 'the Admiralty.' "

The division of labour that put Canada's "Y" experts in charge of the western Atlantic resulted from the Washington Radio Intelligence Conference. The ties that increasingly bound Canada to the Western intelligence community were drawn tighter as operational practice was formalized in written agreements. By 1943 an effective transatlantic alliance had been forged. In May of that year, at Bletchley Park, the Americans and the British signed a formal pact for full co-operation, the Britain–United States Agreement on Signals Intelligence (BRUSA). It laid out detailed guidelines for operational co-operation on signals intelligence, as well as for the exchange of personnel and the standardization of codewords and terminology. More important, the document spelled out the strict security regulations that were to apply — regulations that neither side could unilaterally modify without running the serious risk that vital intelligence from its ally would suddenly dry up. From this sprang the pressures that led to the tightening centralization of Canadian operations at the end of the war.

Canada was a de facto member of the BRUSA community from the beginning. In January 1943 the principle SIGINT actors in Canada visited Washington to take part in an inter-Allied conference to co-ordinate the interception of various kinds of diplomatic and military traffic. As a result of this meeting, work on *Abwehr* material was discontinued. A year later, in March 1944, Edward Drake, now a lieutenant-colonel in charge of the Discrimination Unit that analysed the frequency and direction of radio communications, travelled down to Virginia to take part in the second Joint Allied Conference on Signals Intelligence held at Arlington Hall, the headquarters of the American codebreakers. One result was greatly improved co-ordination between Drake's Unit and the U.S. Signals Security Agency (SSA), with the latter becoming the co-ordinating centre for this type of work. A few months later Drake noted with satisfaction that, as a result of visits of SSA officers to Ottawa, all unnecessary duplication of work would be eliminated.

Drake's presence at this second major meeting of the BRUSA community not only marked Canada's full participation as a junior partner in the Western SIGINT network, it also illustrated the continuity between war and peace that characterized the history of Western SIGINT.

For all the talk of winding down or even disbanding the Examination Unit, the success of SIGINT in the war against Germany and Japan guaranteed its survival in the Cold War. Other wartime Allied intelligence agencies disappeared, but SIGINT agencies lived on.

In September 1945, President Truman gave his blessing to peace-time U.S. SIGINT operations and the need for "collaborating in the field of communications intelligence between the United States Army and Navy and the British." The decision also included Britain's Commonwealth allies. In Ottawa, top officials discussed the future of Canadian SIGINT operations. At an afternoon meeting on New Year's Eve 1945, Norman Robertson and other top External Affairs officials met with the chief of the general staff, General Charles Foulkes, and C.J. Mackenzie and decided that SIGINT operations would carry on.

The compelling reason was political, best expressed in the words of Foulkes. "The position of Canada," he wrote, "in respect of defence and peace time economy, on the one hand, as a member of the British Commonwealth and, on the other, as an essential economic and military partner of the United States is a paramount political factor. This position . . . indicates the need for Canada sharing the fruits of the intelligence activities of the two other Powers in keeping Canada in their confidence . . . if a pooling of intelligence is in the best interests of Canada, it will be enhanced by Canada's making a contribution to the pool." The choice to head Canada's SIGINT was Edward Drake.

The final step in the formal creation of the Western SIGINT community came in 1948. To prepare the way, Travis organized an imperial SIGINT conference in London over the winter of 1946–47. Drake led a Canadian delegation to Britain and here, along with other Commonwealth countries such as Australia and New Zealand, he laid the foundations for the Commonwealth SIGINT organization, headed by GCHQ, the peacetime successor to Bletchley Park. A year later, in a still classified top-secret agreement, Canada joined with the United States, the United Kingdom, Australia, and New Zealand in signing the so-called UKUSA pact — otherwise known as the U.K.–U.S.A. Security Agreement.

UKUSA outlined spheres of cryptographic influence and divided responsibility among the five participating nations. The United States and the United Kingdom were designated as first parties, and the remainder as second parties. Canada was assigned the task of covering the northern Soviet Union and part of Europe. As in the

BRUSA, considerable attention was paid to uniform security arrangements, the standardization of codewords, and agreed procedures of the handling and distribution of SIGINT material. In 1990, Canada, like all signatories, remains bound by these agreements and regulations. All are detailed in a top-secret handbook, kept constantly updated, entitled *International Regulations on SIGINT*. A year after signing UKUSA, Canada signed the CANUSA agreement, a separate bilateral pact with the United States on signals intelligence. Similar in content to BRUSA, it defined the terms for bilateral exchanges of signals intelligence between the two allies. Canada, it need hardly be added, accepted the role of junior partner in the alliance.

The decision to carry on with Canadian SIGINT after the war owed much to two men. The first was Norman Robertson, who alone was able to convince a reluctant Mackenzie King that such peacetime operations were useful. The second was Igor Gouzenko.

3.
THE MAN WHO STARTED
THE COLD WAR

D uring my residence in Canada," defector Igor Gouzenko wrote in his own hand on October 10, 1945, "I have seen how the Canadian people and their government, sincerely wishing to help the Soviet people, sent supplies to the Soviet Union, collected money for the welfare of the Russian people, sacrificing the lives of their sons in the delivery of these supplies across the ocean — and instead of gratitude for the help rendered, the Soviet government is developing espionage activity in Canada, preparing to deliver a stab in the back to Canada — all this without the knowledge of the Russian people." What this amounted to was "double-faced politics" that endangered "the security of civilization and," he concluded, "I decided to break away from the Soviet regime and to announce my decision openly." Igor Gouzenko signed his name to the statement he had composed in his secret and guarded hiding place, and the young cipher clerk continued telling his story to the security officials interrogating him and working their way through the sheaf of 109 documents he had brought with him from the Soviet embassy when he had defected one month earlier.

Before the dust of the Second World War had barely begun to settle, the Cold War between the Soviet Union and the West had begun. Incredibly enough, Igor Gouzenko's defection, the first of a string of postwar Soviet defections, had begun the new struggle for international domination in Ottawa.

The Soviet Union had no embassy in Canada until Hitler's invasion of the USSR on June 22, 1941 made the two countries allies. Soon after, Moscow sent a trade mission to Canada and, as relations warmed between the two allies, the two nations agreed in June 1942 to open diplomatic relations. There had been some lingering concern in Ottawa that to exchange diplomats might be an invitation to Moscow to use the Communist International, or Comintern, to propagandize in Canada, but those fears were apparently put to rest after Novikov, the counsellor of the USSR embassy in London, told George Ignatieff of Canada's High Commission there that there should be no such worries. According to Ignatieff, Novikov had said "with emphasis that it had been widely believed that Soviet diplomats were agents of the Comintern and were employed in conducting Communist propaganda in countries to which they were accredited. . . . nothing could be further from the truth."

The first diplomats from the USSR soon arrived in Canada. With the establishment of their mission in Ottawa, the Soviets now had in place for the first time the firm base on which they could build the embryo of a spy network.

Of course, the Russians had not been entirely without assets in Canada. The tiny, weak Canadian Communist party, though banned early in the war, was an arm of Moscow that did almost nothing without authorization from its masters, and Sam Carr and Fred Rose, two of its leaders, acted for Soviet intelligence in the country. Joseph Stalin, as British historian Hugh Thomas noted, looked on "foreign parties as intelligence-gathering agencies, or spy recruiters, rather than as institutions to take decisions of their own." Thus, both Rose and Carr had served the NKVD (the precursor of the KGB) for years, both had received payment for their work, and both had reported to Moscow on factionalism within the Canadian party, the activities of Trotskyites and other Communsit dissidents, the attitudes of Russian immigrants and disaffected émigrés in Canada and, when it fell into their hands, occasional information about Canadian public life and military-diplomatic activities. There were, in truth, few reports on the last-named: until the Second World War, Canada had almost no armed forces to speak of and its diplomatic activities, despite its legal autonomy in foreign policy, remained completely unimportant.

The war was changing all that. Canada had raised armed forces of a million men and women; its factories were producing advanced munitions, and its scientists worked on research on radar, high explosives, and the atomic bomb. Canadian diplomats had close links with London and Washington, and they were privy to much of the alliance's secret information. Moreover, Canadian codebreakers and intelligence analysts had begun to unlock the secrets of German and Japanese wireless traffic. For the first time ever, there was secret information in Canada that could interest another country.

The Russians were interested. When the trade mission arrived in Canada in 1942, one of its members was a Major Sokolov. Ostensibly a commercial counsellor with an interest in industrial production, Sokolov in fact was an officer of the GRU, Soviet military intelligence. (Curiously, Major Sokolov's son, Sasha, born in Ottawa in 1944, became well-known in the USSR as a dissident novelist in the 1970s and 1980s. His Canadian birth and Canadian citizenship gave him the right to leave the repressive Soviet Union of the Brezhnev era — and led to his denunciation by his father. After President Gorbachev's *glasnost* policy liberalized Soviet society, Sokolov returned to the USSR with his American wife.) His first task was to meet with Fred Rose and then to secure permission from Moscow Centre to take him and Sam Carr into the GRU net. As the two had been under NKVD control, this required special dispensation from the party's Central Committee, which took time, but was eventually granted, probably because the NKVD assets in Canada were rich enough to withstand the loss of two highly placed members. With Rose's help, Sokolov and his assistant Sergei Kudriavstev recruited the nucleus of a network — three or four people in Ottawa and Toronto and a similar number in Montreal. In August 1943, Rose ran for Parliament under the banner of the Labour-Progressive party, the Communist party's new — and legal — name, and won a Montreal by-election. His new, higher profile was an unexpected benefit.

Two months earlier, the newly named Soviet military attaché, Lieutenant-Colonel Nikolai Zabotin, and his staff had arrived in

Ottawa after an arduous flight across Siberia, Alaska, and northern Canada, followed by a long train ride. Zabotin was an artillery officer, a magnetic personality of intelligence and charm, and he brought with him several officers as well as codes and a cipher clerk, twenty-four-year-old Lieutenant Igor Gouzenko, to handle transmissions to and from Moscow. Before his departure for Canada, Zabotin had been thoroughly briefed on his duties by NKVD headquarters, or Moscow Centre, and by Georgi Malenkov, a senior member of the Politburo. As was usual, his orders were to keep his espionage work secret from the ambassador, who was to see none of his correspondence and never to learn the names of any of his agents. If he uncovered information about Canadian policy that might be of use to the ambassador, then Zabotin was told that he could pass on the information if he carefully protected his sources.

At the same time as Zabotin and his staff were taking over Sokolov's tiny existing networks, the embassy's naval attaché was creating his own small network, based mainly in Canadian port cities. The NKVD was also setting itself up in the embassy and expanding its own existing espionage operations. The NKVD networks, or so Gouzenko later told his interrogators, were likely bigger than the GRU's. The NKVD had its own cipher officer, Farfontov, and he was always much busier coding and decoding than Gouzenko, suggesting a greater volume of information; moreover, the NKVD had more officers in the embassy than did the GRU, a fact that suggests more contact men were necessary to keep in touch with the NKVD's agents. The head of the NKVD operation in Canada was Vitali Pavlov, nominally the second secretary of the embassy. Pavlov was a "really tough guy," as Fred Soward, a wartime External Affairs officer, remembered. After a dinner Pavlov attended with a number of External Affairs officers, Charles Ritchie wrote in his diary that Pavlov was "very cocky and on the offensive — looks like Harpo Marx but with fanatical eyes and a false mouth, nimble-witted and entertaining — the only one from the Embassy who talks freely."

But there was one person with whom Pavlov never talked freely — his colleague Zabotin. The GRU and the NKVD in Moscow were rivals in the collection and dissemination of intelligence, rivals for

Generalissimo Stalin's ear, and so they were in Ottawa, though the responsibility for keeping watch on all the embassy officers rested with Pavlov. Zabotin and Pavlov led their own separate spy nets; no information passed between them; and in telegrams to Moscow, the GRU referred to the NKVD as "the neighbour."

The two competing agencies had to share the embassy's facilities. Although Zabotin occupied a house on Range Road, the chancery, located at 285 Charlotte Street, in a large old mansion, was where both intelligence organizations operated. The embassy had its main public rooms on the ground floor. Secure facilities were on the second floor: secret rooms with steel doors, barred and painted windows, a concealed button under the banister to secure entrance past the ever-present guards, codes held under tight security measures, incinerators for the disposal of classified waste, and photographic equipment. Here in their separate workrooms, the NKVD and GRU cipher clerks did the coding and decoding of the messages Zabotin and Pavlov sent to Moscow (ironically using the Canadian Pacific and Canadian National telegraph for this purpose); here the files were kept secure. In his code room, Room 12, Gouzenko worked, surrounded by safes and secret documents, and under the GRU's rules, he could deny access to the room even to Zabotin if he was in the midst of code work.

The military attaché's men began immediately to expand the networks they had inherited and to set up new ones. This was slow and cautious work, both out of fear of running afoul of Canadian security, however rudimentary and trusting it was in its assumptions that all the Allied powers were working together in a common cause, and because of Moscow Centre's own cautious bureaucratic concerns. Possible recruits were carefully screened by the GRU staff in Ottawa, Moscow was told about them and undertook its own lengthy checks and, if the Centre duly approved, they were enlisted and assigned a Centre-selected codename that was to be employed in all correspondence. This process could take several months. In the embassy, a file card was maintained on each agent, listing name, codename or pseudonym, address, place of work and position, financial condition, and biographical data. Zabotin also kept a secret notebook with more personal comments about his agents.

The GRU's system sometimes assigned leadership roles to Canadians. Fred Rose and Sam Carr, for example, were recruiters of agents, assigners of tasks, and transmitters of information to Zabotin and his officers. Another typical network had been organized by Lieutenant-Colonel Rogov, the assistant air attaché and one of Zabotin's team. His network consisted of four Canadians — Gordon Lunan, an employee of the Wartime Information Board and its successor, the Canadian Information Service; Israel Halperin, a mathematician working on artillery for the Canadian Army Research and Development Establishment; Dornforth Smith, an engineer with the National Research Council; and Ned Mazerall, also of the NRC. Each of the four, even the reluctant Halperin (who appears to have drawn back once he realized the information he was asked to provide was being collected for the Soviet embassy), had been assigned a codename beginning with the letter "B" — respectively, "Back," "Bacon," "Badeau," and "Bagley." Lunan was the leader, the only one in contact with Rogov, and he was the only one in direct touch with the other three, collecting their documents and information. It was a simple system, but one that protected security. Even if a member of the net other than Lunan were caught, he could give the authorities only one name.

By 1945, the GRU's network had seventeen officers and diplomats at the embassy and approximately twenty Canadians in its clandestine employ. Two of the GRU staff posed as trade-mission officers, one was secretary of the embassy, one was a Tass correspondent, one was a translator, two were doormen, and two were chauffeurs; most of the rest were military officers. The GRU officers ran the networks; directed the Canadians, most of whom were civil servants or military officers in sensitive positions; and served as "go-betweens," picking up documents, photographing and translating them, and passing them on to Moscow, usually by the diplomatic bag for bulky materials or by wireless for urgent matters.

As was the case for every bureaucratic organization in every country, the GRU and NKVD in Ottawa were subject to inspections from head office. In mid-1945, two inspectors arrived in the guise of diplomatic couriers: "Mikhail Milsky," or Milstein, the deputy to the head of the GRU, and Grigori Kosarev, a senior official of the NKVD. The two were pleased with the work that Zabotin and Pavlov had accomplished in Canada, so much so that Milsky telegraphed Moscow to that effect, and the GRU inspector even met with Sam Carr, then involved in a scheme to secure Canadian passports for Soviet agents. And more NKVD and GRU agents were coming. In August 1945, Zabotin told the Department of External Affairs of his plans for a major expansion of the Soviet trade mission from fifty to ninety-seven officials and for the establishment of an office in Montreal. Events, however, were to intervene to cut short Zabotin's plans — and his life.

When Lieutenant Igor Gouzenko left the Charlotte Street building at 8:30 p.m. on Wednesday, September 5, 1945, taking with him a sheaf of documents, he knew that his evidence would expose the operations of the GRU's spy network in Canada. He also expected that the Canadian government would immediately take him to its bosom and protect his family. Initially, the government reaction was very different.

Astonishingly, the cipher clerk, perhaps because he was so clearly agitated and because he spoke broken English with a thick accent, met only complete indifference when he tried desperately to persuade Canadian journalists and officials to believe that he had critical information and that he would be killed if his embassy caught up with him. At the *Ottawa Journal*, his first port of call, the staff sent him away, telling him to come back in the morning. The scoop of the century had been sent packing. At the Department of Justice on Wellington Street, where he went next, everyone in authority had gone home hours before, and the by-now panicky Gouzenko returned to his apartment at 511 Somerset Street, knowing that he would have to persuade his pregnant wife, Svetlana, that the decision they had jointly made to defect was still the right one.

In September 1945, Igor Gouzenko was twenty-six, a blond, good-looking man of high intelligence who had been born in Rogachovo, near Moscow, while Lenin's Russia was in chaos and in the throes of civil war. His father, killed on service with the Red Army during the civil war, had been an accountant; his mother was the well-educated daughter of bourgeois parents. Gouzenko, the third son and youngest of four children, received his early education in Rostov-on-Don and in Moscow, studied drawing for a year, and then entered the Architectural Institute of the University of Moscow where he met the then-beautiful Svetlana, soon to be his wife. The German invasion interrupted Gouzenko's studies, prevented him from taking up a major fellowship, and put him in the Red Army. By 1942 he was a cipher clerk in the Moscow headquarters of the GRU, where he worked until his 1943 posting to Ottawa.

It was life in Ottawa that persuaded the young and idealistic Gouzenkos that there was something terribly wrong with the Soviet system. The material comforts that Canadians took for granted, even with housing scarce and food and fuel rationed during wartime, stunned the two Soviets who had long been accustomed to peacetime privation, shortages of food, and few luxuries. So, too, did the freedom of speech that Canadians had, not to mention their vigorous elections. The federal campaign of 1945, for example, came as a revelation to Gouzenko. And the young officer was appalled by the oppressive, secretive atmosphere within his embassy, by the casual talk about the inevitability of war between the USSR and the West, and by the spying run from the embassy on the Canadians who, Gouzenko genuinely believed, wanted nothing more than an end to the bloodletting of the Second World War. But the cipher clerk said nothing about his feelings — "nobody had any chance to accuse me of any political weakness which is considered a grievous crime," he said later. Then Moscow sent orders for the Gouzenkos to return to the Soviet Union, apparently because the young officer had committed a minor breach of document security. In any other nation, such recall orders were a regular occurrence, even for cipher clerks; in the GRU, however, recall orders could also mean severe punishment, or even death. The Gouzenkos decided not to take the chance.

Their decision to defect was not made lightly. Gouzenko and his wife realized the consequences that would certainly fall upon them if they failed; they knew what would happen to their relatives in the USSR if they succeeded. (As Gouzenko told Arnold

Smith, an External Affairs officer with service in the USSR, who questioned him on February 16, 1946, he expected the NKVD to try to murder him — "It is vital for them to give a lesson to others who might think of following my example." He added: "It was not easy for me to sacrifice my mother and sister," and Smith agreed that it was likely they had already been shot or deported to the Gulag.) But how could the Gouzenkos ensure that the Canadians would welcome them? Shrewdly, Gouzenko realized that the telegrams and files he saw every day were the key to his reception, and he prepared carefully for the break, selecting the most important and revelatory telegrams to Moscow and documents written by Canadian agents, from the green canvas sack in which they were kept in the safe in Room 12. As he said later, "During the course of about half a month I examined the materials so as to select the best ones that would disclose the operative work, leaving the informational telegrams on one side. . . . The telegrams which I wished to take out I marked by bending over slightly one of the corners, so it would not be noticed by Colonel Zabotin . . . when I finally decided to take the documents I would lose no time. . . . I could take them out . . . in two or three minutes."

His preparations had been clever and thorough. But, so far, he had failed completely to get anyone in authority in Ottawa to take him seriously.

The next morning, September 6, the two Gouzenkos, this time with their young son, tried again. Once more, the Minister of Justice's aides sent him away; so, too, did the editors of the *Journal*, again passing up the story of all stories; officials at the Ottawa Magistrate's Court were more helpful but no more successful in getting anyone to believe the Gouzenkos' story. Then, literally shaking with fear, Igor and Svetlana returned to their apartment on Somerset Street, where they soon realized with mounting horror that two men were watching their flat from a park across the road.

In fact, Gouzenko's pleas for asylum had roused a hitherto unsuspecting and somnolent Canadian government, if not yet to the realization of Soviet espionage, then at least to the fact that Gouzenko was a problem. Within thirty minutes of Gouzenko's second visit to the Justice department, Norman Robertson and Hume Wrong, the two senior officials of the Department of External Affairs, went to see Prime Minister Mackenzie King. As King wrote, "Robertson said to me that a most terrible thing had happened . . . that this morning . . . a man had turned up with his wife at the office of the Minister of Justice. . . . He said he was from the Russian Embassy. That he was threatened with deportation and that once he was deported that would mean certain death. That the Russian democracy was different from ours." King also learned that the Russian had documents taken from the embassy vaults. Robertson thought the documents might be so important that they should be seized and examined, even if they had been stolen. But the prime minister, a politician who had made a career out of caution, did not want the Canadian government to do anything that might cause repercussions in the diplomatic negotiations then underway between the victorious Allied powers. In fact, King even contemplated with a certain equanimity the possibility that the defector might commit suicide: "If suicide took place," King wrote, "let the city police take charge . . . but on no account let us take the initiative."

By chance, however, William Stephenson, the Canadian-born head of British Security Co-ordination (BSC) in New York, was at the Seigniory Club in Montebello, Quebec, close by the capital. Robertson and Stephenson had worked closely together during the war, and it was natural for the Canadian official to consult Stephenson about Gouzenko; it was also no surprise that Stephenson's advice was, "Get your man at once" along with his documents. While the bureaucrats and politicians decided what they would do, two officers were sent to watch over the Gouzenkos' apartment building.

That was just as well, for Vitali Pavlov of the NKVD soon came to call. By the night of September 6, Gouzenko's absence and the fact that documents were missing had been noted by Colonel Zabotin, who was soon in a panic. The colonel knew the implications for his career — indeed, for his life — of a defection by one of his staff. The immediate result was that Pavlov, whose own well-being was just as threatened, took over the case.

Fortunately, for Gouzenko, he and his family had sought the assistance of Canadian neighbours and were sheltering in another apartment in the building. Even before Pavlov and his colleagues beat on the Gouzenkos' door and then kicked it in, one of those neighbours, an RCAF sergeant named Maine, had sent for the Ottawa police, who confronted the NKVD men in the Gouzenkos' apartment. The police called the RCMP, and by the middle of the night, the Gouzenkos were in safe hands, giving a statement to the RCMP. The documents were soon being translated.

That evening, the Canadian government had begun to realize just what it had on its hands. Robertson saw the prime minister and told him

> that everything was much worse than we would have believed. . . .
> [The documents] disclose an espionage system on a large scale.
> He said it went lengths that we could not have believed. Not only
> had [U.S. Secretary of State] Stettinius been surrounded by spies,
> etc., and the Russian government had been kept informed of all
> that was being done from that source, but that things came right
> into our country to a degree we could not have believed possible.
> He then told me that they went into our own Dept. of External
> Affairs, that in the cypher room there was an agent of the Russians
> who had seen and knew all our cyphers. . . . The same was true
> at Earnscliffe [the British High Commission]. In the cypher room
> at Earnscliffe [High Commissioner] M[alcolm]. MacDonald's
> despatches were all seen, read and known. In our Research
> Laboratories here at Ottawa, where we had been working on the
> atomic bomb there is a scientist who is a Russian agent. In the
> Research Laboratories in Montreal . . . there is an English scientist
> who is pro-Russian and acting as a Russian agent.°

The Soviet net had been widely cast, and the Russians' interest in atomic research, having been exposed just one month after the bombing of Hiroshima and Nagasaki, stood out like a sore thumb.

°External Affairs later concluded that Emma Woikin, the Soviet agent in the department's code room, had not passed secrets of Canada's "Typex" system to her masters. "Apparently Mrs. Woikin's interest was solely in the actual typed result from the machines and not in the various Tables used to arrive at such result," or so the under-secretary was told on March 23, 1946.

Some of the information that the "atomic scientist," quickly identified as British nuclear physicist Alan Nunn May, had at his disposal was considered very valuable.

By this point, Mackenzie King had changed his mind about Gouzenko: "I said I felt that at all costs we must not let him come into the hands of the Embassy people." Gouzenko and his family soon were housed and guarded at Camp X, the training base and communications centre near Whitby, Ontario, used during the war by William Stephenson's BSC.

The RCMP was neither equipped nor trained to handle a major spy case such as that revealed by Gouzenko's materials. The Mounties, George Glazebrook of the Department of External Affairs said later, "didn't know what the hell to do." The British did, however. The year before the permanent under-secretary at the Foreign Office, Sir Alexander Cadogan, had told Prime Minister Churchill that "we are weeding out remorselessly every single known Communist from all our secret organisations. . . . We did this after having had to sentence two quite high grade people to long terms of penal servitude for their betrayal, in accordance with Communist faith, of important military secrets." The British were soon called in, Peter Dwyer and Jean-Paul Evans being sent to assist from British Security Co-ordination headquarters in New York and from Washington. Moreover, as the communications through External Affairs and the British High Commission were compromised, recourse was had to BSC, which provided a telekrypton ciphering machine of its own and specially trained Wrens to operate it. The FBI also sent the head of its Communist desk to Canada at Ottawa's request. At the same time, Malcolm MacDonald was told of the spy in his office and word was passed to the American ambassador.

As that suggested, the international ramifications of the "Corby" affair — so-called because Norman Robertson kept the documents relating to Gouzenko out of his department's filing system and in a Corby's whiskey case in his office — soon came to dominate the prime minister's thinking. Naïvely, King assumed that Soviet spying would be as great a shock to the British and Americans as it was to him. More shrewdly, he feared that precipitate action by his government against the Soviet espionage networks could have implications not just on Canada–USSR relations, but also on those between the Soviets and Canada's senior partners. By the end of September, therefore, King had journeyed to Washington to brief President Harry Truman on the affair, and early the next month, he and Norman Robertson went to London to meet with Prime Minister Clement Attlee and officers of MI5 and MI6. Attlee and his colleagues were very keen to arrest Nunn May, the nuclear physicist implicated in the spy ring, but King persuaded Attlee to delay action until after a mid-November meeting in Washington between the American, British, and Canadian (or "ABC") leaders on atomic energy would allow a chance for their officials to discuss the proper way to proceed.

The result of those discussions was a tripartite agreement on the procedure for dealing with the "Corby" case. The wartime allies agreed that, while Soviet espionage could not be tolerated, they did not want their action to disturb "the continuance of normal diplomatic relations with the U.S.S.R.," especially as vital discussions on the future of Germany were then underway. The intent, as Hume Wrong of External Affairs later noted, was "a surgical operation" against the spying in Canada, and the U.S. and U.K. ramifications of it that would not impair "an effort to reestablish working relations." Nor did the ABC discussants want the Russians or anyone else to be able to claim that "counter-action has been taken for ideological reasons." The plan called for action against those suspected in the week of November 25, 1945 in all three countries. "In the first place, it should consist of the interrogation of agents, accompanied when legal power exists and this is considered desirable, by temporary detention." Then prosecution should follow. In Canada, the agreement noted, an *in camera* royal commission might also be set up. Such an enquiry was the method preferred by both Justice minister Louis St. Laurent and the RCMP.

But the American FBI was not yet ready to move. The Soviet networks there were bigger and more highly placed than had been feared — "The information is so grave," the RCMP commissioner told the prime minister, "that Mr. Hoover . . . has instructed the F.B.I to concentrate all their activities on this case" — and more time was needed to unravel them. Thus November 25 came and went. In fact, it was not until February 4, 1946, that action was finally forced on Ottawa. That night, American radio and newspaper columnist Drew Pearson told his audience of a vast Soviet spy network in Ottawa. Pearson's source may well have been the BSC's Stephenson or, more likely still, FBI director J. Edgar Hoover, both men apparently fearing that the Canadians might allow this opportunity to expose Soviet espionage to slip away. The next day, Mackenzie King told his astonished Cabinet for the first time of the evidence revealed by the "Corby" case, and he read his ministers an order-in-council naming Robert Taschereau and R.L. Kellock, two justices of the Supreme Court of Canada, to be royal commissioners to take evidence. The justices were to begin their work the next day.

For a week, Taschereau and Kellock reviewed the evidence brought by Gouzenko *in camera*. On February 13, they took evidence from Gouzenko himself in a long session, the Russian proving a most impressive witness, with full recall of names, dates, and events. The next day, the royal commissioners advised the government that the arrests of some of those named in the documents and evidence were justified, the Cabinet was consulted and formally agreed, and the RCMP knocked on the doors of twelve men and women at 7:00 a.m. on Friday, February 15. The police had initially intended to make their swoop in the middle of the night, but as King's private secretary, Jack Pickersgill, recollected, Norman Robertson persuaded the Mounties that "we are not going to behave like the Soviets" — a more civilized hour would look better to the world. Among those picked up were Dr. Raymond Boyer, an explosives expert with the National Research Council; Emma Woikin, an External Affairs code clerk; Scott Benning, an official in the Department of Munitions and Supply; Kay Willsher of the British High Commission; and Gordon Lunan, an army officer seconded to the Wartime Information Board. More arrests followed as the royal commission heard further evidence.

The same day, the prime minister issued a statement on the affair, giving the public its first inkling of what had happened. The Soviet Union's attachés and diplomats were nowhere named as the guilty parties, but press speculation quickly focused on them. Five days later, Moscow admitted that "certain members of the staff of the Soviet Military Attaché in Canada received, from Canadian nationals with whom they were acquainted, certain information of a secret character." That was an almost unprecedented admission of guilt — though the Moscow statement ludicrously suggested that the secret information acquired in Canada was virtually worthless "in view of more advanced technical attainment in the U.S.S.R."

Moscow's statement also noted that Colonel Zabotin had been recalled because of the incident. In fact, the military attaché had left Ottawa in December 1945, secretly and without the usual courtesies being shown to his host government. Zabotin was never heard from again; one report had it that he jumped overboard from the ship returning him to the Soviet Union, another that he died of "heart failure" shortly after his arrival in Moscow. For its part, Ottawa served expulsion orders on the members of Zabotin's staff who were implicated in the affair. The ambassador, however, was allowed to remain, the Canadian government concluding that he was not involved in the spy rings.

Public attention focused on those Canadians who were involved as the royal commission released, first, preliminary reports and, in July 1946, a very thick final report. Names, dates, and activities were set out in detail, the commissioners going fully into the ways and means by which Canadians had broken their oaths as civil servants and military officers to pass secret information to a foreign power. A few, the commissioners observed, were interested in the small sums the Soviets paid them; more were ideologically committed Communists who owed their first allegiance to the party; still others were Jews, appalled by North American anti-Semitism and somehow fooling themselves into believing that the USSR, which had played so great a role in destroying Nazism, must be different; one or two were of Russian origin; and one or two were simply lonely people who had joined Communist study groups in the hopes of meeting friends and had been drawn into espionage almost without knowing why or how it had happened.

The commissioners, their report largely drafted by Arnold Smith of External Affairs, who had formed a very dark view of Stalinist aims during his posting at the Canadian Embassy in Moscow, took the occasion to warn Canadians and the West generally of the dangers of Communist entrapment. Certainly that was there. But what was even more striking was the normalcy of those who had been caught — they were plain unvarnished Canadians, no brighter, no more stupid, than most of their countrymen.

Perhaps it was this fact that helped shape the Canadian response. After the first shock had worn off, the press and the Opposition parties turned their attention to the extraordinary, but completely legal, procedures employed by the royal commission. Many of those accused of spying had been denied the most basic civil liberties: most were held incommunicado for long periods — to keep them from getting orders not to talk, officials admitted — and put before the commissioners without legal counsel; many, badgered by the inquiry's lawyers, confessed quickly and found their testimony used against them in subsequent trials; others, tougher-minded, simply refused to tell Justices Kellock and Taschereau anything other than their names, and they were almost all acquitted for lack of evidence. The simple truth was that, beyond Gouzenko's documents and their own confessions, there was little hard evidence against those who were accused of spying. None of the spies had been caught in the act, and the embassy documents were stolen materials and, some lawyers believed, of doubtful legal validity. As a result, only eleven of the major figures named in the royal commission report were found guilty after all legal proceedings had concluded; seven of those named were acquitted. The guilty, whose sentences ranged from two years' to ten years' imprisonment, included Fred Rose, the MP whose arrest might have posed knotty legal problems had he tried to hole up in the Parliament Buildings and claimed his privileges as a Member, Raymond Boyer, Gordon Lunan, Alan Nunn May (who was tried in Britain), Kay Willsher, and Emma Woikin. One of those named in the royal commission report, Freda Linton, secretary to film-maker John Grierson who headed the Wartime Information Board, and mistress of Fred Rose, fled before she could be arrested. Sam Carr, who had escaped to the United States, was not caught until 1949, and was then tried and convicted in Canada. It should also be remembered that only the GRU network was cracked by Gouzenko's defection; the

NKVD's "powerful organization in Canada," or so the royal commission report described it, remained untouched. And in 1989, a Soviet author, Stanislav Pestov, bragged in the Moscow press that highly placed Canadians in the Department of National Defence, Parliament, and "research circles" were never uncovered.

The impact of the whole Gouzenko affair was substantial in creating the atmosphere of crisis, betrayal, and fear that heralded the coming of the Cold War. In the United States, the case created a hullabaloo of major proportions that played directly into the hands of those who wanted their government to take a hard line against domestic and foreign communists. In Britain, the Attlee government ordered the purchase of 4,400 copies of the report for distribution to officials and for public sale. The Foreign Office's "Russia Committee" considered it in detail, and London drew implications for its own internal security from the Ottawa experience. And in Canada, the age of innocence ended. Canadian perceptions of the Soviet Union swung round quickly, and the public-opinion polls registered the sea change in attitude. During the war, a majority of Canadians had expressed the belief that the Soviets could be trusted to "cooperate" with the West; after the Gouzenko affair, however, larger numbers now thought the Soviet Union sought world domination. The Cold War had come to Canada with a vengeance; to a substantial extent, the Cold War had *begun* in Canada.

Gouzenko's documents and the knowledge of Soviet codes that he brought with him from the Charlotte Street embassy obviously had major implications for Canada and its senior partners, and the ripples from the wave the Soviet cipher clerk started in Ottawa have not yet disappeared in London or Washington.

The immediate ramifications were British. Gouzenko's documents pinpointed Alan Nunn May, who had worked in Canada on research on the atomic bomb intimately linked with that underway in the United States. Indeed, Nunn May had visited the Chicago research laboratories three times in 1944, and he had passed to his GRU control a small sample of enriched uranium. The scientist was allowed to return to England, his voyage arranged before the Gouzenko defection. He was watched for a while, then questioned initially on February 15, 1946, and he soon confessed. His trial lasted one day, and he was convicted and sentenced to ten years' imprisonment.

For the United States, Gouzenko's documents provided little direct information. Much more important was what the defector said in his debriefing. As Prime Minister King put it to President Harry Truman on his brief visit to Washington on September 30, 1945, Gouzenko had told his interrogators that "an assistant secretary of the Secretary of State's Department was supposed to be implicated."

In fact, two American officials were implicated — Harry Dexter White, a brilliant economist who was assistant secretary of the Treasury, and Alger Hiss, who had been assistant to the assistant secretary of state, then special assistant to the director of the Office of Far Eastern Affairs, then special assistant to the director of the Office of Special Political Affairs, and finally director of that office.

Gouzenko's sources for his fingerpointing were evidently conversations in Moscow and in the Ottawa embassy, most notably with a Lieutenant Kulakov who had arrived in Ottawa as Gouzenko's replacement — incredibly, GRU and NKVD agents apparently gossiped about the identities of their high-placed sources just as teenagers trade tales of unrequited love and spurned passion. In fact, the Truman administration had received some confirmatory information about White from FBI investigations and from the revelations of Elizabeth Bentley, a one-time courier for a Soviet espionage ring who had told all to the FBI. An investigation of Hiss was soon begun, and it too produced some confirmatory information which was presented to the president on November 8. Perhaps out of fear of the political consequences or perhaps because the circumstantial evidence was thought to be unlikely to stand up in court, the Truman administration chose not to prosecute White and Hiss; instead both were allowed to find employment outside the government, White as a member of the board of executive directors of the International Monetary Fund, an organization he had been instrumental in creating, and Hiss as president of the Carnegie Endowment for International Peace. Hiss later was named by journalist and former communist Whittaker Chambers as a Communist party member and as a Soviet agent, and the subsequent investigations and perjury trials riveted Americans for decades — and made the career of a hitherto unknown California congressman named Richard M. Nixon. Although he was found guilty and served time in prison, Alger Hiss still stoutly maintains his innocence. Apparently, Harry Dexter White was never directly confronted with the suspicions about his role before his death in 1948.

There was one other important, indeed absolutely vital, aspect of the American side of the Gouzenko case. Though nothing whatsoever has been said publicly to this point, the defecting cipher clerk's knowledge of Soviet codes, cryptonyms, and techniques proved invaluable to Western cryptanalysts. The telegrams and documents he brought from the embassy were extremely useful in unravelling GRU codes; some believe that Gouzenko also brought codebooks with him, something that would have been entirely logical for the very intelligent defector who had prepared so carefully.

Where there remained deciphering difficulties, Gouzenko could and did advise on how they might be overcome. When what Gouzenko knew was added to other sources, including intercepted Soviet diplomatic traffic and a Soviet codebook captured by the Finns in the Winter War of 1939, then Western intelligence services had a bonanza — and the Soviets, as British defector Kim Philby later admitted, suffered a "disaster."

One aspect of that disaster was what Gouzenko knew about Operation "Candy," the crash NKVD–GRU effort to discover everything possible about the Manhattan Project, the Americans' atom bomb venture. "Candy" had been a great success, a brilliant intelligence coup. The weakness of the operation was that some information had to be transmitted to Moscow by radio and in code. Like most secret services, the Russians believed their codes to be unbreakable. So they had hitherto proven. But Gouzenko had accelerated the process of unwrapping "Candy," and his information on ciphers helped the FBI uncover the American spy rings. The codebreakers in Washington unravelled cryptonyms in telegrams by cross-checking on the information passed to Moscow by the spies, and the trail eventually led to a couple named Julius and Ethel Rosenberg in New York City.

The Rosenbergs' execution for treason in 1953 was a major cause célèbre of the Cold War, and their defenders to this day persist in believing that the two were framed. They weren't, although the FBI played fast and loose with the law and the whole business reeked of anti-Semitism. In a very real sense, the uncovering of the Rosenbergs' treason can be traced back to the information an obscure GRU cipher clerk carried out of the Soviet embassy in Ottawa in September 1945, both in his hands and in his head.

The ripples from Gouzenko's defection made as major an impact on the British, though it took far longer for the outlines of the story, if not yet its ultimate truth, to become known. The origins, however, are clear. Gouzenko's documents contained references to a spy whose cryptonym was "Elli," subsequently identified as Kay Willsher, who worked in the Ottawa High Commission. But Gouzenko also told his debriefers that he had seen a telegram either at GRU headquarters in Moscow or in the embassy in Ottawa (the sources are contradictory) that referred to a spy with the same cryptonym working in London. He said that he had confirmed this in a conversation with a fellow GRU cipher clerk in Moscow, Lieutenant Lev Lubimov, who had handled the radio traffic of the mole and who had told him that the spy "has something Russian in his background."

Gouzenko said much the same thing to the royal commission. Commission counsel E.K. Williams asked him if he knew "whether Elli was used as a nickname or cover name for any person other than Miss Willsher?" "Yes. There is some agent under the same name in Great Britain." "Do you know who it is?" the counsel asked. "No." The next day one of the commissioners returned to this point, and Gouzenko's testimony was again the same. Six years later, in a memorandum he wrote for the RCMP, Gouzenko (who had been given citizenship, a new identity, and the chance for a new life in Canada after his appearances before the royal commission) expanded on his 1945 and 1946 evidence. Now he was certain that the mole was not just in London, but in MI5. Whether this was correct remains unclear. Like many other subsequent defectors, Gouzenko was interested in "spinning" — providing ever-new information to keep the security services happy and to keep their limelight focused on him. In fact, he may have suffered from what has come to be known as "defector syndrome," a combination of resentment, paranoia, and self-righteousness. The embellishing of the record and the recollection of facts that he had totally omitted or glossed over in his first interrogations, as well as Gouzenko's notorious willingness to sue those who wrote about him unfavourably, might well have been part of this.

But Gouzenko still had the power to set the public, press, and security services a-twittering, and most especially in Britain where his stories of Soviet spies in the Secret Intelligence Service caused an enormous ruckus in the early 1980s.

What has been largely forgotten, however, is that there was British involvement in the Gouzenko case from the very beginning. The RCMP had called for assistance and, because Cyril Mills, the MI5 representative in Ottawa, was on his way back to England, London had notified its nearest available officer, Peter Dwyer, late of BSC but now an MI6 representative in Washington who was also temporarily wearing the MI5 hat in the American capital (MI5 handles Britain's domestic security, MI6 foreign security). Dwyer and another officer, Jean-Paul Evans of British Security Co-ordination, came to Canada on Sunday, September 9, to work on the case and to assist in Gouzenko's interrogation. Apparently, or so Evans said and wrote in his private memorandum of his involvement in the affair, neither man saw Gouzenko face-to-face, their questions being passed to the defector. Nonetheless, it was in response to Dwyer that Gouzenko apparently first mentioned the existence of the second "Elli." MI6 in London would normally have handled the British end of the Gouzenko defection but, according to some accounts, Kim Philby, the head of its Section IX, the Soviet department, was busily involved in handling another Soviet defection in Turkey. Others suggest that Philby could have gone to Ottawa, the Turkish case not arising until September 19; instead he chose to stay in London where he could better track the Western response to Gouzenko. Thus, Philby received from his superiors authority to pass the file to his counterpart in MI5, Roger Hollis, the director of "F" division. Hollis promptly came to Canada and saw Gouzenko briefly in the company of an RCMP officer. Hollis was not impressed with Gouzenko the man or with the information he was providing, or so his report to London, submitted on his return, evidently suggested. The British secret services, perhaps in consequence of Hollis's report, did not press the search for "Elli" in MI5.

There should be no suggestion that Hollis suppressed the information Gouzenko had given. Even if he had wanted to, this would have been beyond him. The reason is twofold: first, Peter Dwyer was on the spot in Ottawa and passing information back to London as it emerged; and, second, Mackenzie King went to Britain in October 1945 to discuss the Gouzenko case with the British government. Certainly, Hollis was much in evidence on that trip, the MI5 officer even meeting the prime minister when his liner first docked at Southampton. But in King's party was Norman Robertson, the under-secretary of state for External Affairs and, as we have seen, one of the major figures in handling the Gouzenko case. Robertson spent substantial time discussing the Gouzenko case in various meetings that included, among others, the directors general of MI5 and MI6, personally briefing them on the ramifications of the case. The one memorandum of October 8, all that appears to exist in the available Canadian records, makes no mention of a Soviet mole in MI5, though it does refer to MI5's eagerness to proceed to arrests. Nonetheless, it is scarcely credible that Robertson would not have referred to Gouzenko's evidence about a mole in MI5. If no notice was taken of the defector's evidence, therefore, the blame for that cannot rest on Hollis alone.

All of this became important years later. In 1951, Guy Burgess and Donald Maclean of the Foreign Office defected to the USSR. Both had been Cambridge undergraduates in the 1930s and their treason spread doubt within the ranks of the British Establishment and concern in MI5 and MI6, not to say in the American and other Allied intelligence agencies. Who had tipped off the two and warned them to flee? In the late 1950s, suspicion that he had done the job and that he was a Soviet spy fell on Kim Philby, another Cambridge man. The security services questioned Philby inconclusively, then shunted him off to Beirut where he worked as a journalist. Philby eventually defected to the USSR, cheerfully admitted that he had been a long-term mole, and became a high-ranking officer in the KGB. The damage he had done was incalculable.

Were there still more moles to be uncovered? Numbers of journalists and spywatchers thought so and wrote about them in books that continued to appear throughout the 1970s and 1980s — names like Sir Anthony Blunt, Roger Hollis, and Charles Ellis were thrown around, public accusations and denials issued, and still more books written.

None of the books, none of the revelations, could definitively determine who was the mole, if indeed anyone was, in the British secret services. Unless they are caught in the act or confess, spies can rarely be definitively uncovered. And with Blunt, Hollis, and Ellis dead and buried, no such final answer will be reached unless the Soviet archives are opened to research. The real point, however, is the way in which Igor Gouzenko's revelations of September 1945 have continued to reverberate. In the labyrinthine world of espionage, spies and defectors may die, but the echoes of their doings ring long after them.

For Canadians, the Gouzenko affair had its most important implications in Ottawa. The day the news of Soviet espionage became public, Norman Robertson attended a dinner with a number of British officials in Ottawa to negotiate another huge loan from the Canadian government. "Norman was quite grave on the consequences of finding that public servants could have a split loyalty to their country and to the C[ommunist] P[arty]," one of the visitors wrote back to England. Another senior officer in External Affairs, Escott Reid, was just as blunt. "We are now up against an ideological conflict without parallel since Elizabethan times," Reid told a friend. "The Communists today are the papists of the last half of the seventeenth century. . . . You have citizens who give an allegiance elsewhere and your normal system of justice and individual rights breaks down."

Those two comments encapsulated the problem in which the federal government found itself. During the Second World War, Ottawa had operated on the perfectly correct assumption that the entire public service was of one mind on the need to defeat the Axis powers. Security had, of course, functioned on a need-to-know basis, but it was generally not heavy-handed, as virtually everyone's loyalty never seemed to be in doubt. But Gouzenko's documents had demonstrated that some military officers and civil servants could simultaneously serve Canada and another power. That was a wholly new idea in Canada and in the Canadian public service.

In May 1946, a few weeks before the royal commission issued its final report on the Gouzenko case, the country's new security machinery was in gestation. Robertson had played a key role in its design, his set-up closely resembling that existing in Britain. After consulting with George Glazebrook and others in his department, Robertson had proposed that an advisory interdepartmental committee, soon to be named the Security Panel, be established in the Privy Council Office, be given a permanent secretariat and chaired by the secretary to the Cabinet, Arnold Heeney. The Cabinet Defence Committee accepted this on May 4 and instructed the Security Panel to "advise on the coordination of the planning, organization and execution of security measures which affect government departments." For the first time in Canada, efforts would begin to shape a security policy.

Very quickly, the Security Panel produced a guidebook on security for departments. It began at once to wrestle with the thorny problem of "vetting" public servants — considering "security measures which would be practical to prevent the infiltration into positions of trust under the government of persons likely to commit acts such as those in the [royal commission] Report." Before the end of 1946, the Security Panel had recommended that the RCMP, which had been collecting information on left-wing elements since the First World War, act as the agency to investigate the "antecedents of applicants for government employment to determine their suitability from a security point of view." The Cabinet approved this recommendation in January 1947.

The bureaucrats making these policies were not insensitive men. Nor were they anti-communist fanatics. Instead, they were all too aware that Gouzenko's documents had revealed a situation that had to be dealt with. Ideology evidently could make men betray their oaths to Canada and that was a problem to be faced. G.G. Crean in External Affairs, for example, wrote to the under-secretary in

September 1946 of his concerns: "As the subject is one which is likely to cause considerable public feeling if it becomes known that the Government has laid down, as a matter of policy, that persons in certain categories should be vetted," he wrote, the Cabinet had to be aware of this and make the decision. As we have seen, the Cabinet agreed with the recommendations, the dimensions of the security problem apparently outweighing the political risks.

One difficulty was that vetting could not be kept entirely secret. The RCMP did two kinds of checks. The first simply entailed a file check that focused on any police record or "any known subversive activities." The second, a "character investigation," was broader in scope: "a complete personal investigation through all sources available." That meant that RCMP constables questioned family, teachers, neighbours, and co-workers; by its definition, that was a very public process. In September 1949, in fact, *Maclean's* magazine had sneered at the Mounties' inability "to devise no more subtle method than ringing back door bells to gather up gossip of the neighbourhood." And some RCMP reports that featured an illegitimate child or the failure to pay a debt suggested just that kind of prying.

Another problem was that the Security Panel had decided that government departments, not the RCMP, were to be responsible for deciding whether to vet an employee and what action to take on the reports produced by the vetting process. That, naturally enough, troubled the Mounties, who also feared that vetting reports were kept in open departmental files. On balance, however, some such system seemed to be necessary and, as Arnold Heeney, the Cabinet secretary, told Prime Minister Mackenzie King on January 6, 1947, the Security Panel had tried to create a process "which will uncover (in advance, wherever possible) persons whose records render them untrustworthy and, at the same time, avoid any system which would be capable of improper application or anything in the nature of victimization."

The Cabinet Directive on the Security Investigation of Government Employees that was ultimately approved on March 5, 1948, was a sophisticated document. There was no intention of creating "precise and rigid standards for determining the 'loyalty' of government employees," as the United States had done. Some departments had greater need of security measures than others, the directive observed, and the existing terms of the Civil Service Act were broad enough "to permit rejection of an applicant for employment on security grounds" or the shifting of a civil servant from a sensitive to a less-sensitive position. Nonetheless, as Reg Whitaker has noted, "The screening criteria . . . were highly ideological and decisively anti-Communist in their thrust." A Cabinet directive on April 6, 1948, was explicit: Communists or Fascists "should not be employed by the government in positions of trust or upon work of confidential character." In effect, an open or suspected member of the Communist party or one who associated with party members was no longer likely to be hired, and certainly not for a sensitive department such as National Defence or External Affairs. Very few Canadians would have disagreed with the intent of the policy. Had they known that no appeal procedure was built into the regulations, however, Canadians, and not just civil libertarians, would have been outraged.

Vetting was not a perfect answer to security. The April Cabinet directive sensibly noted that it was open to doubt if any of the individuals named in the Gouzenko royal commission "would have been discovered by any conceivable system of 'screening.'" Only "alert and continuous supervision of departmental staffs" could guarantee security, and that was true enough. But the directive nonetheless ordered that full security investigations were to be made on all persons with access to Top Secret and Secret files, while record checks would be done on civil servants with access to files with lower security classifications.

The Gouzenko revelations had forced changes on the public service. The automatic assumption of bureaucratic loyalty to the nation had been shaken, and the RCMP had entered the scene in a major way. Everyone in a sensitive position was to be subject to vetting and, for the first time, security became a fact of everyday life in the public service.

The genuine difficulty was in determining who was a security risk. Did past membership in the Communist party constitute a security threat? What if one had been a party member but had nonetheless served Canada well and fairly? And what about sexual weaknesses? Was a philandering male open to entrapment, and should that lead to his release from the service or a denial of access to classified materials? Was homosexuality a "character weakness" that opened a public servant to blackmail and hence one that should forbid employment? And were the members of the RCMP, quasi-military constables of the ultimate straight-arrow organization, politically sophisticated enough to pass judgment on questions of this sort? These issues would soon bedevil Ottawa.

So, too, would a "red scare." As the Cold War that Igor Gouzenko's stolen documents had helped to create began to intensify and as the United States, in particular, began to search for tinges of communism in the pasts of army dentists, civil servants, school teachers, and film directors, it was inevitable that anti-communists would begin to press for similar action in Canada. The Conservative Opposition, particularly after 1948 when it was led by George Drew, pressed the Liberal government of Louis St. Laurent to take action to ban the Labour-Progressive party and to root out Communists and their sympathizers from the public service. The government stoutly resisted driving the party underground, surprisingly, perhaps, since St. Laurent as wartime Justice minister had kept the ban on the Communist party in effect until 1943, long after Canada and the Soviet Union had become allies and exchanged diplomatic recognition. And Ottawa refused to remove the passports of known communists, a bureaucrats' committee objecting to the erection of an "iron curtain of our own."

One favourite Opposition target was the National Film Board, some of its war and postwar films being seen as too sympathetic to the Soviets and the Chinese and some of its staff thought to be active party members. The name of its founder, John Grierson, had come up in the Gouzenko royal commission and his secretary, Freda Linton, had fled to avoid arrest. Though no overt suspicion fell on Grierson, he and his agency had an aura of leftism that took time to dissipate. In fact, the Department of National Defence became so alarmed that it actually refused to allow the NFB to make training films, instead contracting them to the nascent private film industry. That provided critics with ammunition, and the business press, led by the *Financial Post*, took up the cry. "That the NFB is a group 'with a message' is no secret to Canadian viewers of its products," the *Post* editorialized on November 19, 1949, adding that the labour movement complained that the NFB's films promoted communist unions. The pressure on the government mounted, but the NFB's executives resisted any wholesale purge, insisted on seeing the evidence collected by the RCMP on thirty-six NFB staff members, and only under duress reluctantly agreed to the compulsory release of three employees.

This was no glorious moment in the history of the Canadian public service. However, neither was it any great purge. As Whitaker says, the government had "an official aversion to McCarthyism or anything which smacked of freelance witch-hunting." Some careers were affected by the Red Scare — physicist Leopold Infeld, hounded by Conservative leader Drew, had his passport seized by the Canadian government and opted to live and work in Poland; historian Harry Ferns, denied a post at the Canadian Services College Royal Roads in Victoria, B.C., spent his career in Britain; and a female worker at the A.V. Roe aircraft factory at Malton, Ontario, lost her job because of her association with "left-wing elements in the union" to which she belonged. No overall numbers of those released from the public service are available, though approximately 150 civil servants were fired in a seven-year period between 1956 and 1963, two-thirds of them for "character weaknesses" such as homosexuality. Most of the remainder were discharged because of questionable loyalty, including suspicions of communism or of support for Quebec independence.

Fear of the Soviet Union and of domestic communism had existed in Canada ever since "Bolsheviks" and "aliens" had allegedly inspired the Winnipeg General Strike. But the Soviet Union's astonishing resistance to Hitler had largely overcome those fears; indeed, admiration had become the dominant aspect of the Canadian public's reaction to the USSR. Igor Gouzenko changed all that. The defecting cipher clerk had brought the evidence of Soviet espionage from his embassy, and in the process he had sparked the beginning of a great Cold War that was destined to shape the relations of East and West for more than forty years. The forces Gouzenko unleashed helped to ruin the careers of high-placed civil servants in Canada, the United States, and Great Britain and changed the way those governments — and others — dealt with their citizens. For a little man who simply wanted his wife and children to be able to live in freedom in Canada, Igor Gouzenko had certainly made his mark on the history of the twentieth century.

4.

THE MAN WHO NEVER WAS

The Second World War and the defection of Gouzenko did not lead only to the Cold War — they produced a strange footnote that says a lot about Canadian dreams of glory in international espionage. Facts about the war were twisted to create a national hero who never was — or, at least, was not the hero he was made out to be.

When Norman Robertson and Arnold Heeney were considering proposals for establishing intelligence and security systems in the wake of Gouzenko, they encountered the name of a person supposedly ideally suited by his wartime record to head the new service: William Stephenson, the director of British Security Co-ordination (BSC).

Submitted initially to Robertson and Heeney by Charles Vining, a close friend of Stephenson and former head of the Wartime Information Board, the proposal was followed up by at least one personal visit by Stephenson to Ottawa to lobby Robertson. Douglas LePan, then a junior diplomat working in London, was on leave in Ottawa over the winter of 1945–46. He later recalled that, walking outside the Centre Block one day, he encountered Robertson in company with Stephenson. The latter, Robertson told LePan, was there "on a purely routine visit" to discuss some security issues. Although in reality far from routine, the visit saw Stephenson's hopes of becoming master of intelligence in Ottawa come to nothing. That his bid was seriously considered indicates the weight his name carried in Ottawa by the end of the war. That it was ultimately rejected throws light on the curious relationship that lasted until Stephenson's death in 1989 between the Winnipegger enshrined in myth as "the man called Intrepid" and those who ran Canada's intelligence affairs.

Stephenson leveraged his bid to become boss of a revamped postwar Canadian intelligence service on his wartime reputation. His efforts were considerably assisted by a happy accident of timing that briefly placed him at the centre of the Gouzenko affair. He was on a private visit to Ottawa the very day that Gouzenko walked out of the Soviet embassy with his bundle of secrets. Urgently consulted by Robertson, he insisted that Ottawa give the cipher clerk refuge and take seriously his allegations of widespread spying in Canada. Over the ensuing crucial weeks, he made available BSC communications, personnel, and other facilities to help with the case. As a result, he accumulated a lot of credit among grateful Ottawa officials. This added to the lustre accumulated during his five years of wartime work in New York.

Stephenson was not by profession an intelligence officer, and his name would never have entered the realm of espionage mythology had it not been for the Second World War. Born in 1896, he spent most of his first forty years accumulating a private fortune as a successful entrepreneur and company promoter. Leaving Canada during the First World War to fight against the Kaiser, he won for himself a distinguished war record. He served with the Royal Flying Corps, shot down several German aircraft, and was awarded the Military Cross and Distinguished Flying Cross. Afterwards he settled in Britain, married an American heiress, and did well as a financial speculator. It was the approach of war in the 1930s that brought him into the orbit of the intelligence world. As a businessman with interests in Germany, he began to pass on bits of gossip to Lieutenant-Colonel Claude Dansey of the British Secret Intelligence Service (SIS). Through his connection with Dansey, who specialized in developing contacts in the business world and later became wartime assistant chief of the service, Stephenson became involved, in winter 1939–40, with a scheme by SIS to sabotage German iron-ore supplies from Sweden. Although the plan failed when Swedish police unmasked attempts to recruit Swedish agents,

Stephenson proved his mettle by escaping. The affair made him a known quantity and trusted in the corridors of SIS.

The Dansey connection, combined with his entrepreneurial flair and transatlantic business associations, made Stephenson an ideal candidate when the collapse of France and the accession of Churchill as prime minister made secure Anglo-American relations a top priority. In the First World War, the SIS's station chief in the United States had been Sir William Wiseman, a dashing entrepreneur with business interests throughout North America and Mexico. Wiseman's job, which he carried out with great flair and some success, had been to report on pro-German activities and efforts to sabotage Allied arms supplies. In spring 1940 what the SIS needed was another Wiseman, a figure with ambition and contacts who could work with Americans and motivate them to build an effective transatlantic security and counter-intelligence alliance. Stephenson, the successful Canadian businessman, was the right man in the right place at the right time. After he had made a preliminary reconnaissance visit in April 1940 to FBI chief J. Edgar Hoover to win his support, he was appointed by SIS director Sir Stewart Menzies as station chief for the United States, based in New York. There, on Friday, June 21, 1940, he and his wife arrived on the SS *Britannic*. He gave the Waldorf Astoria as his address and his length of stay as "indefinite."

Stephenson's mandate, like that of Wiseman before him, was to counter enemy activities in the United States, especially those that threatened British war supplies. Since this meant working closely with the FBI, a first priority for Stephenson was to establish good relations with Hoover. There was a great deal to do. American security precautions were lax, and U.S. opinion was far from unanimously pro-British. Gradually, as Anglo-American relations grew closer and developed from a casual relationship into a formal marriage, Stephenson took on more and more tasks. His New York staff grew accordingly, many of them recruited from Canada. Practically all the secretarial and administrative support staff, for example, were women spotted by Stephenson's business friends in Vancouver, Ottawa, Montreal, and Toronto.

Countering enemy efforts in North America meant opposing their propaganda, and at London's request Stephenson was soon running an effective secret public-relations campaign to win over American opinion to the British cause. This involved clandestine subsidies to certain American newspapers and radio stations and the careful cultivation of some selected journalists. Early in 1941 he added to his responsibilities that of representing the Special Operations Executive (SOE) throughout the Americas. The SOE ran British sabotage and subversion operations — "dirty tricks" — and British Security Co-ordination, as Stephenson's New York office was now officially called, began to recruit agents for use behind enemy lines overseas and actively carry out operations against German and Axis activities in Central and South America. The SIS also put Stephenson in charge of the administrative and financial management of their many stations throughout Latin America, although they kept their agents under direct control. In addition to all this, Stephenson, again on orders from London, temporarily took on some tasks of MI5 (British Security Service). As a result of a bureaucratic division of labour with the SIS, MI5 was responsible for security and counter-intelligence matters throughout the British Empire. Within Stephenson's geographical orbit lay Britain's various Caribbean posessions, Newfoundland, and Canada. Much of his job involved the co-ordination of all the British agencies he represented and effective liaison with the many local governments and authorities involved.

As fixer and facilitator, Stephenson did an effective job, although he never reached the heights of influence enjoyed by Britain's intelligence chief in the United States during the First World War, Sir William Wiseman. As long as the United States remained neutral, the BSC worked well with the FBI and also did excellent work in the propaganda field. Later on, however, Stephenson fell out with Hoover, and MI5 ceased to use him, sending out their own representative to North America. After Pearl Harbor, when the United States began to develop an independent capacity for secret intelligence and special operations in the form of the Office of Strategic Service (OSS) under General William ("Wild Bill") Donovan, Stephenson arranged for doors to be opened for Donovan in London so that the Americans could learn first-hand from British intelligence experience.

The BSC–OSS relationship now formed the principal axis of Stephenson's relationship with the Americans. For Donovan, Stephenson provided access to British expertise in intelligence affairs that was lacking in American experience. For Stephenson, Donovan provided a valuable ally in Washington, and in addition, through the OSS, access to materiel resources that were badly needed by the British. A graphic example of the mutual advantage the two men found in their relationship came in an arrangement that involved Canada. Late in 1941 a BSC-administered special-operations training school, designed to instruct Americans in the British arts of secret warfare, began its work in Whitby, just outside Toronto. "Camp X," as it has become known, opened its doors just as Pearl Harbor finally ended U.S. neutrality. Donovan flung himself into creating his secret intelligence service with enthusiasm. Many of his earliest recruits found themselves initiated into dirty tricks at the Canadian school, and its expert instructors, provided directly by SOE, in turn helped establish similar schools in the United States. As a result, the British acquired considerable credit in Washington. Most of this accrued to Stephenson in New York.

Canada and Canadians played an important part in the BSC story. To create the staff for his New York headquarters, Stephenson needed British subjects, and the recruiting drives he carried out for the SOE to find agents for service overseas involved hundreds of Canadians. Not only was Camp X built in Ontario but Canadians formed the bulk of its administrative staff and kept it running for its British commandant and instructors. From the beginning Stephenson gained the support of top Canadian officials such as Norman Robertson, the under-secretary at External Affairs, the Canadian military brass, and Commissioner Stuart Wood of the RCMP, who also provided Stephenson with a liaison officer in New York.

Canada gained in return. At Camp X, several RCMP officers received instruction in British security and counter-sabotage techniques that later stood them in good stead. Among these were Terry Guernsey and George McClellan, both of whom played an important part in the later history of Canada's security service. One important operation at Camp X was "Hydra," a wireless communications centre that the British used for the transmission of top-secret communications across the Atlantic. "Hydra" was linked by land lines to Stephenson's headquarters in New York. Eventually, in 1946, to protect the security of this link, the telekrypton or "TK" machine was introduced. One of the principal uses of the TK system was to safeguard the intercept raw material analysed by the Examination Unit in Ottawa, the bulk of which came from British sources.

The BSC was not involved in actually decoding enemy messages. Instead, it channelled and distributed intercepts shared by Canada, Britain, and the United States. For example, messages sent by German agents in South America to Hamburg, intercepted by wireless operators working from various British embassies throughout the region — many of them Canadians trained at Camp X — were sent to the BSC in New York. Here they were sorted and sent on to Britain, or to the Examination Unit, or to the Americans, for decryption and translation. For material sent on to Ottawa, the TK link established by the BSC provided a vital secure channel. This more than anything endowed Stephenson with authority and mystique in Ottawa.

His reputation was enhanced in other ways. British intelligence officials on business in North America invariably made the BSC their first port of call, and often their visits were orchestrated and arranged by Stephenson. Stephenson's number two at the BSC, Colonel C.H. ("Dick") Ellis, was another frequent visitor to Ottawa. A professional SIS officer since the 1920s, Ellis ran the BSC's Intelligence Division. In 1944 he visited Ottawa to brief RCMP Commissioner Stuart Wood on British perceptions of the Soviet and communist threat. Another SIS officer based at Stephenson's HQ, Gerald Wilkinson, an expert on the Pacific, spent considerable time in 1944–45 talking to Canadian officials about SIS plans in the Far East.

In 1945, having convinced the government of the importance of Gouzenko, Stephenson provided support in the handling of the defector by sending to Ottawa two of his counter-intelligence experts, Peter Dwyer and John-Paul Evans, to help with the preliminary investigation. Further, to bypass regular communications between the High Commission and London that had been compromised by the recruitment to the Soviet network of one of its members, Stephenson made available the BSC telekrypton link between Ottawa and his office in New York. And as a temporary hide-out for Gouzenko and his family, he put the now mostly disused facilities at Camp X at the disposal of the RCMP.

Yet, Stephenson himself was soon being bypassed and pushed aside by British intelligence. The war over, BSC's days were numbered, and by mid-1946 Stephenson no longer represented SIS in the United States. In the Gouzenko affair, despite later claims that he played a major role, Stephenson became increasingly peripheral once British Intelligence and the FBI got directly involved. One of his last acts as director of BSC was to insert a special supplement about the Gouzenko affair in the secret internal history of BSC in the hope that he could use the case as a lever to convince others of his postwar value. This was the document that Vining left with Robertson and Heeney. As we have seen, it failed to accomplish its purpose. Nonetheless, Stephenson did not give up, nor did Robertson cease to consult him. Four years later, in 1950, when there was another bout of discussion in Ottawa about a reorganized Canadian intelligence community, Robertson sought Stephenson's opinion. Not surprisingly, Stephenson replied with a similar response. There was need for much greater centralization, and someone powerful to run it, he told Robertson. "There are several good cooks," he said, "without a master chef to control the final brew." Again, this barely concealed bid for a top-level position in Canada was spurned — and Stephenson returned to focusing on the lucrative business enterprises he conducted from his homes in New York and Jamaica.

For the next decade or so Stephenson remained in obscurity, his name scarcely known to Canadians. But, in the late 1950s, he made the first of many moves that would eventually place him at the centre of international attention and controversy as "the man called Intrepid."

Stephenson had never had much time for the professional bureaucrats who ran Britain's Secret Intelligence Service. A junior member of the SIS staff in New York when Stephenson took over in 1940 later recalled how "he took one look at the office and then fled to set up his headquarters in his own private apartment" so as to avoid the deadly routine of daily SIS life. More seriously, his independence as a wealthy outsider caused clashes with SIS headquarters at Broadway in London. At one point, in 1943, it even seemed as though SIS chief Sir Stewart Menzies might get rid of him. Although this did not happen, Stephenson came to nurture a grudge against Broadway, a grievance that was probably exacerbated when he was first pushed aside during the Gouzenko affair and then failed to get a postwar job in intelligence. This, combined with a growing desire to gain recognition for his wartime career, led him to seek publicity for his case by commissioning a book that would tell the story of BSC.

To secure his place in history, Stephenson first approached his former second-in-command at BSC, Dick Ellis. Although recently officially retired, Ellis continued to work part-time at SIS headquarters as a "weeder" of out-dated files. With time on his hands, Ellis agreed to Stephenson's request. But the prosaic manuscript that he finally produced failed to satisfy his former boss. So, in 1960, Stephenson turned to another former member of his staff, Harford Montgomery Hyde.

Hyde was another ex-SIS man, and from 1941 to 1943 he had run BSC's censorship division in New York. Later, in 1950, he had become a Unionist MP, and at the time Stephenson got in touch with him he had established a reputation as a successful writer of popular biographies and was teaching history at the University of Lahore in Pakistan. Hyde agreed to do what Stephenson asked, which was, according to Ellis, to write a book that would show Stephenson as an initiator and innovator who overcame official obstruction in London, especially from Broadway, to build BSC into an agency that was vital to the war effort and to the cementing of Anglo-American relations.

Hyde's book, *The Quiet Canadian* (in the United States *Room 3603*), appeared in 1962. It lived up to Stephenson's demands, emphasizing Stephenson's entrepreneurial flair and his relations with J. Edgar Hoover and with "Wild Bill" Donovan, and highlighting dramatically many of BSC's most colourful operations. In turn, it downplayed Stephenson's subordinate relationship to his superiors in London and ignored his relatively secondary role in the wider picture of the Second World War.

This was perhaps no worse than many wartime biographies appearing at about that time.

Unfortunately, but significantly in view of the later vast exaggeration of Stephenson's wartime role, the book also included claims that were untrue. One was that BSC had broken enemy codes. Another was that Stephenson had played a role in one of the most dramatic deceptions of the Second World War — "Operation Mincemeat." This was the operation designed to mislead the Germans about Allied plans for the invasion of Sicily by planting misleading documents on a dead officer strategically placed to drift ashore on the Spanish coast, a plan immortalized in the 1955 film *The Man Who Never Was*, starring Clifton Webb. Hyde's book, whose principal source, besides an internal secret history of BSC, was Stephenson himself, claimed that Stephenson had been consulted in advance of the operation by the officer in charge, Commander Ewen Montagu. Montagu subsequently denied that Stephenson had been involved. Also misleading in *The Quiet Canadian* were exaggerated assertions about Stephenson's personal career — most notably that he had shot down more than twenty German planes in the First World War and that he had been awarded the French Legion of Honour. Official records in London and Paris that have since been checked bear out neither claim.

Lost in the larger body of information that made up Hyde's book, these errors attracted little notice at the time. But they were doubly portentous for the process that soon got under way of magnifying Stephenson's wartime role. They exaggerated his personal achievements and linked BSC quite erroneously with some of the most dramatic operations of the Second World War.

Stephenson was the source for these stories, all of which and more he came sincerely to believe were true. The explanation is simple. Already by the time Hyde's book came out he was in poor health and — according to Ellis — "very forgetful." Within a year, he suffered a major stroke, which completely jumbled his memory and meant that he frequently placed himself — and others —

at the centre of events when, in reality, they had never been involved at all. It also meant that he lost any real sense of the proper
chronology of events — so that, for example, a chance meeting with
Churchill in London after Britain's wartime leader had lost the 1945
election became in Stephenson's mind a special appointment two
years earlier to discuss some top-secret affair of state.

The next and decisive step in magnifying Stephenson's career
came in 1976 with the publication of the international bestseller
A Man Called Intrepid. It dramatically portrayed Stephenson as the
mastermind of Western intelligence, the supreme spymaster who
was constantly at Roosevelt's and Churchill's side, supervising all
the major operations of the clandestine war against Hitler and his
allies. The book claimed, for example, that Stephenson had been
Churchill's principal intermediary with Roosevelt; that he had personally been given the codename "Intrepid" by the prime minister;
that he had masterminded the assassination of ss leader and brutal
slavemaster of the Czechs, Reinhard Heydrich; that he had delivered the secrets of the German "Enigma" coding machine to the
Allies; that he was responsible for defeating Nazi attempts to acquire atomic weapons; and many other exploits that fell far beyond
the range of bsc's responsibilities. Later a sequel appeared, under the title *Intrepid's Last Case*, that claimed for Stephenson a
major and continuing role in the Gouzenko affair.

In Canada, reception of the claims for "Intrepid" was eager and
enthusiastic. Long accustomed to the prosaic image of Mackenzie
King being upstaged by Churchill and Roosevelt, Canada suddenly
appeared to have its own wartime superstar to equal those of its allies.
Besides, the time was right for the emergence of a hero cast in such
a mould. One of the proudest symbols of Canada's past, the revered
RCMP, was by the late 1970s mired in scandals surrounding the activities of its security service. The McDonald Commission was about to
recommend major liberal reforms that would make the service both
more accountable and respectful of the civil liberties of Canadians,
changes that many conservatives strongly resisted on the grounds that
they would weaken national security. By the time *A Man Called Intrepid* had been transformed into a TV movie starring David Niven and

Michael York in 1979, the eagerness for a hero of national security had been sharpened by the swelling conservative tide in North America that brought Ronald Reagan to the White House and — briefly — Joe Clark's ill-fated government to Ottawa. Early in 1980, Governor General Edward Schreyer flew to Bermuda and presented Stephenson with the Order of Canada, the first official Canadian honour for his war work that Stephenson had received. Canadian universities awarded him honorary degrees. At the site of Camp X, Ontario's lieutenant-governor unveiled a special plaque. One participant at the ceremony, in a fit of hyperbole, hailed Stephenson as "perhaps the greatest individual Canada has produced in the past century."

Praise was even more lavish in the United States. The climax came at a glittering ceremony in September 1983 when Stephenson flew to New York to receive the William J. Donovan Award. This top U.S. honour, named after the oss founder, included among its previous recipients several former directors of Central Intelligence as well as two distinguished Britons, Earl Mountbatten of Burma and Prime Minister Margaret Thatcher. At the head table with Stephenson sat CIA chief William J. Casey, along with former director Richard Helms and Canadian ambassador Allan Gotlieb. Ronald Reagan sent a personal message, read to the several hundred guests by his close friend and adviser, Edwin Meese III. "Your career . . . adds up to one of the great legends," the president wrote. "As long as Americans value courage and freedom there will be a special place in our hearts, our minds, and our history books for the 'Man Called Intrepid.' "

Ronald Reagan, the man who himself frequently confused the fiction of Hollywood for reality, spoke more accurately than he undoubtedly knew. For legend, while popularly believed to be history, does not have to be authentic. "Intrepid" is a classic case in point. Stephenson's mandate never stretched beyond the Western Hemisphere — North, Central, and South America — he played no part in breaking the "Enigma" secret, and in the Roosevelt–Churchill relationship he was much less prominent than now widely believed.

The truth was understandably resisted by many "Intrepid" fans in Canada. Critics who raised doubts about the legend either went unread or encountered popular hostility as ill-motivated antagonists of a true Canadian hero. It was even suggested that such attacks were part of a Soviet disinformation campaign carried out by "leftist" dupes. This was desperation *in extremis*, for the majority of critics were well-established experts in intelligence with no political axe to grind. Even when he died in January 1989, it was clear that Stephenson was still being credited in Canada with imaginary achievements. The *Globe and Mail* entitled its obituary "Winston Churchill's Spymaster," while the country's largest circulation newspaper, the *Toronto Star*, described him as "Churchill's master of espionage." It was both symbolic and illuminating that the man widely applauded as a heroic Canadian spymaster should in reality have worked for British Intelligence from a base in the United States. Nothing better could have illustrated the point that during the Second World War Canada became an integral part of the ABC intelligence alliance. And of the three transatlantic allies, Canada was undoubtedly the junior partner.

5.
CASUALTIES OF THE COLD WAR

T he documents that Igor Gouzenko had given to Canadian security officials demonstrated that Canadian civil servants and military officers could be swayed by ideology, financial gain, or simple loneliness to betray their country. That ought not to have been a surprise, but it was. Canada's enemies, before Gouzenko, had been thought to be ones that unified the whole nation — except for a few readily identified individuals or immigrant groups. But how could a Communist be easily identified? A Soviet spy could look and act like anyone else. Security measures and vetting might prevent the hiring of the "doubtful," but skilful spies could readily overcome such screening. How could spies be rooted out in Canada? How could the suborning of Canadians abroad be prevented? And what damage to individuals could the search for spies do to the lives of men and women?

The Senate committee room in Washington was blisteringly hot that August day in 1951 as Dr. Karl Wittfogel, professor of Chinese history at the University of Washington, gave his testimony. Wittfogel agreed that he had been a member of the Communist party from 1920 until 1932 or 1933, and that even after he turned in his membership card he stayed "within the Communist periphery." During the late 1930s, the professor said, he had participated in a communist study group in New York, "a discussion among a group of friends, of people who belonged to [the same] political creed."
"Who were some of the other students in the group?" asked

Robert Morris, counsel to the Internal Security Sub-committee of the U.S. Senate's Judiciary Committee.

> *Dr. Wittfogel:* There was a talented and pleasant young man who was studying in the Japanese department at Columbia. His name is Herbert Norman.
> *Mr. Morris:* Was he a member of this study group?
> *Dr. Wittfogel:* Yes.
> *Mr. Morris:* To your knowledge, did he know it was a Communist study group?
> *Dr. Wittfogel:* Yes, it was obvious.
>   . . .
> *Mr. Morris:* Was it obvious therefore that he was a Communist?
> *Dr. Wittfogel:* Yes.

Suddenly, Egerton Herbert Norman, though a Canadian citizen, was in the soup, labelled a communist before the Senate Internal Security Sub-committee. In the witch-hunting 1950s, in the American era of Joe McCarthy and the Korean War, an allegation of that sort could spell the loss of a job and hounding by press and "patriots." For a senior and trusted officer of Canada's Department of External Affairs, this was not a comfortable position. Until his suicide in 1957, Herbert Norman lived a tormented life as allegations about his past political beliefs and current loyalties swirled around him. More than three decades after his death, the controversy has not abated, and conclusions remain extraordinarily difficult to reach, so much so that the Department of External Affairs in late 1989 commissioned political scientist Peyton Lyon to examine the government's files with a view to answering the persistent questions raised about the Norman case.

Born in Japan in 1909 to Canadian Methodist missionary parents, Norman was educated there and at the universities of Toronto, Cambridge, Harvard, and Columbia. Fluent in Japanese, he became one of the great Western scholars of Japanese history. His PhD dissertation, published in 1940 as *Japan's Emergence as a Modern State*, still ranks as a major study, although one critical scholar has vigorously attacked his use of sources — by putting

Norman's paragraphs side by side with those from other works —
and charged him with the academic crime of plagiarism.

Blond, bespectacled, and slender, a quiet, calm intellectual,
Norman had emerged from the missionary and Methodist Social
Gospel traditions. If he soon rejected the religion of his parents, he
still sought a system of beliefs that could explain the cruelties of the
material world. First, in his late teens, he was a Christian socialist;
then a social democrat; then, at Victoria College, at the University
of Toronto, a Trotskyite and, after his time at Cambridge, an ortho-
dox Stalinist. All this suggests a certain ideological mobility that was
not unusual for a young man on the left in an era of depression, war,
and revolution. At Cambridge, where he fell under the powerful influence of the charismatic young poet John Cornford, who later died
in action in the Spanish Civil War, Norman appears to have joined
the British Communist party. As he put it in a letter to his brother
after Cornford's death, "I was influenced by him more than any of
my friends there and under his tutelage I entered the party."

Did this mean that he became a card-carrying member? The
evidence is unfortunately unclear. What is certain is that in the
early years of the 1930s, with the industrial world in the grip of
the Great Depression and with the Nazis entrenching themselves
in power in Germany while the smug and conservative West did
nothing, joining the Communist party was understandable. Joseph
Stalin's Soviet Union seemed to be a bulwark of anti-fascism in a
world of weak, cowardly democracies. Moreover, the Communist
creed promised greater equality for all peoples than seemed possible under a decayed, corrupt, depression-ridden capitalism.

But Norman did more than just join with the Communists. His
assigned party task was to recruit Indian students at Cambridge and
so to help the party take over the Majlis, the Indian students' organization at the university. To perform this task, he ended his
attendance at cell meetings. Michael Straight, a wealthy American
who was at Cambridge at the same time, recalled it this way: "Soon
after I joined the Trinity cell, [Norman] stopped coming to our meetings. James Klugmann [the leader] explained that Norman would be
working with Indian students and, since they were watched over by

the Colonial Office, he would have to be discreet. Norman had, in our terminology, become a 'mole.' "

This smacks of more than youthful enthusiasm, and as James Barros, Norman's sternest academic critic, has noted, his actions were consistent with those of other Cambridge undergraduates of the early 1930s, such as Kim Philby and Anthony Blunt, who either hid their party allegiances or claimed to have put them behind, and later burrowed into the British civil service and intelligence bureaucracies.

(After he was identified as a Soviet mole, Sir Anthony Blunt would later be quoted — by the less-than-completely reliable British journalist Chapman Pincher — as remarking that "Herb was one of us," a statement that is tantalizing, but remarkably imprecise. So imprecise was it that, early in 1990, the British press began to suggest that Norman might have been "the fifth man," the last spy in the chain of Burgess, Maclean, Philby, and Blunt who did such damage. In fact, according to Peyton Lyon's report for External Affairs, what Blunt had told his British interrogators was that Norman was "definitely in the game." That again is imprecise, but not if Blunt was a reader of Kipling's *Kim*. Lyon adds that John Cairncross, another Cambridge contemporary of Norman's who did become a Communist mole in the U.K. Treasury, "thought" that Norman had been in the "Circle," but could recall no specifics.)

Moreover, when Norman left Cambridge in 1935 after some success as a recruiter of Indians and after seeing party stalwarts win control of the Majlis, he persuaded Victor Kiernan, another party member who later became an academic in Scotland, to take over his work with the Indian students. And at one point Norman also tried to persuade Robert Bryce, a Canadian student at Cambridge who eventually rose to head the Canadian public service, to join the party. Here, at least, he had no luck — Bryce had already realized that being a communist meant sacrificing everything for the party, and he wasn't prepared for that; nor was he an admirer of Soviet policies.

Back in Canada, Norman immediately sought entry to the Department of External Affairs, but there was little growth in the public service in the 1930s, and his name remained on a list of bright young men who might be brought in when financial stringency eased. After a year teaching at Toronto's Upper Canada College and working for the Canadian Communist party, which, according to Alexander George Heakes, a fellow student at Toronto and Cambridge, he had joined and for which he had helped to set up a front group, the Canadian Friends of China, Norman went off to the United States to do his doctorate in Japanese history. At Harvard University, where he studied from 1936 to 1938, he belonged to a Marxist study group; at Columbia University in 1938–39, he participated in the communist-oriented study group mentioned by Karl Wittfogel. Then, in the summer of 1939, External Affairs finally accepted his foreign-service application. In those still-innocent days the department conducted only the most cursory of checks, which Norman, a son of missionaries and a graduate of great universities, easily passed. Almost certainly no one asked him if he had ever been a communist. And Peyton Lyon's very positive report on Norman's loyalties for the Department of External Affairs asserts bluntly that Norman "would never have been accepted" into the department had there been a serious clearance procedure.

Was he still a true-believing Marxist when he joined the department? There seems no doubt that he was. Was he a card-carrying member of the Canadian party or had he kept up his membership (if indeed he ever had formally signed on) in the British party? The evidence again is completely uncertain, although Lyon is convinced that he was not.

External Affairs posted Norman to Japan in 1940, and after Pearl Harbor in December 1941, he was held under house arrest as were other Allied diplomats. Exchanged in 1942, he worked in Ottawa as the head of External Affairs's newly created Special Intelligence Section on vital, secret counter-intelligence duties relating to the Pacific theatre, work that intimately involved him with the Examination Unit. In his office in the house next door to Prime Minister Mackenzie King's residence on Laurier Avenue, Norman saw all the intercepted messages, was aware of Japanese codes, and had ample opportunity to see top-secret Canadian and Allied files. By every account, Norman was very good at his work, brilliant enough, in fact, that William Stephenson wanted him to work for British Security Co-ordination in New York.

As that suggests, no suspicion attached to Norman during the war. He was openly a leftist, but so were many others. His friend and fellow academic Harry Ferns, then working in the Prime Minister's Office, wrote later of this time that "he was just as much a Marxist as I was." No one seemed to worry about this when the real job was to beat the Nazis and the Japanese, and when the Soviet Union was an ally and, moreover, the ally bearing the brunt of the fight against Hitler.

But Norman nonetheless got himself in difficulty that would come back to haunt him. During his Harvard days, he had been introduced to Shigeto Tsuru, a Japanese studying there, by Robert Bryce, his compatriot from the University of Cambridge who was coincidentally studying in Boston at the same time, and spending most of his time spreading the Gospel according to John Maynard Keynes. Tsuru was a communist, and he participated in a free-wheeling study group on the problems of American capitalism to which Norman was quickly invited. The two men became friendly, and when Norman came down the gangplank of the neutral liner carrying repatriated Allied diplomats in 1942, he bumped into Tsuru, who was waiting to get on board to be returned to Japan. The two Harvard men, their nations now at war, had a brief word together, and Tsuru asked Norman to recover the library of scarce Japanese books he had left in Boston. Norman dutifully went to Tsuru's flat soon after his return to Canada but found the FBI there. Then he stupidly blustered that he was on official Canadian government business. Challenged by the agents, he apparently owned up to the personal nature of the visit. What interested the FBI was that Tsuru was a secret Communist party member who had run a study group and his papers contained party material. There would now be a file on E. Herbert Norman in Washington.

As Lyon has established, Norman told his masters at External Affairs of this incident, the FBI's paranoiac treatment of the Canadian diplomat was duly dismissed, and Norman's career blossomed in the heady atmosphere of wartime. As one of the very few experts on Japan in the government, he had genuine influence in ensuring that Canadian official views were forward-looking and liberal about the way a defeated Japan should be treated. After V-J Day, Ottawa assigned him to the staff of the Allied Supreme Commander,

General Douglas MacArthur, in Tokyo where he again held crucial counter-intelligence positions and where his liberalizing influence on policy was once more important. He also forged a close relationship with MacArthur, which Ottawa considered to be extremely valuable and most definitely in the Canadian interest.

Some of the general's staff worried about Norman, however. Major-General Charles Willoughby, his intelligence officer, had seen Norman urge the imprisonment of some right-wing Japanese figures as war criminals and arrange the freeing of important communists in the autumn of 1945. That concerned this militant anti-Marxist who was trying to check burgeoning communist influence in Japan. So, too, did Norman's close connections with the Institute of Pacific Relations, an academic organization that had had some distinguished figures in its ranks before the war (including John W. Dafoe of the *Winnipeg Free Press* and Vincent Massey, the future governor general), but one that American right-wingers believed to be crammed with communists and their sympathizers. In an American and Asian atmosphere soon to be poisoned by Mao Tse-tung's Communist victory in China, leftist connections, past or present, were becoming dangerous.

Then, in 1950, Norman's name turned up in some belated investigations being run by the FBI arising out of the Gouzenko case. First, there was a telegram, brought from the Soviet embassy by the Soviet cipher clerk, in which Moscow asked Colonel Zabotin whether he knew "Norman." Norman could have been a first name, a last name, or a codename, but the FBI and the RCMP, their cooperation in the search for communists already close and growing closer, considered Herbert Norman to be one of the possibilities. Moreover, one of those arrested after Gouzenko's September 1945 defection was Israel Halperin, a mathematician and a former classmate of Norman's in Toronto. As might be expected of old friends, Halperin listed Norman's name and telephone number in his address book. Although Halperin was never found guilty of anything, that too had to be investigated, particularly as Klaus Fuchs's name was also included in the address book. The German refugee Fuchs had already been identified as a valuable Soviet spy who had worked on

94

atomic research in North America during the war. Norman's name also turned up in the desk file of Frank Park, another communist and wartime civil servant and, by 1950, an employee of the National Council for Canadian–Soviet Friendship. Again, that by itself was not especially suspicious; but again, it was checked out.

The RCMP file on Herbert Norman was growing fast. And by then Ottawa had heard via the FBI of the Tsuru incident, and the FBI for its part was poring over the information on Norman that the Mounties had dutifully passed to Washington. By this time Minister to Japan, Norman was recalled to Ottawa in October 1950 for the first security check of his career. George Glazebrook, External Affairs's security specialist, told his minister, Lester Pearson, that Norman had had connections with communists, but he was not thought to be a spy by the Canadian security people. He did note that "we are . . . far from hopeful that we can persuade the Americans, particularly [FBI director J. Edgar] Hoover, to reach a similar conclusion." That was an indication of the evidence that had flowed from Washington to Ottawa; it was also a sure sign that the American security apparatus had enormous influence in and on Canada.

Norman Robertson, the former under-secretary of state for External Affairs and then the Cabinet secretary and Clerk of the Privy Council, along with Arnold Heeney, the under-secretary, questioned Norman. Both men knew and liked their younger colleague, and their questioning was far from rigorous. Robertson for one, as Glazebrook remembered years later in an interview not long before his death, simply would not believe that Norman could ever have been a party member. And Robertson was almost certainly gratified when Heeney asked the $64 question about party membership and Norman "categorically" denied it, admitting only to having associated with radical undergraduate groups. This stretching of the truth was almost certainly an error: Robertson had had his own flirtations with socialism and had supported the General Strikers in England in the 1920s when he was a Rhodes Scholar at Oxford (his friend Heeney, also a Rhodes Scholar, had supported the government), and he would likely have been disposed to be charitable if Norman had come clean about his communist activities.

Norman repeated his story when he was questioned by the RCMP, though the somewhat more sceptical police did raise the possibility that Norman's connection with Tsuru's study group at Harvard, whose purposes he must have known, suggested that he was either "politically naïve, or worse, a fool." But then the police often found academics, like Norman, to be naïve, and for its part, the Department of External Affairs then or later never had any regard for the political sophistication of the Mounties. For whatever reason, the RCMP did little or no cross-checking of the information Norman provided, and the result of the investigation was that "no evidence [was] uncovered which would indicate disloyalty. . . . The worst possible conclusion we can arrive at is the very apparent naïveté in his relationship with his fellow man."

The mandarins of External Affairs essentially had protected one of their own. Robertson and Heeney were not prepared to believe that Norman had been a party stalwart and, even if he had sympathized in the 1930s with the communists, his good work for the department since 1939 had to be set against those previous leanings. And, of course, there was absolutely no evidence suggesting disloyalty that could discredit Norman. In the circumstances, the decision was understandable — and correct.

Norman soon was put in charge of the American and Far Eastern Division in the Department of External Affairs, a particularly sensitive position with the Korean War raging and with Canada rearming as fast as it could. There was genuine concern about the possibility of Stalinist aggression against Western Europe at the time; there was also deepening concern about Soviet moles, fed by the May 1951 defections from Britain of Guy Burgess, a senior intelligence officer, and Donald Maclean, head of the American desk at the Foreign Office. Both men had been at Cambridge in the 1930s.

All this was in the air when Norman's name turned up in the Senate Internal Security Sub-committee's hearings in August 1951. Men and women of distinction were paraded before the committee, put under oath, and ordered to incriminate themselves and their old friends. Many did; others refused to answer questions and were usually charged with contempt of Congress and often jailed; as a minimum, "Fifth Amendment" witnesses were ordinarily hounded from their jobs and suffered from persecution and denunciations. Professor Wittfogel evidently was not prepared to risk jail, and he decided to name names. His testimony to the committee that Norman had been a Communist in the late 1930s was unequivocal. What made it devastating for Norman was that it clashed with his fervent avowals that he had not been a Communist.

Perhaps alerted by the congressional testimony, the British security services were soon in the act, MI5 sending on to Ottawa a compromising letter involving one "E. Norman" who had apparently been at Cambridge in 1934 and 1935. Additional information came from MI5 on December 28, 1951, in a top-secret report, the effect of which evidently was to nail down the allegation that Norman had recruited Indians for the party.

Inevitably, the result was a second interrogation and investigation in January 1952, this time one that was tape-recorded, apparently without Norman's knowledge. Again Norman was less than truthful. When he was asked by Inspector Terry Guernsey of the RCMP what he would say "if a high executive of the British Communist Party stated that you, and none other than you" were in charge of recruiting Indian students into the party at Cambridge, Norman denied the claim. He did not know where such an idea could have come from. He had "never volunteered to do any such work — I certainly didn't do it." This was simply untrue. The questioning then shifted to Norman's time teaching at Upper Canada College in the mid-1930s, and again Norman denied having been a party member. "You never have been a member of the Communist party?" Guernsey asked. "No," Norman replied once more.

The questions took Norman back and forth through his years in Britain, the United States, and Canada, probing his connections with friends and acquaintances. The most that Norman would concede was: "In my Cambridge time I came close to [joining the party] and if I had stayed there another year I might have." A few minutes later, he repeated, "I didn't accept any posts or responsibilities." If that was untrue, Norman was likely on firmer ground when he maintained stoutly throughout the questioning that "I am not aware that I ever violated my duty to my government. . . . Nor have I engaged in what might be called conspiratorial activities, trying to pass secret messages off or anything of that sort." No evidence to the contrary has ever emerged. It is also worth remarking that neither then nor later did Norman ever incriminate his friends, something that seems wholly honourable.

The RCMP conclusion after all this was that despite Norman's denial of "all the serious implications [*sic*] directed against him," there were "far too many from various sources to discount them all." Norman had agreed that in the 1930s some could have seen him as a communist, but he claimed to have since rejected that ideology. "Whether or not this is true remains unanswered," the Mounties' report concluded. "In fact there are numerous points to which no answers have been found." The unofficial position of some RCMP security officers was far harsher: Norman was a security risk, a man who had concealed information about his past and who had never been forthcoming. And as the police saw it, the Department of External Affairs's duty was clear: where there was a risk or possible risk to the security of the state, the individual concerned should either be released from the public service or put in a position where he had no access to secret materials.

George Glazebrook, who recalled that he had sat in on the RCMP interrogation at Norman Robertson's insistence, was if anything harsher in his comments on some aspects of Norman's responses than the police had been. Norman had been, "in effect, a Communist in opinion" and an "active member of the Party with a particular job," Glazebrook said, completely discounting Norman's denials. He concluded that his departmental colleague had concealed his communist links when first interrogated in 1950, and he added that he had been "a Communist or fellow traveller in 1935 with no certainty on when this belief changed." Glazebrook, a Canadian historian of some distinction and a fair man, noted that there had been no suggestion of disloyalty by Norman during the years he had served in External Affairs; he did note that the department "should consider whether Norman attempted to influence policy to the left in the period before this case broke."

Glazebrook's comments seemed basically sound. There was not the slightest evidence that Norman had ever been a spy. No one had ever observed him holding clandestine meetings with Soviet diplomats; no one had ever seen him leaving microfilm in dead drops. That was scarcely surprising, of course, even if Norman had been a spy; only rarely is someone caught in the act. But there was the possibility that Norman might have been an "agent of influence," someone who tried to influence policy in directions helpful to the other side.

Arnold Heeney, the under-secretary, however, saw no reason for any exhaustive inquiry into the files to track down Norman's policy prescriptions. No one had ever suggested examining the files to see if some External Affairs officers had tried to tilt policy towards the Nazis in the 1930s, for example, or towards the Americans in the late 1940s. Why should Norman's memoranda be subjected to a screening of this sort? And even if Heeney had agreed to this review, the picture was almost certain to be blurry. Norman had, for example, wanted Japan to be treated in a liberal manner after V-J Day — was that a sign of Red leanings? or was it the wisest policy to ensure the creation of a democratic Japan? The result of all these considerations and of his examination of the evidence was that Heeney concluded that "from my knowledge of Norman, Norman had been, is and is likely to continue to be a trustworthy officer of the Department and that we sh'd reaffirm our confidence in him on the basis of the evidence." Years later, in his memoirs, Heeney indicated that his opinion remained the same, though it "was not possible to produce irrefutable proof" of Norman's loyalty. Irrefutable proof of loyalty, of course, is almost impossible to find.

Lester Pearson agreed with Heeney's judgment and decided to keep Norman in his department. This was not surprising, especially as the RCMP had never done a thorough-going check into Norman's past. "In the light of the primitive security apparatus in External Affairs," former ambassador to Moscow Robert Ford wrote, "and the tendency to assume that someone of Norman's background and intellectual brilliance could not be guilty as charged, it was inevitable that Pearson would accept the findings of the Department based on Norman's word."

(In 1951 a U.S. Congressional Committee was told by one-time Communist agent Elizabeth Bentley that Pearson himself might have had communist connections and, indeed, had knowingly passed information through an employee of the Canadian Legation in Washington. Further allegations are made by James Barros in his study of Herbert Norman, *No Sense of Evil*, but these and Bentley's are convincingly refuted by John English in *Shadow of Heaven: The Life of Lester Pearson, Vol. I: 1897–1948*.)

Pearson did indeed accept those findings. He told the RCMP on March 31, 1952, of his conclusion that Norman had been a communist at Cambridge (whether Pearson meant a sympathizer or a party member was unspecified), but that he had subsequently changed his opinions. Now, Pearson said, Norman was "a loyal Canadian and an efficient and trustworthy member of the Department." Certainly there was no hard evidence to the contrary. As far as the Canadian government was concerned, the case was closed. Norman's security clearance was soon restored.

But there remained concerns in External Affairs that the British and the Americans might be reluctant to deal with Norman now. As a result, just as Herbert Yardley had been pushed aside a decade earlier because of the U.S. reaction to his employment by Canada, so Ottawa shunted Norman off to head the department's Information Division and then to the backwater of New Zealand as High Commissioner.

In 1956, Norman became Canadian ambassador to Egypt and Lebanon, a posting that became critically important after the Anglo-French-Israeli invasion of President Nasser's country and the subsequent creation of the United Nations Emergency Force (UNEF). Mike Pearson's role in creating the force won him the Nobel Peace Prize; a substantial share of the credit for that fell on Herbert Norman, who played a key role in persuading Nasser to let UNEF into Egypt and to permit Canadian troops to be a part of it.

Norman's glory lasted only a short time. On March 12, 1957, a witness before the Senate Internal Security Sub-committee in Washington raised Herbert Norman's name in a wholly innocent way and was stunned when the senators professed to be astonished to learn that Norman, a man the committee had earlier "identified" as a communist, was now Canada's ambassador to Egypt. The "Norman case" hit the headlines once more, and Opposition leader John Diefenbaker raised it in Parliament by urging Ottawa to protect its diplomat against the insinuations of the senators. On April 4, 1957, a depressed Herbert Norman jumped from the roof of an apartment building in Cairo, his death instantaneous. A suicide note (one of several) he left behind set out Norman's final position: "I am innocent on the central issue, that is, I have never conspired or committed an act against the security of our state or another state. Never have I violated my oath of secrecy. But I am tired of it all. The forces against me are too formidable, even for an innocent man, and it is better to go now than to live indefinitely pelted with mud — although so much of it will be quite incorrect and false."

One Member of Parliament expressed the feelings of many Canadians when he charged that Norman had been "murdered by slander." Diefenbaker said in the House of Commons that Norman was "a victim of witch-hunting proclivities." And Pearson told Arnold Heeney that the wave of anti-Americanism produced by Norman's suicide exceeded anything in his experience.

More than three decades after Herbert Norman's suicide, there are still few firm conclusions that can be drawn. That he was a victim of witch-hunting who was hounded to his death by the U.S. Senate is almost all that is certain. No such clarity exists concerning other aspects of the Norman case. Was he a spy? There is no evidence available in Canada, the United States, or the United Kingdom that suggests so, but that question is unlikely to be answered definitively until the Kremlin opens its archives. Was he an agent of influence? No evidence exists to support that allegation and Peyton Lyon's apparently systematic search of his memoranda and telegrams has turned up no evidence to suggest that he was. Was he a communist in the 1930s? Undoubtedly. Was he a communist after that? There is no hard evidence.

What Norman's defenders forget is the pattern of untruths that enmeshed their man. He initially lied to the FBI in 1942 in Tsuru's apartment. He fudged the truth when speaking to Robertson and

Heeney in his first interrogation in 1950, and he did the same under questioning by the RCMP in 1952. His sympathetic biographer, Roger Bowen, discounts those latter untruths: "With a full decade of External Service behind him and communism an abstract and academic concern equally far removed in time, Herbert spoke to what was relevant to him there and then, and not to what Cold War fears deemed to be of more than mere historical interest." Peyton Lyon says much the same.

But in the early 1950s, the Cold War was at its fiercest, Canadian soldiers were being sent to Western Europe and dying in Korea, and the evidence of Soviet spying and moles seemed to be everywhere. The only possible conclusion is that Norman's lies about his past Communist party involvement aimed to protect him from dismissal from the foreign service. Anyone can understand the human impulse to save oneself by hiding behind denials, but it is less easy to comprehend why Heeney and Pearson did not press the investigation more rigorously to determine once and for all the truth or falsity of Norman's claims — and those of the British, American, and Canadian security services. Still, as decent liberal men, Heeney and Pearson detested the idea of witch-hunting and preferred to base their judgment on their own assessment of Norman and his departmental work.

What Norman's attackers forget, on the other hand, is that the RCMP, the FBI, and MI5 — with all their voluminous security files — are far from infallible. The sins of the secret police have been so well aired in all three countries that no one can any longer automatically assume that the security services are correct in their judgments. Moreover, the pages of rumours, half-truths, and outright misinformation that make their way into secret dossiers have ruined countless careers, and unquestionably Norman suffered from this. It must also be remembered that whatever he may have believed about the weaknesses of capitalism and the virtues of socialism, and whenever he believed it, ought to have been his own business in a society that professes to defend freedom of thought. Belief is no crime today, not even for public servants, and it was no crime in the early 1950s. But in the Red-hunting atmosphere of that era, Herbert Norman was evidently damned if he did admit to being a 1930s communist and, as unfortunately became his fate, damned if he lied in a vain attempt to protect himself.

Norman was a Canadian victim of the dark, dirty decades of the 1930s and 1950s. Many others had seen communism as the right path to follow in the Depression years, an attitude that was then wholly understandable, but less so years later when Stalinism threatened the democracies as much as Hitler ever had. And Norman was a victim of the U.S. Senate's Internal Security Sub-committee, not the first, not the last. He was hounded and reviled *in absentia* by senators and committee counsel, treated abominably and smeared with suspicion in a public forum where justice was bent out of all normal shape. But it is worth remembering that the U.S. government had some reason to be concerned about Herbert Norman. As Ambassador Ford put it: "He had [been a student] for four years in the United States, but more important he had occupied in the Canadian government a series of positions which made him privy to American political and military secrets." Neither Ford nor any Canadian would ever concede that an American assessment of the loyalty or otherwise of a Canadian should automatically prevail over that reached here. But in a world of alliances, every member had an interest in every other nation's affairs, and Norman's access to American "secrets" naturally concerned the United States.

The tragedy of Herbert Norman has about it a feeling of terrible inevitability. And the one certainty, after all the evidence that is now available has been pored over and after the Lyon report, is that the full story has yet to be told.

Another of Norman's colleagues in External Affairs also came under suspicion within a few years of the ambassador to Egypt's suicide. This was John B.C. Watkins, a gentle, scholarly man who rose rapidly through the ranks and served with distinction in the Soviet Union. Watkins was a secret homosexual, and in the less liberal days in which he lived, homosexuality was a private vice and a public crime. It was also of great concern to the Canadian government.

103

"The case of the homosexual is particularly difficult," the memorandum "Security Cases Involving Character Weaknesses, with Special Reference to the Problem of Homosexuality" prepared for the
government's Security Panel in May 1959, noted. Certain characteristics of homosexuals stood out: "instability, willing self-deceit,
defiance toward society, a tendency to surround oneself with persons of similar propensities, regardless of other considerations —
none of which inspire the confidence one would hope to have in
persons required to fill positions of trust and responsibility."

However alarmist and absurd that conclusion, it was very calm
compared to the views of Admiral Roscoe Hillenkoetter, in 1950 the
director of the CIA. The admiral had written that "the moral pervert
is a security risk of so serious a nature that he must be weeded out
of government employment wherever he is found. Failure to do this
can only result in placing a weapon in the hands of our enemies."

Comparatively low-keyed the Canadian assessment may have been,
but its practical result was not much different than the CIA policy. As
the security panel memorandum put it:

> Much as they may wish to give the employee the benefit of any
> existing doubt, our security policy, as well as that of our allies,
> has always been that any such doubt must be resolved in favour
> of the security of the information for which the department is
> responsible. As there is no method of ascertaining whether the
> facts of a homosexual's private life will be exploited by hostile
> intelligence agencies, employing departments are left with no
> choice but to ensure that no such person is permitted access to
> classified information.

This attitude remained unaltered for years. When Lester Pearson
became prime minister in 1963, he soon received a briefing paper
on Soviet espionage. The Russians, he was told in this June 1963
document, concentrated on "suborning people through greed or illicit sexual behaviour, and in effect forcing them to cooperate. Their
techniques of blackmail are highly developed, imaginative and quite
ruthless." Robert Bryce, Pearson's first secretary to the Cabinet and
then his deputy-minister of Finance, a man with long experience

in security questions, didn't disagree with a word of that. "The situation in those days was that homosexuality was a crime and it was also regarded as immoral," he told the Montreal *Gazette* in 1985. "We had to regard it as dangerous because of the dangers of blackmail." Regrettably, that was simply true.

Without question, the attitudes and practices of mid-century were different from those of 1990. Forced into secrecy by a stern heterosexual morality, however hypocritical it may have been, homosexuals were always in danger of discovery, especially as the RCMP Security Service rooted them out of the public service whenever they were found. Between 1956 and 1963, to cite only one period, more than a hundred homosexuals were fired. No one seems to have considered that acknowledging homosexuality as "normal" would remove the possibility of blackmail or make it no more likely for a homosexual than for a philandering husband or an adulterous wife to be compromised in government service.

Homosexuality existed all the same in the Canadian public service, and some senior diplomats were gay. One of these was John Watkins, a distinguished scholar of Icelandic sagas and Norse literature, who joined the Department of External Affairs in 1946 as a first secretary. A heavily built man with undistinguished facial features lost in a doughy complexion, the linguistically gifted Watkins was head of the European Division in Ottawa until his appointment as chargé d'affaires in Moscow in 1948 at the height of the Cold War. He remained in that repressive Stalinist society until 1951. After service in Ottawa and Oslo, Watkins returned to Moscow as ambassador in early 1954, not long after Stalin had died, and stayed there until 1956 when he took a posting in Ottawa as assistant under-secretary of state for External Affairs. His final post was as ambassador in Copenhagen from 1958 to 1960, after which, his health failing, he had a number of long medical leaves that concluded when he retired at age sixty-one.

Watkins was, his friends and colleagues recalled, a small-l liberal who was willing to bend over backwards to understand the Soviet position on issues, a humanist, an iconoclastic intellectual, a bohemian at heart. He bought books in wholesale lots, read everything during bouts of insomnia, and was greatly interested in art. During his time

in the USSR he built up a good collection of paintings, greatly assisted by George Costakis, a locally engaged half-Greek, half-Russian
embassy employee who was officially allowed to collect the mod-
ernist work of otherwise banned artists. Watkins was also "rather
an innocent" about the harsh and sometimes ruthless politics of the
Cold War, one colleague recalled. Another remembered his tendency to make light of the necessity for security in the embassy.

In short, Watkins enjoyed a distinguished career of public service,
one notable for the genuine affection with which his subordinates
regarded him and for the high regard of his superiors for his intelligence, brilliant reporting on life in the USSR, and the quite unusual
entrée he had made for himself into Moscow's cultural circles. But as
a homosexual, Watkins had behaved indiscreetly in the Soviet Union,
and the KGB, always ready to trap diplomats who engaged in sexual
peccadilloes with the tempting young men or women who were dan-
gled before them, quickly had their hooks into him.

This first became public knowledge in 1980 when American writer David Martin published his book on the CIA, *Wilderness of Mirrors*,
and further details emerged in British writer Chapman Pincher's
Their Trade Is Treachery the next year. According to Martin, a
succession of Soviet defectors had revealed that Watkins had been
compromised. The first, KGB Major Anatoly Golitsin, who defected
to the CIA in Helsinki in December 1961, spilled the beans about a
number of Soviet operations. One involved the KGB's blackmail of a
Canadian ambassador in Moscow. Golitsin said that he didn't know
the ambassador's name, and he wasn't sure of the precise time period, but he knew that a homosexual trap had worked. The RCMP's
security service was duly informed of Golitsin's story, apparently during the visit to Ottawa of two MI5 representatives around Easter 1962.
And after the American, British, French, German, and Dutch intelligence services had had their chance at Golitsin, the head of the
security service's Soviet Intelligence desk, Leslie James Bennett, finally managed to see the defector in August 1962 (see Chapter 7).

Soon after, Golitsin's information was confirmed twice more.
Yuri Krotkov, a good-looking Soviet writer sometimes used by the
KGB to seduce potential foreign female recruits, defected in London

in autumn 1963 and mentioned the gossip he had heard about a suborned Canadian ambassador. More important still was KGB Captain Yuri Nosenko, who jumped the fence in Geneva in February 1964 with the same story. According to Nosenko, who like Golitsin had spent much of his career in the Second Chief Directorate responsible for actions against foreign missions in and visitors to the USSR, the Canadian ambassador's case officer had arranged for Foreign Minister Pearson to see General Secretary Nikita Khrushchev at his dacha in the Crimea in October 1955. Moreover, he added, after an evening of heavy drinking, Khrushchev had proposed a toast to women, pointedly remarking that not everyone — and here the General Secretary was said to have looked at the Canadian ambassador — loved them. If there had been any doubt before Nosenko about the ambassador in question, there now was none: John Watkins was the ambassador in Moscow when Pearson visited the Soviet Union.

Martin's account was a mixture of truth and falsity. There was no doubt that Watkins had a close relationship with a more than slightly mysterious Soviet official he referred to in his despatches home as "my friend Alyosha." This man, Alexei Mihailovitch Gorbunov of Moscow's Institute of History, as he was known to Watkins, was in fact Oleg Gribanov, the number-two officer in the KGB's Second Chief Directorate. Watkins realized that he was well connected with the Soviet leadership, but he clearly did not know his precise status, though he ought to have had some suspicions. After Pearson's trip to the USSR, Watkins told Ottawa that Alyosha had attended the Crimea dinner "with Messrs. Bulganin and Khrushchev, but which of these he works for I do not know — perhaps for both. In any case he has a direct enough line." That he had.

Watkins also told his department guilelessly that Alyosha had helped to smooth over details during Pearson's visit: "Alyosha said that he thought that the fact that we had been able to discuss certain details of the trip together on a friendly and confidential basis had contributed a good deal to its success. It sometimes seemed a rather devious mode of operation," Watkins admitted, thinking perhaps of one meeting he had with his friend on a street corner, "but

I can see now that with the curious mentality of these people it was probably quite useful."

Watkins had another acquaintance of importance, one Professor Anatoly "Tolya" Nikitin, also of the Institute of History. Nikitin was Anatoly Gorsky, another senior KGB officer who had served in London and Washington running spies (including Kim Philby and Donald Maclean) and who worked for Gribanov. The three "friends" socialized together, had discussions on policy questions, and their conversations and the tidbits of information the Russians offered formed the heart of many of Watkins's most valuable reports back to Canada. On one occasion Alyosha "wondered how foreign diplomats in Moscow reported to their governments on Soviet conditions and opinions since they did not associate much with Russians." Watkins replied, as he told Ottawa in June 1955, that "they had to base their reports largely on the press," not a good source in a tightly controlled society. Then Alyosha and Tolya came to the point: "it had now been agreed at the top that it had been a great mistake to cut the foreign representatives in Moscow off from contacts."

In effect, Watkins was being offered favoured treatment, and he accepted it. Alyosha "tells me what's going on," George Ignatieff of External Affairs remembered Watkins having said. In mid-1950s Moscow, where Soviet citizens could not ordinarily talk to Westerners, Watkins should have known or at least suspected that Alyosha and Tolya were KGB. (But as one Canadian security official recalled later, "to whom do you speak in Moscow but the KGB? They're the *crème de la crème*. When the Russians want to learn something," or when they want you to learn something, "they haul out their KGB front types.")

And what of the famous dacha dinner? That there were endless vodka toasts was certainly true. In his diary, Pearson referred to the toasts and to the ordinarily light-drinking Watkins as looking "less and less healthy" as the long evening wore on. The Russian-born Ignatieff, who accompanied his minister, added that after eighteen toasts he had thrown up three times. But neither the Pearson nor the Ignatieff account makes any mention whatsoever of Khrushchev alluding to Watkins's sexual orientation. Common sense indeed suggests that only a complete fool, and Khrushchev was far from that, even in his cups, would have said any such thing with the Canadian Foreign Minister present. Common sense also strongly suggests that if the Soviet leader had made any such comment, the Canadian government would promptly have removed the compromised Watkins from Moscow.

But Watkins was compromised, though no one in Ottawa yet knew this. As Robert Ford, Canada's veteran Soviet expert, put it: "During my entire stay in Moscow, the Soviets kept up constant pressure on the Canadian staff in an effort to find out some weak spot. Most of them stood firm, but inevitably there were a few who permitted themselves to be ensnared." Watkins was one.

In January 1955, nine months before Pearson came to the USSR, Watkins had taken a trip into Soviet Central Asia, a rare privilege for a diplomat in this period of the Cold War. In Tashkent, however, this lonely man had a brief homosexual liaison with a poet, and in Stalinabad (now Dushanbe), he had a more intense affair with an eighteen-year-old collective-farm clerk named Kamahl. The KGB, never far from a travelling ambassador, knew at once of these affairs, even if it had not arranged to put Watkins in the way of temptation; certainly the KGB brought the boyish clerk to Moscow some time later and secretly photographed his hotel-room tryst with Watkins. The Canadian, who had been thoroughly briefed before his appointment to Moscow, as were all diplomats sent to Soviet-bloc countries, had violated one of the fundamental rules of security in the Soviet Union. As the wife of the British naval attaché put it to the Canadian ambassador's spouse in the 1980s, the rule for affairs in Moscow was "keep it white and keep it in NATO." She might also have added, "keep it heterosexual." Watkins knew the risks and acted despite them.

The KGB now had all it needed to put pressure on Watkins. But Moscow was very clever. Instead of squeezing Watkins all at once, it tried to make him indebted to Alyosha and Tolya. The two Russian friends repeatedly opened otherwise firmly shut doors for the ambassador, all of which was useful in helping Watkins in his reporting on the Soviet Union. As we have seen, Gribanov facilitated Pearson's visit to the USSR and was instrumental in arranging the interview with Khrushchev. This raised Watkins's standing at home, as did his remarkable access to bureaucratic circles that ordinarily were closed to Western ambassadors.

One example of this could be seen in a despatch that Watkins sent to Ottawa in February 1956. In it he recounted the conversation over "supper at Alyosha's apartment with him and Anatoly" the previous night. The discussion had begun with the Russians attacking Watkins about remarks that Lester Pearson was supposed to have made, remarks that condemned the Soviet Union for its aggressive aims and its imperialism and that tried to frighten Canadians "by telling them that the Soviet Union would attack them across the North Pole." Watkins, who had seen nothing beyond a brief *Pravda* article, was at a disadvantage, but fended off the attacks. Then the two KGB men dropped a small gem, telling Watkins that their government was soon to protest to the United States "against the sending of balloons equipped with photographic apparatus over the territory of the Soviet Union. . . . Alyosha was only telling me about this," Watkins said, "because they would soon be sending a note about it." There were minor pay-offs from the special relationship.

But the price would soon be extracted from Watkins. In spring 1956, when he was due to return to Ottawa to take up the senior post of assistant under-secretary, Alyosha finally made his pitch. Even then he moved with a care that showed the thought that had been put into the best way to handle Watkins. He had learned that the KGB had entrapped Watkins in Central Asia, Alyosha said, and he wanted the ambassador to know that he thought this was outrageous. But he, Alyosha, had managed to get the file, and so long as he had it his friend Watkins was safe. But, Alyosha said, he hoped that Watkins could repay this friendship in Ottawa. The Soviet ambassador to Canada, Dimitri Chuvakhin, had a difficult task and needed help. "Be friendly to Chuvakhin," Watkins was told.

Even the naïve Watkins now must have realized that he had been mousetrapped. One word from Alyosha leaked to the press or to a Western intelligence service would end his career in disgrace. But Alyosha/Gribanov's skilful handling of his pinned butterfly had been so well managed that Watkins could scarcely complain, even to himself, of being blackmailed.

What the unhappy Watkins may have done for the Soviets in Ottawa, if anything, remains unknown, though there is no doubt that he failed to inform his superiors of the KGB's grip on him. Author and journalist John Sawatsky, whose intelligence contacts are first-rate, suggested that the new assistant under-secretary avoided Chuvakhin and other Soviet-bloc diplomats like the plague and did absolutely nothing of benefit to the interests of the USSR. Certainly he blocked a Soviet attempt to increase the complement of their embassy, ordinarily viewed by the security services as a transparent ploy to put more spies onto the street. That may be so, though Robert Ford stated flatly that the KGB "enrolled him as an active collaborator." He recalled that Watkins unilaterally, and without Soviet reciprocity, recommended an increase in the distance Soviet-bloc diplomats could travel outside Ottawa without permission. That greatly aided Soviet intelligence operations, upset the RCMP, violated NATO policy, and overrode Ford's advice. In his memoirs Ford called Watkins a "sad case," then added: "I do not think he was a spy for the KGB in the sense of transmitting documents or information. He was probably used as an agent of influence, which he was in a position to be."

Watkins's secrets died with him, but he certainly was in a position in which he could have done damage. John Starnes, a senior official in External Affairs and director general of the RCMP security service from 1970 to 1973, wrote a number of spy novels after his retirement. In one, *Deep Sleepers*, he has a spy ruminate on the kinds of information she could pass on to her masters:

> She had been surprised at the extent of the rivalries she had encountered. They existed not only between Canada and its allies, but between different government departments. . . . Different divisions within External Affairs often held opposing views, which division officers defended fiercely. . . . There were often strong rivalries between individual officers . . . [and] an unspoken, but no less sharp, rivalry between senior bureaucrats and Ministers and their staffs. She selected examples of how the rivalries affected the development of

policies, and committed them to memory to relay to Viktor Aleksandrovich.

The controller, Viktor, is also used by Starnes to suggest the kinds of information an embassy officer might be told to provide: "information about the embassy staff and their families. . . . We are especially interested in the stenographers, the cypher staff, the security staff, the staff handling the archives and the couriers. . . . We would like to have the duty roster of the security guards, with emphasis on the quiet hours and holidays and week-ends." Watkins, or anyone in his position, could have been a valuable man to the KGB.

Whether or not he succumbed to the KGB's blackmail, Watkins must have been relieved when he was posted away from Ottawa to the pleasant backwater of Copenhagen as ambassador in 1958. He was even more relieved to leave the service. As he wrote to a friend in 1963 (in words that derive their real meaning only now that most of Watkins's story is known), "I just didn't like being an ambassador. . . . I didn't want another post anywhere and hoped I'd never go to another national day party as long as I lived." In 1964 Watkins's tragic life came to its end.

Until 1981, he was largely forgotten. Then author Ian Adams revealed that Watkins's death had occurred while he was under interrogation (the investigation was named "Operation Rock Bottom") by Leslie James Bennett and Corporal Harry Brandes of the RCMP. Bennett ran the Russian Intelligence desk, and Brandes was thought to have a good head for counter-intelligence work. The two had talked to Watkins at length early in 1964 in Paris where he lived in increasingly precarious health after his retirement, and then in London, England, and in Canada. Bennett and Brandes clearly came to like Watkins and they had just about concluded that he had resisted the KGB's blackmail. Then, on October 12, Watkins collapsed and died of a heart attack during an after-dinner interrogation in a Montreal-area hotel room. The RCMP hushed up the details and a death certificate was duly issued.

After Adams's book appeared, the Parti Québécois government of René Lévesque — which had its own scores to settle with the RCMP

— ordered a new inquest, which began in October 1981 and reported the next June. Its conclusions, however, declared that Watkins
had died of natural causes. The RCMP interrogators were declared
blameless. John Watkins's story was over at last.

The real question that remains is why Ottawa would have sent a
middle-aged homosexual to Moscow in the darkest days of the Cold
War. The answer is clear: no one in authority knew (or, if they did,
no one said) that Watkins was a homosexual, and Moscow was such a
hardship post that External Affairs thought it too cruel to inflict it on
a diplomatic family. Moreover, the department naïvely believed that
the Russians, while they might try to snare junior officers in sexual-
ly embarrassing situations, simply would not aim at an ambassador,
whatever his sexual orientation. The potential for embarrassment to
the KGB was too great, or so Ottawa believed. Perhaps that explains
why Watkins's lacklustre successor as ambassador was David Johnson,
another bachelor, a one-time Olympic athlete, and a secret homosexual, who held the post until his recall in 1960. At the very least, the
Canadian government has to stand convicted of utter naïveté.

As we have seen, by 1959 the Canadian government had become
deeply concerned about the danger posed to security by homosexuals
in government. Prime Minister John Diefenbaker's secretary of state
for External Affairs, Howard Green, in particular, was unsympathetic
to "deviants" in his department, and his under-secretary, Norman
Robertson, had to deal with the problem, if possible without let-
ting the puritanical Green intervene. Robertson was an intellectual, a powerful man of great sensitivity who was not personally
offended by the idea of homosexuality. As his successor, Marcel
Cadieux, remembered with a half-smile, Robertson had read Proust
on homosexuality. The under-secretary had also lived through the
McCarthyite attacks on suspected leftists in the late 1940s and
1950s, and he had been involved in the tragic case of Herbert
Norman; Robertson was not one to persecute his colleagues. But
he had also been a key figure in the unravelling of the Gouzenko
case in 1945–46, and he was exquisitely conscious of security and
its needs. To him, the security of the state was paramount and, although he agonized over each case that came before him, his usual

conclusion was that doubt had to be resolved in favour of the nation's security.

Thus, after 1959, at least two External Affairs officials were either allowed to resign or moved to non-sensitive posts when their sexual orientation was discovered. One was David Johnson, whose case must have especially grieved Robertson who had known him since they were Rhodes Scholars at Oxford in the 1920s and who had brought him into External Affairs in 1947. Although in 1963 the Canadian government of Lester Pearson did put a more liberal policy towards homosexuals in place, it would take a major change in public morality and attitudes before gay men and women finally were recognized to be no more or less susceptible to blackmail than heterosexuals.

The Cold War, then, had many victims, and not least in Canada. Herbert Norman was one, a man who suffered for his beliefs and evasions and who was hounded to his death by American senators and congressmen concerned that a trusted ally should employ someone so self-evidently untrustworthy as a communist. John Watkins was another victim, a man whose sexuality and naïveté put him in a position that made him susceptible to blackmail. So far as we now know, neither Norman nor Watkins passed information to the Soviets; even so, both were undoubtedly casualties of the Cold War. The 1960s would produce still more victims, but for the first time, they would be exploited by Canada's political parties for partisan ends.

6.
SPIES, SEX, AND
PARTISAN POLITICS

The headlines screamed out the key words: Sex, Defence Minister, Germany. The *Ottawa Citizen* had a scoop in its February 12, 1985, edition, and the newspaper played it for all it was worth.

In November 1984, the newspaper said, Brian Mulroney's minister of National Defence, Robert Coates, had visited the Cabaret Tiffany, a sleazy bar-cum-brothel in Lahr, the small German town where the Canadian Forces in Europe are headquartered. The minister had been on a twelve-day inspection trip to visit his country's forces in NATO and meet fellow defence ministers. After a dinner in the officer's mess, he, his chief of staff, and his press aide had slipped out of the base at midnight, without any accompanying security, to visit the clip joint. Although the two aides, as the *Citizen* reported it with a barely disguised nudge and a wink, "disappeared with two other women to another part of the establishment," the fifty-six-year-old minister, a married lawyer from small-town Nova Scotia, and a twenty-seven-year veteran of the House of Commons, had apparently passed his time drinking, watching the club's pornographic movies, and talking at the bar with a stripper named Micki O'Neil. According to the Ottawa newspaper, Coates's visit to Tiffany's might have posed a security risk by opening him to blackmail.

A minor tempest in a ministerial teapot? Yes, except that Coates submitted his resignation the same day, apparently in response to Mulroney's request. The minister apparently believed that he had done nothing wrong, but he had left the government, the story went, to spare the prime minister any embarrassment. As for Mulroney, he had learned of the Tiffany incident on January 22 when the secretary to the Cabinet, Gordon Osbaldeston, briefed him on it. Just where Osbaldeston, a respected former deputy in Trade and Commerce and External Affairs, had heard the story was unclear, though speculation focused on a disgruntled Coates aide, Duncan Edmonds, who had resigned a month before the *Citizen* story broke.

Still a minor tempest except for its impact on an unpopular and ineffective minister's career, but anything involving sex, security, and a politician is newsworthy and, while no one except Mulroney knows what the Cabinet secretary told him, the conversation can be easily conjured up.

"Prime Minister, your Defence minister has acted stupidly in Germany. He went to a sex club with two of his aides, men who are supposed to keep their boss out of trouble, not drop him into it. I regret to tell you, sir, that there is a possibility of blackmail, and the military police are now keeping the club under observation. So far we have no evidence that security was breached, although the possibility exists, and my recommendation is that a security investigation be launched at once." Mulroney's reply also can be imagined: "Get that investigation underway now, Gordon, and let me know as soon as it's complete." The *Citizen*, tipped off either by one of Coates's aides or by a senior and disgruntled military officer, broke the story at roughly the same time that Mulroney received the report on the incident. The security investigation, Mulroney claimed, established to his complete satisfaction that "at no time and in no circumstances was the national security of Canada compromised in any way," although it was obvious that the minister had made "an error in judgment."

Once the incident was public, once the Opposition parties in the House of Commons got their teeth into the story, Coates was doomed; if it had stayed secret, he might have survived for a time — until some other foolish incident inevitably brought him down.

Unfortunately, the possibility of blackmail was real. Sexual indiscretions, homosexual or heterosexual, or simply voyeuristic, as Coates's seemed to be, offer easy prey to hostile intelligence agencies. John Watkins had found that out to his cost thirty years earlier and there had been a host of incidents in every Allied nation in the intervening years. In the circumstances, it was reasonable for the secretary to the Cabinet and the government's security officers to believe that a sex club adjacent to the Canadian NATO base might be routinely watched by Soviet or East German agents; it was similarly reasonable for the government's security officers to assume that secret photographs of the minister and his aides might have been taken in the club.

And it does not stretch credulity very far to imagine a situation in which a plain brown envelope, marked "Personal," might have been slipped under the minister's Ottawa apartment door. Any politician eager to maintain his Cabinet post and perks who opened that envelope and found photographs could have panicked and, blackmailed, done whatever the KGB or one of its satellite agencies demanded. If Coates had been minister of state for Multiculturalism, the danger would have been there, but minimal; as he was minister of National Defence, however, no risk could be taken. Osbaldeston had acted prudently and properly; by seeking Coates's resignation, Mulroney too had acted correctly (though the suspicion exists, and it is largely confirmed in the autobiography of Erik Nielsen who claims to have found it necessary to urge the prime minister repeatedly to get rid of Coates, that he would not have acted if the *Citizen* had not published its story). The only person who acted improperly, of course, was Robert Coates.

Secrets about the Canadian Armed Forces are few. Anyone who reads the newspapers or *Hansard* has a pretty fair idea of the lamentable condition and equipment of the Canadian Forces. But as a NATO member and as a close ally of the United States, as a country that exchanges intelligence information with the British and the Australians and other friendly countries, Canada has access to secrets that are well worth the minor effort of blackmailing a minister; Coates undoubtedly knew things of international importance, and any betrayal of them might have had serious consequences for Canada and its allies.

The Coates affair also demonstrates the avidity with which political opponents and the press feed on ministerial indiscretions, especially when they involve security questions. Nothing so excites the politicos and public, it seems, as stories about spies.

Progressive Conservative politicians, like Robert Coates, ought to have been aware of that. During the administration of Prime Minister John Diefenbaker, from 1957 to 1963, two spy cases occurred to trouble, torment, and perplex the government. Both cases, however, emerged into the harsh glare of publicity only after Diefenbaker had been driven from power, and Prime Minister Lester Pearson had to bear the responsibility of action. But John Diefenbaker and his party were active participants in the parliamentary mud-slinging about the two cases; neither left any of the political participants in good odour.

George Victor Spencer, a middle-aged, nondescript, and completely ordinary postal clerk from Vancouver, met two Soviet diplomats at a seedy motel in suburban Ottawa on October 8, 1960. The Russians, cultural attaché Lev Buriukov and his colleague Rem Krassilnikov, had followed a circuitous route to the rendezvous, actually heading south to the town of Brockville, sixty-five miles away, before doubling back for the meeting. Buriukov had varied his speed, made repeated U-turns, and taken dusty, little-travelled back roads. He and his colleague had also been accompanied by another embassy vehicle, presumably to keep an eye out for an RCMP tail and, if one was found, to divert the police. The precautions amounted to good tradecraft, but in this instance the Mounties' Watcher Service, probably the most professional arm of the RCMP and very skilled at its work of keeping track of and tailing USSR Embassy personnel, had prevailed.

The clandestine meeting was observed and the Watchers followed Spencer from the time he left the motel for Ottawa airport in an operation that came to be called "Moby Dick." The police followed Spencer again when he disembarked in Vancouver. Then, Mounties followed him to and from work, watched him on the job, and observed him whenever he went on holiday. The RCMP, of course, kept tabs on each of the seven meetings he held with his controllers in Ottawa. His conversations with the Soviets were also bugged on several occasions.

Spencer had no access to state secrets. His job in the Post Office was a minor one, though he was presumably aware of details of the Post Office's security system. What Spencer gave the Russians was material for the construction of "legends" — credible backgrounds, backed by genuine documents. He photographed cemetery headstones, collecting birth and death dates so that Soviet spies could secure Canadian passports. He collected the detail and minutiae necessary to secure drivers' licences, birth and death certificates, and the knowledge of Canadian life that an undercover agent would need to be able to pass him- or herself off as a citizen. All this sounds trivial, completely unimportant. It is not.

Ottawa's Royal Commission on Security in 1969 noted that "Canada has acquired a dubious international reputation with regard to her passports, and there is evidence that hostile intelligence services have concentrated on the acquisition of Canadian documentation because of this relative ease of procurement." The commissioners may well have been referring to the Spencer case or to another well-known case involving the improper use of genuine Canadian passports and documents.

That case took place in Britain where the security services in 1961 had unmasked one Konon Molody or "Gordon Lonsdale" and charged him with leading a Soviet spy ring out of Portland, England, the site of a large Royal Navy base. Lonsdale claimed to be Canadian, and his passport attested to his birth in Cobalt, Ontario, in 1927. But all the Lonsdale family documents had been destroyed in a forest fire that all but wiped out the town of Haileybury, Ontario, and no one was left to recall the death of the real Gordon Lonsdale. Some Canadian information-gatherer working for the Soviet embassy in Ottawa had provided the necessary details and KGB legend-makers had made the Lonsdale vital statistics fit their man Molody. The work was high-quality, and Molody's authentic passport had withstood countless tests. The information Spencer had gathered for his masters was designed to be put to similar use.

To zero in on George Victor Spencer was a minor feat, one that reflected credit on the Watcher Service. But the Canadian government nonetheless thoroughly botched the case, especially if its intent was to prosecute the hapless postal clerk. The Mounties had bugged the conversations between Spencer and his controllers in March and August 1961. As an official in the Justice department told his deputy-minister in September 1965,

> a playing of these tape recordings indicated that while the one
> related to March is reasonably good, the one relating to August is
> of extremely poor quality. Our discussions with the R.C.M. Police
> personnel directly involved in the surveillance of Spencer
> and the recording of his conversations with the Russians
> disclosed that they did not retain notes as is ordinarily done
> in the course of a criminal investigation so that, in most cases
> they have no material from which they may . . . refresh their
> memories. These witnesses are naturally weak . . . they did
> not appear to us to be strong witnesses who may stand up
> well under cross-examination.

Moreover, the RCMP now had possession of only two of the four sets of tapes and were unable to account for the continuous custody of those two. The courts, the official said, were leery of taped evidence and insisted on being satisfied that tapes had not been altered. That could not be guaranteed, and in the circumstances the official had to conclude that there was "very serious doubt as to the likely success of any prosecution." The Justice minister agreed.

It might seem to be merely a botched case, one for the file labelled "Errors of RCMP Procedure." Ordinarily that would be true. But in mid-1965, the RCMP was under attack in Parliament and in the press, denounced for slack procedures in their investigation of a political scandal that had enmeshed ministerial aides and criminals. What better way to divert attention from the police's failings than to show how the Mounties had caught Soviet spies in the act. Not for the first time, and certainly not for the last, domestic political imperatives determined the timing of the expulsion of Soviet spies. The two embassy officials who had run Spencer's activities were expelled from Canada with much publicity for "activities incompatible with their official status." External Affairs said that the two had been caught buying secret information from Canadians, one of whom had assisted "in the establishment of espionage activities in Canada and other countries and to perform economic intelligence tasks." Spencer himself was never named.

In the House of Commons, curious Opposition members asked about the affair, only to draw an evasive response from Prime Minister Pearson. The suspected Canadian, Pearson said, would likely not be charged because he was dying of cancer. Little more was heard of the matter until Tom Hazlitt, a reporter for the Vancouver *Province*, speculated that the man in question was a low-level civil servant in Vancouver. Ingeniously tracking his quarry by checking on local civil servants recently treated for cancer, Hazlitt unearthed George Spencer, who promptly and voluntarily confessed.

Even so, the case soon disappeared. Late in November 1965, however, Justice minister Lucien Cardin stupidly confirmed during a TV interview that Spencer was the man. More important, he said that Spencer had been fired and stripped of his pension rights and was to be kept under surveillance for the remainder of his life.

The issue of spying was quickly forgotten as civil libertarians rushed to Spencer's defence. Had the prime minister not said the man would not be prosecuted? How then could action be taken against him? The *Montreal Star* editorialized that the government thought it could "deal with people as if we were living in a police state." From critics on the right, the demand was to fling the spy into jail at once, cancer or not. For three months and more, the issue made headlines. Despite some wobbling by the prime minister, the Justice minister rejected all demands for an inquiry, his defence against the attacks boiling down to the simple fact that Spencer had not asked for one. Nonetheless, the Opposition pressure continued in the minority House of Commons, part of the daily war of charges of scandal and improprieties that had been waged between Prime Minister Pearson and his vengeful antagonist, John Diefenbaker, ever since the 1963 election put the Liberals into power.

Feelings had risen so high in what journalists called the "scandal session" of Parliament that in November 1964 the prime minister asked the commissioner of the RCMP, through the Justice minister, for a search of the police files. What Pearson wanted, he wrote later, was "evidence, if any, of other cases they had investigated in which Members of Parliament, whether Ministers or not were involved. I wanted to get information on the nature and magnitude of this problem. To remove any impression that I was concerned only with trying to implicate the Diefenbaker Government, I told the Police to go back as far as 1954." That extraordinary request, surely unprecedented in Canadian history, produced only one important case in the report delivered in early December by Commissioner George McClellan. "It was really shattering," Pearson wrote, "because it showed, with supporting and detailed evidence, that a woman, who had been a Russian agent in Germany and later a 'call girl' in Montreal, had established a close association with the Canadian Associate Minister of National Defence." It was, he added, "a particularly sordid affair" with a security aspect that had to be followed up.

The minister was Pierre Sévigny, a decorated Second World War veteran who had lost a leg in the Canadian army's struggle to cut off the remnants of the *Wehrmacht* in Normandy and to close the Falaise Gap in August 1944. Sévigny had been summoned to see Diefenbaker when the RCMP informed the prime minister of its evidence. The Chief read him the Riot Act and sent him on his way and back to his sensitive ministerial post. As Pearson noted, Sévigny "had certainly by now become a vulnerable person from a security point of view"; that was absolutely true. Pearson added: "how great was the temptation to use this knowledge at a time when we were being subjected to every kind of slimy attack on grounds of corruption." Instead, Pearson sent a hand-delivered note to Diefenbaker, asking him if he could throw "further light" on the case.

Diefenbaker met with Pearson on December 10, 1964, the Opposition leader seeming "tired and more than usually nervous," or so Pearson wrote. "He knew of the Sévigny case, had interviewed his minister, had satisfied himself that no security had been violated." Pearson was not impressed, noting that "I shudder to think what he would have done to a Liberal P.M. who kept a Defence Minister on the job in these circumstances."

But Diefenbaker, not unreasonably, believed that Pearson's raising of the Sévigny affair was an attempt to blackmail him and his party into silence on the series of scandals with which the Tories had been mercilessly bashing the government. Had he come out openly and confronted Pearson with this, his moral position for once would have been unassailable. Instead, Diefenbaker tried his own blackmail, or so Pearson recorded it, "by telling me that when he took office [in 1957], there was a very important secret file — from Washington — in which I was involved. He was surprised, I think, when I identified it, said I knew all about it, would have no worry whatever if it were ever made public and had, years ago, told the U.S. State Department just that! This ended the subject." The file in question involved the testimony before a witch-hunting congressional committee by a long-time Communist and Soviet courier, one Elizabeth Bentley, in which Pearson, first the number-two man at the Canadian embassy in Washington and then the ambassador to the United States, had been mentioned glancingly and in a second- or third-hand way.

This extraordinary interview between the present and former prime ministers was nothing less than one of the most disgraceful encounters in Canadian political history. One prime minister tried to blackmail another into silence with the threat of a sex-and-security scandal, only to be countered by a threat of revealing alleged communist connections.

More than a year was to pass before the Sévigny and Spencer cases came together in a way that almost destroyed the credibility of Canadian politicians and the credulity of the public. Reeling under the Opposition's continuing assaults about the Spencer case and other issues, Liberal government ministers searched desperately for any weapon at hand to counter or defuse their political enemies. In late February 1966, Guy Favreau, the president of the Privy Council, warned Conservative MP Davie Fulton, a former Justice minister in the Diefenbaker government, that the Sévigny affair might be used in retaliation. Favreau had seen the RCMP report prepared for Pearson in late 1964; Fulton had officially been privy to the facts of the case at the time the Mounties had initially investigated it, and he had believed that there were serious security implications in the affair. Favreau's warning was a clear attempt at blackmail, made all the more shocking by the fact that the minister was widely considered to be a decent and honourable man. Moreover, Favreau had been a civil servant under Fulton and the two were friends. Nonetheless, Fulton appreciated the warning and understood that the Sévigny file would be employed if the government thought it necessary. The Conservative told Favreau that he could take no responsibility but he would tell Diefenbaker that the Liberals had the file. He did, and Diefenbaker said, "Let them use it."

There was more to come. On March 4, 1966, Justice minister Cardin and John Diefenbaker fell into a shouting match about the Spencer case in Parliament. The Leader of the Opposition demanded an investigation of security matters from 1944 onwards, something that was surely unwise, given his knowledge that the Liberals were completely aware of the Sévigny case, and accused the minister of erecting "a labyrinth of deception" about the Spencer case. Cardin, a nervous man and one now driven to distraction by the continuing charges, shook his fist at Diefenbaker and said: "Of all the members he, I repeat he, is the very last person who can afford to give advice on the handling of security cases in Canada." Diefenbaker shouted back, and in the hubbub Cardin, believing that he was challenged yet again, shouted out that he wanted "the right honourable gentleman to tell the House about his participation in the Monseigneur case when he was prime minister." Pearson and Cardin both later maintained that the Justice minister had simply blurted the name out, that it had been in no way planned ahead of time. But Cardin did admit that he, Favreau, and Pearson earlier had discussed using the case against the Tories. Pearson had refused. Even so, though he understood his prime minister's position, Cardin decided to raise the "Monseigneur case" if he was pressed.

While reporters rushed out of the Press Gallery to try to determine who or what "Monseigneur" might be, David Lewis of the NDP was rising in the House to wave a telegram from Spencer's lawyer officially asking for an enquiry into the disposition of his pension rights. Cardin was quick to deny the request, but after consulting him and other ministers, the prime minister that afternoon overruled his Justice minister and accepted it. Pearson wrote that Cardin had agreed to the volte-face, but the embattled minister nonetheless brooded about the humiliation he had suffered and submitted his resignation to Pearson. Eventually he was persuaded to withdraw it, primarily by warnings that, if he went, a flood of other ministers would follow him and the government might fall. Many Liberals were appalled at the way Pearson had folded in the face of Opposition pressure, for so it was perceived.

The next act came on Thursday, March 10, when the Justice minister told a press conference more about the "Monseigneur" case. The journalists had now tracked down enough information to be sure that the case concerned a German woman named Gerda Munsinger (though Cardin would tell them her name was Olga) who had lived in Montreal from 1955 to 1961 and worked as a prostitute. But none of the media were ready for what Cardin told them. The case was "worse than the Profumo case," a British sex-and-spy scandal that, the year before, had resulted in enormous publicity and produced the resignation of John Profumo, the Secretary of State for War. Profumo had lied to Parliament about his sexual relations with Christine Keeler, a gorgeous tart who simultaneously was seeing the Soviet assistant naval attaché (and others listed in *Burke's Peerage*). Moreover, Cardin said, Munsinger had been a Soviet spy before coming to Canada, and her association with Conservative cabinet ministers had threatened national security. Worse still, Cardin said, Diefenbaker knew of the case and mishandled it by failing to refer it to the legal officers of the Crown. Munsinger, he added, had died of leukaemia in East Germany, or so the RCMP had told him. The more titillating Munsinger case instantly replaced Spencer's on the front pages.

The country was already agog at the stories coming out of Ottawa. Now the pace quickened with Cardin's insistence that ministers were involved. Pearson felt that his caucus "could hardly help but feel some exhilaration at seeing the Tories squirm in the gutter where they had chosen to fight." That Liberal exhilaration increased for a time when Robert Reguly, a reporter from the *Toronto Star*, found Gerda Munsinger, not dead of leukaemia, but alive and well and living in Munich. When he knocked at her door, the slightly faded but still attractive barroom worker said huskily, "I suppose you want to ask about Sévigny." Before long, Gerda had named George Hees as a second Tory minister with whom she had been involved. And she was selling her story to any who would pay. In the *Neue Illustrierte* in Germany, Munsinger breathlessly said, "I will not be quiet about it. I will tell you how it was. How it really was in my fast-living restless life . . . where I met the men of society who wanted to have my love." It didn't sound like the Ottawa Canadians knew and despised.

The *Star* headlines on March 11 rocked the country. In Parliament, while MPs shouted, Pearson promised another enquiry. The television screens over the weekend featured an angry Pierre Sévigny defending his home by hitting Larry Zolf of the CBC over the head with his cane. As for Pearson, according to journalist Peter Newman, he was appalled by the outcome of his 1964 queries for details on scandals involving members of Parliament. "This is a terrible precedent," he moaned. "Good Lord, we can't have prime ministers investigated when they make a decision on their own. It's a prime minister's prerogative to make a wrong decision, and it's not subject to checks. We can't investigate a prime minister." But investigate a prime minister was precisely what the enquiry, soon set up under Supreme Court of Canada Justice W.F. Spence, would do. As Pearson recalled, he wanted the enquiry's terms of reference to be "wide enough to take in all of Cardin's statements but clear enough to show that Diefenbaker's mishandling of a security situation was the real point at issue; not revelry in Gerda Munsinger's flat." That did not sound like the agonizing reported by Newman. Nor did Walter Gordon, the former Finance minister, find much angst: after a talk with Pearson on March 15, he wrote that he "thinks it will be the end of Diefenbaker."

The Spence Commission soon established that the RCMP had warned Justice minister Fulton in December 1960 that Pierre Sévigny had a sexual relationship with a woman who had underworld connections in Montreal and a dubious security record dating from 1949. The police, who had been warned by Washington about Munsinger's record in Germany and who had been watching her, had eavesdropped on some of her liaisons with Sévigny, making tape-recordings and it appears, casually writing their notes of the bedroom conversations in pencil on the back of envelopes. (One tape was given to Prime Minister Diefenbaker and used to blow Sévigny's protestations of innocence out of the water.) The RCMP file on Munsinger noted that she had worked for Soviet intelligence in West Germany after 1949 and, though married to an American soldier, she had been denied admission to the United States in 1954. CIA evidence later confirmed this. Within a week of getting the RCMP's file in 1960 Fulton took a written report to the prime minister.

The next day, or so the evidence before the Spence Commission established, Diefenbaker had called in his associate minister of National Defence, told him to end the affair, and warned him that he, the prime minister, had still to be satisfied there was no security breach. Two months later, Sévigny, who had been paying Munsinger's rent in Montreal, told the prime minister that the woman had returned to Germany. Nothing further was done, and Sévigny retained his ministerial post until he resigned from the government in its last days in early 1963.

Spence's task was to decide if Diefenbaker and Fulton had acted properly or if they had erred by not referring the case to the law officers of the Crown for advice. The enquiry, in Conservative eyes, was partisan in the extreme, so much so that opposition to Diefenbaker in his party, to that point gaining strength with every passing day, virtually ceased for a time so as not to give any comfort to the Liberals. Diefenbaker and Fulton, between whom no love was lost and who had had serious difficulties in co-ordinating their tactics, even withdrew their lawyers to show their disdain for the Spence Commission and to register their protest at the hectoring tactics employed by the royal commission's counsel.

The royal commission report, released in the fall of 1966, was sharply critical of Diefenbaker. Although it found no evidence of disloyalty on Sévigny's part, the report censured the Chief for failing to dismiss his minister and for placing his own reading of the situation ahead of the security of the state. Incredibly, Fulton was also criticized for accepting the RCMP's conclusions that no security had been breached without further investigation. And George Hees, who claimed that he had lunched with the lady, nothing more, was cited for a "regrettable" lack of discretion. The Liberals, whose behaviour in putting this case into public circulation had been disgraceful, escaped completely unscathed. Pearson's request for information about MPs from the RCMP was "not only a natural but a proper one" and his keeping the Munsinger file in the Privy Council Office from December 1964 onwards was normal. All the allegations made by Cardin at his press conference were substantiated in Spence's report, although it was far from certain that the Munsinger case was "worse than the Profumo scandal."

The whole affair had been appalling from start to finish. The Spencer case, which arguably should have been allowed to disappear since the Mounties' bungling had eliminated any possibility of making a credible case against the postal clerk, had been turned into a political football by the vainglorious efforts of the RCMP, aided and abetted by the Department of External Affairs, to tout its successes against Soviet spying. The Opposition, which ought to have known better, also turned Spencer into a political football. The Pearson government, desperate to resist the scandal-mongering tactics of the Conservatives and the NDP, used an RCMP report on the activities of MPs to beat the Tories. Dredging up past prime-ministerial actions was a new low in Canadian politics. As George Bain wrote in the *Globe and Mail*, "It is now apparent that for 16 months the Government had stood with the Munsinger case held like a pail of slops over the heads of its chief political opponents." The Spence inquiry, he added, had nothing to do with the protection of national security.

Still, the Diefenbaker Tories emerge with no credit. The Chief had countered Pearson's attempt to blackmail him into silence with the counter-blackmailing mention of a 1950s security file on the Liberal leader. Moreover, Diefenbaker ought to have sacked Sévigny in 1960, and he besmirched Canadian politics by the campaign of scandal and smear he directed after 1963. Even so, he (and Fulton even more so) did not deserve the condemnation made by the Spence Report.

As for the RCMP, its actions in supplying Fulton with the details of the Sévigny–Munsinger relationship had been completely proper. Similarly, Commissioner McClellan had no choice but to agree to give Pearson what he asked for in December 1964. Even so, the RCMP's procedures were incredibly slipshod. The inability to produce all the tapes made of Spencer's conversations was a major gaffe; the inability to certify that the tapes had not been doctored was worse; and the absence of notes made at the scene by the investigating officers was a violation of basic police procedure. Some of the same weaknesses in procedures were revealed in the Munsinger case.

If the Mounties ran into repeated calls for the Security Service to be civilianized and hived off from the uniformed RCMP, there can be no doubt that its appallingly sloppy investigative methods, as revealed in the Spencer and Munsinger affairs, played a major role in this. The Security Service had been revealed as inefficient, so much so that it had become the butt of jokes. The RCMP had a great reputation as a police force; even more, it was a Canadian symbol. But handling the interface between politics and security work in the 1960s seemed to be beyond its capabilities. Men trained in horsemanship, in Arctic posts, and in the policing of Saskatchewan towns were not necessarily political sophisticates.

The most important aspect of the Spencer and Munsinger cases, of course, was political. They demonstrated that politicians would hesitate scarcely at all to use security files for partisan political purposes. That was something new in Canada, something that smacked of J. Edgar Hoover's FBI. In this respect, the Cold War had Americanized Canadian politics to an unhealthy extent. Moreover, the Munsinger case demonstrated that the Canadian media no longer had any qualms about dragging sexual peccadilloes into public view. They can scarcely be condemned for that, but Robert Coates, who had been an MP through the whole Scandal sessions of Parliament, should not have been surprised at what happened to him twenty-two years later.

If the media had changed by the 1960s, so obviously had the RCMP and the rest of Canada's intelligence apparatus. The police had been completely unready when the Gouzenko affair had burst on the country, and Canada's wartime intelligence efforts were on the verge of being wound up at just that period. But the Cold War had turned both security and intelligence in new directions, with new enemies — and, sometimes, old friends — to watch and counter.

7.
MOUNTAINS OUT OF MOLEHILLS

I f sex and politics were the stuff of espionage scandals in the 1960s, the 1970s saw the emergence of an obsession with moles — real or perceived. Sometimes, as in the case of Leslie James Bennett, the obsession underlined once again that membership in the Western network could demand the sacrifice of the innocent. On March 13, 1972, Bennett arrived as usual at 7:45 a.m. at his office in RCMP headquarters in Ottawa. Although currently head of "E" branch of the Security Service, the technical-support division that ran secret surveillance operations, he had for several years previously held the super-sensitive post of head of the Soviet desk in the "B" or counter-espionage branch. This was the heart of Security Service operations against KGB and GRU intelligence activity in Canada, and his long tenure there had made Bennett, according to John Sawatsky, "the most influential officer in the history of the Security Service."

Hardly had Bennett opened the safe in his office to take out the day's files when a colleague dropped in to say that the director of the Security Service, John Starnes, wished to see him immediately. The encounter with Starnes was brief and stunning. Bennett heard the former diplomat, who two years before had become the first civilian ever to head the Security Service, tell him that there were serious doubts about his loyalty and that effective immediately his security clearance was lifted. Furthermore, Starnes said, there would have to be an interrogation. Moments later, escorted out of the building on his way to a downtown safe house already prepared for his grilling, Bennett surrendered the pass he had held during seventeen years of service as a civilian with the Mounties. It was the end of a career — and the climax of an attempt by Canada's spycatchers to pin down what they believed had for years been a Soviet mole betraying their secrets to Moscow.

It should be said straight away that the subsequent interrogation of Bennett produced no proof that he had worked for the Soviets. Nonetheless, his career was ruined. Once raised, doubts about his loyalty could never be put to rest. Even if his Canadian interrogators were satisfied, Canada's allies would never work with a man tainted by such grave charges. As Herbert Yardley and Herbert Norman in their own different ways had discovered, absence of proof of guilt was not enough. Bennett was offered a job elsewhere in the federal public service, but declined. Instead, he took a medical pension and left Canada to settle eventually in Australia, where he still lives.

Both inside and outside the intelligence community it is now accepted that Bennett was the victim of a mistake, yet another individual sacrificed on the altar of the state's interest in preserving relations with its allies. This makes his case all the more illuminating and important, a graphic example of the ways in which Canada's security community was affected by forces sweeping the wider Western intelligence network. In brief, Bennett was the scapegoat that Canada offered up in a wider obsession with Soviet moles that swept the West in the 1960s and 1970s.

For Bennett, the story really began in 1954, when at age thirty-four he emigrated from Britain to Canada with his Australian-born wife. He brought with him impressive credentials as an expert in the technical side of intelligence. During the Second World War he had cracked enemy ciphers for both the Signal Corps and the Intelligence Corps of the British army. The war over, he had transferred his skills to the newly established and rapidly expanding Government Communications Headquarters (GCHQ), the peacetime successor to Bletchley Park that was still basking in its secret triumph over German codes. GCHQ was now turning its attention to Soviet ciphers, and Bennett's career took him successively to Turkey, where he helped establish intercept facilities; to London, where he served as secretary to the interdepartmental counter-clandestine committee that brought together representatives from MI5, MI6, and GCHQ to co-ordinate the attack on Moscow's communications with its clandestine agents; to

Australia, liaising with the Defence Signals Division; to Hong Kong as principal GCHQ representative; and then to Cheltenham, the home of GCHQ, as head of the General Search section supervising the analysis of intercepted communications with Soviet clandestine agents.

By 1954 Bennett was becoming bored with his job, and his wife disliked Britain. Expecting to land a job easily with GCHQ's Canadian equivalent, the Communications Branch of the National Research Council (CBNRC), the couple moved to Ottawa. But Canada's codebreakers were already flooded with Brits, and Ed Drake, the head of CBNRC, refused to have any more. Instead, Bennett found himself recruited into the RCMP by Terry Guernsey, head of the "B" branch of the Security Service. Very quickly, Bennett became Guernsey's de facto assistant, helping run counter-espionage operations against the Soviets. After Guernsey left Ottawa to become the liaison officer with MI5 and MI6 in London, Bennett's role became increasingly important. Finally, in 1958, he was officially put in charge of the Soviet desk. It was a position he kept for the next twelve years.

Everyone agreed that Bennett made a valuable contribution in developing new techniques to identify and track the activities of Soviet intelligence officers in Canada. He pushed successfully for all Soviet diplomatic vehicles to be issued with licence plates bearing numbers within the same block for easier identification; he introduced a Vehicle Sighting Programme that circulated these numbers to all RCMP personnel and local police forces so that the whereabouts of any Soviet vehicles could be reported to a central number. An online cipher relay was introduced, linking the observation post outside the Soviet embassy with the Soviet desk so that details of movements to and from the embassy could be instantly tracked. Under Bennett, the Security Service learned a lot more about KGB and GRU activities and tradecraft than it had known before.

Bennett also played a prominent role in some of the cases discussed elsewhere in this book. It was Bennett, for example, who first ordered full surveillance on the Vancouver postal clerk George Victor Spencer, and who authorized his eventual interrogation ("Operation Moby Dick"). Likewise, Bennett was the senior officer responsible for the 1964 interrogation of John Watkins, first in Paris and then in Montreal — and he was present in the hotel room when Watkins suffered his fatal heart attack ("Operation Rock Bottom").

Events outside Canada, however, first inspired suspicions about Bennett's loyalty. In December 1961, KGB major Anatoly Golitsin defected to the Americans in Helsinki, bringing with him tales of Soviet moles in several Western intelligence services, as well as the first lead that eventually identified John Watkins as the victim of a KGB operation. Around Easter 1962, two representatives from MI5 travelled to Ottawa and gave the Security Service a briefing on Golitsin's revelations. Later that year Bennett himself questioned Golitsin in a safe house in Washington, D.C. Bennett had always preached to his colleagues the danger of Soviet penetration of Western security services, and the danger was dramatically highlighted within a few months when Kim Philby, a former high-level SIS officer, defected to Moscow from Beirut. Philby had been only one among a group of Soviet moles who had penetrated British intelligence, and to suspicious minds in MI5 his sudden defection in January 1963 suggested he had been given advance warning of a forthcoming interrogation. In April 1963 the director general of MI5, Roger Hollis, authorized a top-secret investigation ("Operation Peter") of his own deputy. Graham Mitchell, as a possible Soviet mole who had tipped off Philby. At about the same time the head of the CIA's counter-intelligence section, James Jesus Angleton, became convinced by Golitsin that the CIA was also deeply penetrated by the Soviets. In Western capitals the molehunt was on. For the next decade it tore apart the intelligence and security services of the UKUSA alliance.

The close co-operation that Canada enjoyed with its sister services meant that almost every stage of the hunt in London or Washington was known to the Security Service in Ottawa. MI5 officers visiting Ottawa dropped hints about suspicions against high-level figures within the British service, and Hollis himself briefed the head of the RCMP about the investigations of his deputy, Graham Mitchell. When the suspicions against Mitchell got nowhere and were then channelled against Hollis himself — which happened in 1964 — an MI5 source in London was quick to inform Bennett and other top

Security Service officials. The knowledge that Hollis was being investigated by his own service as a possible Soviet mole meant that when the MI5 chief attended a retirement dinner in his honour in Ottawa in 1965 it made the atmosphere, in the words of one participant, "hellishly awkward."

Against this background as well as that of the molehunt masterminded in Washington by Angleton, it was almost inevitable that paranoia would take hold in Ottawa. This was especially so because there seemed no simple alternative explanation for the failure of several Security Service counter-espionage cases against the Soviets. Here, as in Britain, there was a disturbing pattern of cases that had simply died for no good reason.

The first important case was that of "Operation Keystone," an attempt to turn an illegal Soviet agent in Canada who was given the codename "Gideon" by the Secret Service. Gideon had landed in Halifax in 1952 with a false American passport and instructions to establish himself in the United States as a long-term resident Illegal. To "launder" his fake North American identity, however, he was to live first in Canada, where Moscow Centre assigned him tasks in Montreal. By way of preparation for his mission, he visited Vancouver and Toronto to familiarize himself with cities that played a part in the "legend" that the KGB had prepared for him. This presented him as David Soboloff, the son of Russian immigrants. There had been such a person born in Canada, but he had returned with his parents to the Soviet Union in the 1930s and then disappeared. Gideon merely had to acquire his birth certificate to authenticate his false Canadian identity. All this was to give "Soboloff" the perfect camouflage to become one of Moscow's Illegals in North America.

Not even the best-laid plans of spymasters can escape the human factor, however, and Gideon was no exception. In November 1953, having acquired a Canadian mistress and thoroughly enjoying life in Canada, he turned himself in to the RCMP. Guernsey, then the head of "B" branch, seized the opportunity and decided that running Gideon as a double agent would reveal valuable knowledge about KGB tradecraft. It might also, he calculated, help uncover other Soviet spies. This marked the birth of "Operation Keystone," which ran with apparent success until 1955. Gideon, in Guernsey's view, was "the most valuable double agent the West had had since the Second World War." Then, Gideon was summoned back to Moscow for debriefing and further training. After anxious deliberations, his Security Service handlers decided to let him take the risk; after all, if they refused to let him return, the Soviets would become suspicious and his usefulness would be over. Once back in the Soviet Union, however, it quickly became clear that he was under KGB surveillance. Then he disappeared — almost certainly to be executed — and it became obvious that "Keystone" had been compromised for some time.

Another "B" branch operation that failed was "Apple Cider," involving a GRU agent who established himself in Vancouver in 1959. Suspicion fell on Rudolph Kneschke, an immigrant of German origin recently arrived from Brazil. Kneschke ran a small radio-TV repair store that gave him good cover for receiving short-wave transmissions from Moscow. Bennett went personally to Vancouver and lived undercover for a month to monitor any signals from Moscow that Kneschke might receive. He succeeded in establishing the crucial fact that Kneschke was tuning into a frequency at exactly the same time as an enciphered message was being transmitted, and thus determined that he was an agent. But beyond that, Kneschke did nothing untoward. Then, quite suddenly, he took a plane to Amsterdam, transferred to a flight to Rome, and disappeared for good, presumably to some country in the Soviet bloc. "Apple Cider" had also inexplicably failed.

"Top Hat" was yet another counter-espionage operation involving a double agent that came to an unexpected end and became a further item in the file against Bennett. The double agent involved was codenamed "Aquavit" by the Security Service. Of East German origin, he had settled as an immigrant in Vancouver in the 1950s. For a brief period he had worked for U.S. Army Intelligence in Berlin, but after pressure was brought on his parents in East Germany he had agreed to work for the Soviets — an approach that he had immediately reported to the Americans. Then in the hope that he could escape from these complicated entanglements, he emigrated to Canada. Nevertheless, the KGB quickly caught up with him. Not long after his arrival in Vancouver he received a personal visit from the KGB resident at the Soviet embassy in Ottawa, who suggested he could help the Soviets. Having given a non-committal reply, Aquavit reported the incident to the RCMP. The case found its way to the Soviet desk in Ottawa, where Bennett authorized Aquavit to play along with the Russians in the hope that the case would lead to bigger things.

At first, the KGB used Aquavit to supply them with basic economic data about Vancouver. Gradually, they pressed him to provide information that could be useful for the infiltration or recruitment of other agents — material on immigration procedures and the names of German Canadians who were known to have relatives in East Germany (and were therefore susceptible to threats). After a while, he was instructed — as Spencer was to be — to search for information obviously being collected to document legends for illegal agents: dates of birth and death as recorded on headstones in graveyards and in newspaper obituaries, as well as detailed histories of specific residences in British Columbia that could feature in an Illegal's legend. The details of all those missions — usually communicated at clandestine meetings with KGB officers from the Ottawa embassy — Aquavit turned over to the Security Service.

By 1963 the KGB had apparently decided that Aquavit was reliable and skilled enough to receive advanced training as an illegal in Moscow, and they informed him that he should prepare for such a visit. The question now arose for Bennett and the Security Service: should they let him go? The memory of Gideon, who had never returned from such a trip, was fresh in their minds. After considerable discussion, it was decided he should obey Moscow's instructions. The gamble seemed to pay off this time. For a month Aquavit received extensive training in the Soviet capital in Morse Code, short-wave radio procedures, book codes, secret writing, and other elements of basic espionage tradecraft, and then returned to Canada.

Aquavit continued his clandestine meetings with the KGB, encounters that usually took place in and around Ottawa within the seventy-five-mile perimeter zone in which Soviet diplomats had unrestricted freedom to travel. Increasingly he came under pressure to move to

Ontario where, the KGB said, there was important work to do. Finally, he relented and moved into a small apartment in Toronto. All looked set for his transformation into a major Illegal. Then, at his first clandestine meeting following the move, he was abruptly instructed to move back to Vancouver and wait for further instructions. His KGB contact gave him some money and quickly disappeared. After that, Aquavit heard nothing from the KGB. For no apparent reason his Soviet masters had decided to abandon a seven-year investment. Top Hat too had failed.

The failure of these, as well as other, anti-KGB operations being run by the Security Service might have provoked nothing more than greater care in the future — and an even healthier respect for KGB and GRU professionalism — had it not been for the Golitsin revelations, the defection of Philby, and the MI5 and CIA molehunts. Perhaps, some Mounties began to wonder, there was a single and sinister explanation for the series of failures. Perhaps the Security Service itself was penetrated by a mole? Perversely, to some who harboured these suspicions, Soviet penetration provided a badge of maturity for Canada in the league of Western intelligence agencies. "The French have been penetrated and so have the British and Germans," said one Mountie. "The States is having trouble. Yet here we are, the youngest and least experienced and superclean." And increasingly, as talk turned to moles, eyes were focused on Bennett.

Bennett's candidacy as a possible Soviet mole was first mentioned in 1966 by one of his colleagues on the Soviet desk, Staff-Sergeant Don Atkinson. Much of his suspicion centred on Bennett's personality rather than on any hard evidence. This was to be a recurring theme over the next six years as suspicions against Bennett hardened.

In the hierarchical and traditionalist RCMP, Bennett was a natural focus for suspicion once things began to go wrong. For a start, he was a civilian in a service that was still dominated by men trained at the Police academy at Regina. This made him something of an odd man out, a fact emphasized by his appearance. Around the office he wore a battered old tweed jacket and brown suede shoes, and he had long hair. That marked him off ostentatiously from his uniformed colleagues. He also incurred some resentment as a "Brit," a relatively new immigrant who consciously or unconsciously challenged the conventional attitudes of his Canadian colleagues. Bennett was the son of a Welsh coalminer. Brought up in a working-class family with strong Labour-party sympathies, he made no bones about his youthful support for socialism and his family's commitment to left-wing social policies. This in particular focused attention on Bennett when the subject of Soviet penetration came up. So did his professional past. While working for GCHQ in Turkey, he had known Kim Philby, who at the time was the MI6 station chief. Although he had never worked for Philby, and had crossed paths with Moscow's man in SIS merely because of inevitable professional responsibilities, the fact that he had even been in touch with Philby was sufficient in some minds to taint him. Besides, Bennett was resented because he claimed to be the man in "B" division who knew all about the Soviets. He worked excessive hours, refused to delegate, and frequently clashed with colleagues whom he believed were wrong in their assessments of cases.

In 1969, the head of "A" division (responsible for security screening) authorized a secret internal review of past counter-espionage cases to see if any pattern of betrayal could be detected. This search for a possible mole occurred almost simultaneously with a visit to Ottawa by Golitsin, who was brought in by the Security Service to see if he could make any sense of the files on the failed operations. Ironically, the exercise had been stage-managed by Bennett.

Golitsin's visit strengthened the conviction of many Security Service officers that the KGB had deeply penetrated Western capitals. Already, under the impact of the Soviet defector's earlier accusations, the Service had reactivated a file begun in the 1950s. This was the "Featherbed" file, a project begun by Terry Guernsey to identify KGB agents in the federal civil service. For years it received low priority, but in the mid-1960s heightened paranoia breathed new life into it. The Featherbed investigative team was now given a new target: Bennett. To render the exercise, codenamed "Operation Gridiron," more secure, Bennett was transferred out of "B" division and "promoted" to take over "E" division. His new post removed him from any contact with the Featherbed investigators. It also took him away from control of the Russian desk.

Gridiron took two years to complete its work, and involved a thorough review of all the files of the failed counter-espionage cases. Along the way investigators also confided their suspicions to the CIA. Angleton immediately became a believer in Bennett's guilt and lent the Canadian team all the support he could. In Britain, MI5 helped with enquiries into Bennett's family background. Yet no conclusive evidence to link Bennett with the Soviets ever turned up. Finally, the investigators devised what they called "a litmus test" to establish the case one way or another. Bennett was told that a Soviet defector would be making a rendezvous on a certain date at a certain location in Montreal. If Bennett was a mole, it was reasoned, he would tell his KGB masters who would want to identify the (imaginary) defector. RCMP watchers carefully monitored the site in Montreal. At the appointed time, as if to confirm all their suspicions, they spotted a known KGB officer passing through the supposed rendezvous site.

Although it was a poorly conceived and inconclusive litmus test — with a Soviet consulate in Montreal it was more than possible that the KGB officer had come under surveillance merely by coincidence — this operation virtually marked the end of Operation Gridiron. Shortly afterwards, with Starnes anxious to solve the issue one way or another, Bennett received the fateful summons on the morning of March 13, 1972, that abruptly ended his career.

It finished his career because whatever the result of the interrogation, his reputation was tainted and his loyalty could never be proved. In fact, the interrogation, which lasted for several days, was no more conclusive than the researches of the Gridiron team. In many ways it was inept, revealing an embarrassing lack of expertise on the part of the interrogators. Most of the first day was spent ponderously delving into Bennett's working-class youth in South Wales in vain attempts to establish links with organized communism — a quest muddied by the ill-informed belief that the Independent Labour party was somehow a communist organization. Bennett was clearly so unimpressed by all this that he hardly bothered to defend himself, a reaction that only served to heighten suspicion that he had something to hide. There was an equally inconclusive session or two devoted to raking over the coals of failed operations during which Bennett reacted more strongly to suggestions of incompetence than to charges of disloyalty — again, a fact noted against him by the interrogators, but one that was perfectly explicable if Bennett knew he was no traitor and found the charges ridiculous.

It was probably just as well for Bennett that at this stage he remained ignorant of a laughable example of Security Services suspicions against him. During the secret Gridiron investigations into the Welshman, the Watcher Service had spent hours observing him in his spare time placing a cage into the trunk of his car and driving to the grounds of the National Research Council. The surveillance team ludicrously assumed he was releasing carrier pigeons to transmit secret messages to his Moscow controllers. In fact — as they eventually discovered — Bennett was trapping squirrels that were raiding his garden and releasing them a few miles from his home.

Still, despite all the suspicions, after a week the chief interrogator announced that he had come to the conclusion that Bennett was no KGB agent. Director Starnes said the same a few days later after he had read the interrogation report. But he added that Bennett's judgment in some cases had been poor and for that reason the Security Service could no longer use him. After filing a detailed rebuttal of all the charges, and after having successfully passed a lie-detector test, Bennett finally left the Security Service on July 28, 1972. "In the peaceful atmosphere of retrospection," he wrote in his final vindication, "it is so easy to criticize decisions taken in operations, a retrospection so devoid of all essential elements such as atmosphere, ignorance, personalities, policies, information and reasons for those decisions."

Bennett might have added that his case also revealed how far Canada's Security Service had been infected by a general Western obsession with moles and how easy it was in this atmosphere to attribute failures to some single sinister cause. And he could have said as well that, as in medieval witch crazes, he attracted the attention of the witchhunters for the same sorts of reasons that innocent women ended up on the pyres of European villages — a misfit, he became the lightning rod for a multitude of discontents.

One possible explanation for the string of counter-espionage failures was Security Service inexperience that simply failed to match the high professionalism of the KGB and GRU. The Mountie who pointed to Canada's "youthfulness" in the counter-espionage field as a possible explanation for a mole could just as well have said it also provided reasons for the KGB and GRU professionals to defeat the Canadians by sheer "conventional" tradecraft expertise. Several of the cases singled out in the charges against Bennett revealed inept Mountie handling. For example, those involving Vancouver were run without benefit of a "B" branch representative in the city and thus without any officers with expertise in running counter-espionage operations. There was plenty of evidence to suggest clumsy footwork by RCMP surveillance teams in British Columbia, and the Soviets could well have spotted this early on. In other cases where surveillance was involved, it was also more than likely that highly trained Soviet intelligence officers had detected the hand of the Security Service through inexperience or incompetence. This incompetence had also been revealed in Bennett's own interrogation where some of the questions displayed startling historical ignorance. There was, in the mole explanation of events, a tendency to attribute to the KGB tremendous cunning — except in the basic skill of detecting when their own operations had been penetrated by Bennett and his men.

A second possible explanation, on the assumption that all the failures were the result of a single cause, was that there was indeed a mole at work — but that he was not a Canadian mole; rather, he worked in a sister agency that had access to details of operations being handled by Ottawa. The obvious candidate here was the British security service, MI5.

A review of the cases in the Bennett file reveals how closely in this period the fledgling Security Service confided in, depended upon, and worked with the British. There was also co-operation with the FBI and CIA, but at this time the links with Britain still remained particularly intimate.

Operation Keystone, so named because Guernsey believed it vital
to the creation of a reputable Security Service record in counter-
espionage cases, was virtually a shared Canadian-British exercise.
At this time Guernsey was the only Mountie with formal counter-
espionage training (from the British), and throughout the unfolding
of Keystone he confided all its developments to London and frequently relied on its help. Early on in the case, for example, when
he needed to confirm that Gideon was indeed receiving transmissions from Moscow, as he claimed, it was GCHQ that searched the
records of Soviet short-wave broadcasts and demonstrated that they
had taken place at the times and on the frequencies that Gideon
claimed. This search had taken place before Bennett's arrival in
Canada — and it was one of the last assignments he had carried
out at GCHQ. The British, through the Secret Intelligence Service,
also co-operated operationally on Keystone by agreeing to run operations in Moscow once the double agent had returned there on
what proved to be his fateful mission. This meant carrying out
surveillance to pick up signals agreed to with Gideon before his
departure from Canada, and also, if necessary, mounting a rescue
plan to extricate him from the Soviet Union should he indicate he
needed help. The reason for using the British here was, of course,
that the Security Service had no agents operating abroad.

The Security Service sought and received British assistance on
technical tradecraft matters. "Operation Dew Worm," the bugging
of the Soviet embassy in 1956, was carried out by Peter Wright of
MI5 in co-operation with Guernsey and Bennett. Its failure became
yet another item in the file that was turned against Bennett.

The British were also kept fully informed about progress in
Apple Cider, and became operationally involved as well in helping
the Security Service establish the techniques for monitoring Soviet communications that finally pinpointed Kneschke's identity as a
Soviet illegal. Information about Soviet tradecraft was routinely exchanged with London; it was to the British that the Service turned
again in a contentious case where doubt existed about the authen-
ticity of an alleged Soviet defector. This was Olga Farmakovsky,
who in 1965 had worked closely with Canadian journalist Peter

Worthington as his official translator in Moscow. The next year she defected to the West and sought entry to Canada. The CIA believed she was a KGB "plant" and pressured the Security Service to block her entry. To decide the issue, Ottawa asked the British to carry out an interrogation. They did, grilled her thoroughly, and declared her clean. As a result, she was allowed to enter the country — the Security Service clearly at this time still being more inclined to accept a British than an American verdict.

All this close liaison and co-operation meant that the British knew practically everything about the counter-espionage cases being run by Bennett in Canada. And if indeed, as many of MI5's own officers such as Peter Wright believed, the agency was penetrated by a Soviet mole, then this alone would explain many Canadian failures. Not all the cases that appeared in the Bennett file had been shared with or confided to the British. But a large majority had. As for the remainder, in none of these could superior tradecraft by the KGB or GRU be ruled out as an explanation of Security Service incompetence.

Did the Security Service, then, shoot itself in the foot by ridding itself of Bennett? If it did, then the record indicates that it was not alone. Its sister services shared in the collective folly. Canada merely joined in a larger trek into the wilderness of mirrors.

There were two curious epilogues to the Bennett affair.

Gossip about the reasons for Bennett's departure inevitably spread within the Security Service. Soon, rumours that the spycatchers had harboured a Soviet mole reached journalists on the Ottawa circuit. One of these was Tom Hazlitt, a reporter for the *Toronto Star* with some good sources inside the RCMP. On the basis of leads provided by his informants, Hazlitt flew to Johannesburg where Bennett had initially gone after leaving Canada. His mission was to determine whether Bennett was indeed, as Ottawa scuttlebutt suggested, "the Canadian Philby." It was unsuccessful. Bennett maintained flatly that he had left the Security Service for medical reasons and that there was no basis at all to the rumours swirling around his name. Hazlitt was not deterred. Sensing a major story, he teamed up with a younger reporter to dig deeper and produce a full account of the Bennett affair. His collaborator was Ian Adams.

Adams was a radical journalist who had been in Vietnam and South America. Occasionally he had stumbled across covert activities and now welcomed the chance to explore the world of secret service. Before the two men had gone very far in their investigation, however, Hazlitt died of cancer. Adams, alone in unfamiliar territory and with none of the carefully nurtured inside sources enjoyed by Hazlitt, decided to turn the material they had collected into a novel. For him, it would be a vehicle, as he explained later, "to share with readers my perceptions of the role that this secret government [the Security Service] plays within our society." He also believed that a novel could best reveal the role the spy plays in public imagination. "The spy survives as the anima, the fantasy figure licensed to plan and commit all those violent anti-social acts we would like to perform when we are threatened or oppressed by the strains of this life," Adams wrote subsequently. "That the spy can act with such freedom and sanction from the authorities, all under the guise that it is for the protection of our society, makes the role all the more exciting."

In November 1977, just over five years after Bennett's departure from the Security Service — and at the height of public controversy and concern over the behaviour of the Security Service in Quebec — his book, *S: Portrait of a Spy* was published.

Widely promoted as fiction based on fact, the book became an immediate bestseller, with some 15,000 hardback copies sold within thirty days. Several of its major characters were clearly identifiable. "S" was obviously based on Bennett, although Adams presented him as a KGB agent who had been turned by the CIA. Former director general John Starnes, the man who had fired Bennett, was identifiable as Letourneau, and Peter Worthington, the Toronto-based right-wing journalist for whom Bennett had proved on occasions a useful Security Service source, appeared as Hazelton.

These and other character similarities, along with public interest in any scandal surrounding the Security Service, guaranteed steady progress up the bestseller list. It was a climb that was abruptly halted when Bennett — by now in Australia but kept informed of events by Worthington — brought a libel suit against Adams and his publisher and sued for $2.2 million in damages. The book was withdrawn, and the case went to the Ontario Supreme Court. Here Adams was ordered to reveal his sources. Citing the journalist's privilege to protect them, Adams refused. The affair now became a cause célèbre, a freedom-of-speech issue. Writers, journalists, and others around the country rallied to Adams's defence. An Ian Adams Defence Fund Committee quickly raised money to help pay his legal expenses. Preparations began for a lengthy appeal. Then, for no obvious reason, Bennett suggested an out-of-court settlement. Instead of the $2.2 million he had demanded, he accepted $30,000, a sum that barely covered his legal expenses. In addition, he won agreement that Adams's book should carry a distinct disclaimer. It read: "All characters in this book are fictional and any resemblance to persons, living or dead, is purely coincidental and in particular, 'S' is not and was not intended to be Leslie James Bennett."

To the uninitiated reader, this of course merely drew attention to Bennett. To those in the know, or those whose curiosity had been aroused by the Adams case, it was clear that an intriguing non-fiction account remained to be written about the Bennett affair. Despite consistent claims by various government sources that Bennett had left the Security Service for medical reasons, no one believed it. A month after publication of *S: Portrait of a Spy*, Solicitor General Francis Fox repeated the official line to a House of Commons committee. Medical reasons explained his leaving the force, Fox said. "He was not paid off and not ordered to get out of the country." This, while correct, was less than the whole truth. Unfortunately for Fox, his statement was contradicted almost immediately by Starnes's successor as director general of the Security Service, Lieutenant-General Michael Dare.

Dare had already demonstrated that he was inept, and now, before the same parliamentary committee addressed by Fox, he inadvertently revealed that Bennett had been interrogated for several days and that — contrary to Bennett's persistent claim that this was normal procedure on quitting the service — this was not standard practice. "There was a possibility in certain minds," Dare admitted, "that because of certain events he might have been a security risk." This first public admission of doubt about Bennett's loyalty was confirmed during pre-trial hearings in the Adams's libel case. In response to questioning, Bennett, who flew back to Canada from Australia to pursue his case, admitted that the interrogation had revolved around "operational cases of counter-espionage interests which had not developed in the manner expected."

It was investigative journalist John Sawatsky, in his closely researched book *For Services Rendered*, published in 1982, who first revealed the details of the case in an extended study of Bennett's career with the Security Service. And it was this book that precipitated the second epilogue to the Bennett affair.

Sawatsky's book revealed considerable detail about Operation Keystone, and in particular about the ill-fated double agent Gideon who had disappeared in Moscow. In the course of the story, Sawatsky also exposed a Security Service cover-up that had lasted for a quarter of a century. The character at the centre of this scandal was a former Security Service agent codenamed "Long Knife."

In the 1950s Long Knife had been a member of the Security Service Surveillance Unit that kept an eye on the movements of Soviet embassy personnel in Ottawa. A modestly paid corporal, Long Knife nonetheless stood out through his extravagant lifestyle and his unabashed enjoyment of material comforts and status symbols opened up by his marriage to the daughter of a former British naval commander. He sailed his father-in-law's yacht, drove his mother-in-law's Buick, and shared a fashionable house that his in-laws helped to provide. The high living was addictive, and soon Long Knife was in debt. When news reached the Security Service that his cheques regularly bounced, Guernsey recommended that he immediately be transferred out of the service. But Long Knife was a regular Mountie and Guernsey a mere civilian, and his advice was ignored. Soon, the corporal with million-dollar tastes was stealing from the Security Service itself. At this time, Guernsey was regularly paying Bell Telephone to tap the phone lines of foreign embassies in Ottawa. To hide the source and nature of these operations, payment was made in cash, by hand, to the Bell Telephone offices. Long Knife, the delivery man, began to pocket the money. Inevitably, the theft was discovered when Bell began to complain to Guernsey about non-payment. Personally interrogated by Guernsey, Long Knife confessed and was ordered by the then director of the Security Service, Cliff Harvison, to repay the money within a week.

The demand for immediate repayment precipitated Long Knife on to a desperate, and treacherous, course. With all his credit exhausted, his only remaining asset was the secret information he had learned on his official duties. One of these was to carry out surveillance on the movements of Nikolai Ostrovsky, the principal KGB officer operating out of the Soviet embassy — and the controller (or so he thought) of Gideon. That Gideon was in reality a double agent being played by the Security Service against Moscow was known to Long Knife, despite his lowly position in the service and his known penchant for getting into debt that had already marked him as a possible security threat. The reason for this serious lapse of basic security was that once, when Gideon had to be driven in a hurry from Ottawa to Montreal, Long Knife had been the only person available for the job and had been foolishly told the significance of his human cargo. In addition, he knew more than he should have done about other sensitive operations. Some of this he had learned from Bennett. The two men were friends, and their families frequently socialized together. Bennett often selected Long Knife for certain assignments and frequently used him when there was a need to establish clandestine observation posts.

Long Knife turned this knowledge into short-term profit. With Harvison's threat of dismissal hanging over him, he approached Ostrovsky and offered information in exchange for cash. The KGB officer accepted the deal, and for just over $4,000 Long Knife revealed all he knew about Gideon and Operation Keystone. In further clandestine meetings with Ostrovsky, he also provided the names of everybody in the Security Service, including all the civilian members in the Watcher Service that Guernsey was patiently building into a professional organization. Unaware of the betrayal, the Security Service continued to play Gideon as a double agent. And, in innocence, they sent him on his fateful mission to Moscow.

Long Knife in the meantime paid back the money he owed the Security Service, and was transferred to regular police duties and posted to Winnipeg. This was yet another disaster for the high-spending Mountie because it removed him from access to the information the Soviets wanted, and he still needed money. Meetings with Ostrovsky took place on the infrequent occasions Long Knife could get back to Ottawa, but when in 1958 Ostrovsky was replaced by another KGB man, Rem Krassilnikov, and his new Soviet controller told him bluntly that he would have to come up with some real information if he wanted money, desperation set in. The Mountie conceived yet another plan — one that received considerable impetus when he thought he detected RCMP surveillance of his encounter with the KGB officer. To forestall Security Service queries about his Soviet contacts, he decided to offer himself to his former employers as a triple agent — a man in touch with the Soviets who could be used by the Security Service for some counter-intelligence tasks. From his room at the Château Laurier hotel Long Knife contacted the Security Service.

It took little time to see through Long Knife's implausible story. He quickly found himself under arrest and then placed incommunicado in RCMP cells where he was subjected to nine days' interrogation. Finally, he admitted his betrayal of Gideon and his other exchanges of information with the Soviets.

The Mounties were faced with a problem. They needed to get rid of the traitor, but they were desperate to avoid any public revelations about the appalling and tragic breach of security that had occurred. The solution was to charge Long Knife with fraud and expel him from the service. This was relatively easy given his habit of passing bad cheques, and later in 1958 a Manitoba court found him guilty of fraud. He was given a two-year suspended sentence, and ordered to repay his debts at the rate of $100 a month. Dismissed from the RCMP, he failed by only two years to qualify for his lifetime pension. He then virtually disappeared until the early 1980s when he resurfaced as a construction-safety supervisor in Prince Rupert. Few knew of his past with the Mounties and not even his wife and family knew the real reasons for his dismissal from the force some twenty-five years earlier. Then, in 1982, came Sawatsky's book.

Through his Security Service sources Sawatsky had learned the real identity of Long Knife — James Morrison — and had traced him to Prince Rupert. In return for a promise that Sawatsky would not use his real name, Morrison agreed to tell his story. Predictably, publication led to massive media interest, and on November 9, 1982, disguised by a floppy black wig and a false moustache, Morrison appeared on CBC TV's "Fifth Estate" to admit that he had betrayed Gideon to the KGB.

This voluntary confession, combined with a public outcry over the Mounties' unjust protection of one of their own, eventually led to Official Secrets Act charges against Morrison in 1983. A lower court decision to stay the proceedings because of the length of time that had elapsed since 1958 was overturned by the Supreme Court of Ontario, and Morrison, then sixty-nine, came to trial in Ottawa in early 1986. He pleaded not guilty, but after the court was shown a tape of the "Fifth Estate" broadcast and two of his former colleagues identified him as the man in the wig, he changed his plea. On May 26, 1986, Morrison was sentenced to eighteen months in jail.

The Long Knife Affair revealed several things about the Security Service and its counter-intelligence operations in the 1950s. Morrison had clearly been unsuitable for service from the beginning, and his continued employment in such a sensitive position, against the advice of Guernsey, revealed appalling amateurishness and carelessness on the part of those who ran Canada's spycatcher service. This, along with other cases in the Bennett file, showed how ill-equipped Canada was to play hardball in the brutal world of Cold War intelligence. Bennett, in being so open about cases with Morrison, showed poor judgment when he should have known better. So, for that matter, did a number of other Mounties.

When Gouzenko defected, RCMP headquarters had only two commissioned officers on the Intelligence side, the entire Intelligence branch consisted of about two dozen men, and the Mounties quickly turned to the British for help. After Gouzenko, the branch was renamed the Special Branch and put under the command of Superintendent George McClellan. McClellan had worked in Toronto during the war, where he had benefited from his contacts with the British staff that ran Camp X, the secret-agent training school at Whitby. He understood some of the needs of counter-intelligence, and within six months of his appointment had established a counter-espionage branch, "B" branch. In the late 1940s, this section, staffed by three Mounties, was Canada's principal weapon in the counter-intelligence war with the highly professional and long-experienced KGB and GRU. Later on, Guernsey, a civilian, joined the branch. Even with his obvious abilities, however, what Canada could bring to bear against the KGB and GRU was pathetically small. Out of the frustrations that this produced came the search for a scapegoat.

Most important, the Bennett and Long Knife affairs revealed once again how intimately linked with other members of the UKUSA alliance Canada really was. Dependence on the British for tradecraft and analysis remained heavy until the 1960s when the link with Washington began to play a greater role. Membership in the Western security network strengthened Canadian operations, but also made the Security Service more vulnerable. When "mole fever" struck in London and Washington, it was inevitable that Ottawa would catch the disease. And even when Bennett had been cleared, it was obvious to Starnes and others in the Security Service that his usefulness was ended because London and Washington would forever remain suspicious and this would damage vital links for Ottawa. Once again, the responsibilities of being a partner in a transnational community had meant that a "made in Canada" solution was no solution at all.

8.
THE FANTASIST AND
THE FILM-MAKER

I t was, said one observer when it was all over, "as bizarre a
case as you'll find in the murky world of espionage." The Old
Bailey — London's Central Criminal Court, standing in the
shadow of St. Paul's Cathedral — has witnessed all the most
famous British spy trials of modern times. It was here that Dr. Alan
Nunn May, the British nuclear scientist exposed as a Russian agent
during the Gouzenko revelations, was tried and sentenced in 1946.
Klaus Fuchs, another of the wartime atomic spies, had also stood in
its prisoner's dock. So had "Gordon Lonsdale," the Russian deep-
cover agent posing as a Canadian, implicated in the 1962 Portland
Spy Ring Case. Here George Blake had received the longest term
of imprisonment in modern British history — forty-two years — for
spying for the Russians while working for MI6. And as recently as
November 1982 an almost equally severe thirty-five-year sentence
had been passed on Geoffrey Prime for giving to the Soviet Union
top-level secrets from GCHQ, Britain's codebreaking centre.

But the Official Secrets trial that opened in its Number One
Criminal Court on the morning of Monday, November 29, 1982,
only three weeks after the Prime case, was extraordinary on several counts.

First was the prisoner himself. A greying sixty-year-old, he wore
a charcoal suit and horn-rimmed glasses. He was no nuclear scientist, or intelligence officer, or codebreaking specialist privy to the
most up-to-date secrets of state. On the contrary, he was a professor from a provincial university whose main apparent interest in life

was studying Spain's decline in seventeenth-century Europe. He had worked in the same department for eighteen years, but had made no real friends and his colleagues hardly noticed him. How could this unremarkable man have anything to do with the serious charges he faced, charges of passing information for twenty-three years to the Soviet Union?

This, indeed, was the thrust of the defence for the first two days of the trial. Look, suggested his defence counsel to the jury, at the accused's distinguished career for his country in peace and in war. He served with the resistance behind enemy lines during the Second World War, and later had an exemplary career in the academic world as a research economist, sometimes working for government agencies as well as, for a short spell in the 1950s, NATO. Could this man really be guilty of the two specific charges he faced under the Official Secrets Act: of having between 1956 and 1961 (more than twenty years earlier) "for purposes prejudicial to the safety or interest of the United Kingdom ... communicated to a Russian agent information, namely top secret, secret and confidential material belonging to the North Atlantic Treaty Organization ... [which was] calculated to be, or might have been or was intended to be directly or indirectly useful to an enemy"; and the second charge, that between 1956 and 1979, "for a purpose prejudicial to the safety and interest of the United Kingdom he obtained information which was calculated to be, or might have been or was intended to be directly or indirectly useful to an enemy"?

To the initial puzzlement of the press and general public there was added an astonishing claim made by the defendant himself. On the third day of the trial he finally climbed into the witness box. In a slow and rambling manner that made what he had to say even more dramatic, he claimed that, far from being the unworldly professor, in reality he was a double agent in a carefully orchestrated mission to plant disinformation on the KGB. The material he had passed on to the Soviet agents, he said, had been carefully vetted and approved in advance by Western intelligence; he could even identify his two Western controllers.

What added mystery to the drama were two factors that from the beginning had seemed strange. Although being tried in a British court, the defendant had never worked for the British government or taught in a British university. He was a Canadian, born in Ottawa, and now a professor at Laval University in Quebec City. Most curious of all, evidence being used by the British prosecutors had been known to the Canadian government since 1979. Yet no attempt had been made to bring Professor Hugh Hambleton to justice. The Canadian authorities had allowed Hambleton to continue teaching at Laval unmolested as well as to travel abroad. Was this carelessness on the part of the Canadian government, yet another example of bungling by the RCMP Security Service? Or was it something more sinister? Had Hambleton been protected for some reason by higher authority in Ottawa?

Back in the Canadian capital there were people who suggested that fingers should be pointed at the very top. Standing up to denounce the Liberal government of Pierre Trudeau, for example, was Allan Lawrence. Former solicitor general in the short-lived Conservative government of Joe Clark, Lawrence had held the security portfolio when the first suspicions about Hambleton were investigated. But he had lost office before much progress had been made on the case. Now, as headlines about the trial dominated the Canadian press, he suggested to a noisy House of Commons that there had been a conspiracy at work. Had he stayed in office, Lawrence insisted, Hambleton would have been brought to trial in Canada. Obviously there were powerful figures protecting Hambleton. "The woods are full," he claimed, "of Canadian traitors who have been promoted or pensioned off."

The Toronto *Sun* voiced the deepest suspicions. "The only conclusion possible," it proclaimed, "is that [Hambleton] knows too much; that if he was charged names of upper echelon figures would emerge as having worked for the Soviet Union." The reality was, thundered Conservative MP Chris Speyer, "that a parking meter violator or a shoplifter is treated in a far harsher fashion than our spies."

There were plenty of people who shared the puzzlement and outrage. Many were on the Opposition benches. Some were in the Security Service of the RCMP, angry that what they had discovered about Hambleton had been rejected by the Liberal government as insufficient to bring a successful case to court. Others were to be found in the sister security agencies who had worked with the RCMP on the Hambleton case, especially the FBI. On many accounts, it remains one of the most bizarre and unusual of Canadian spy cases. To follow the route that took Hambleton to the Old Bailey, we need first to go back to a story that really began in Toronto more than twenty years earlier. What is particularly interesting about the story is that it reveals so much about the daily life of a spy.

In the early 1960s, Harold's Famous Delicatessen in downtown Toronto was a favourite eating spot for cameramen, technicians, and other employees of the nearby CBC. A small, three-storey brick building, it was five minutes away from the CBC studios on Jarvis Street. It was not just the homemade German potato salad and freshly baked bread made by Inga, the owner's blonde and blue-eyed wife, that drew them to Harold's. Rudi Herrmann, the popular and gregarious proprietor who had bought the place soon after the couple arrived in Canada in 1962, was himself an attraction. He drove a BMW he had specially imported from Germany, he knew how to spin a good yarn, and after hours he frequently entertained his friends with a few glasses of wine and his recordings of old Nazi war songs. A lot of them were German immigrants like himself. For that, as well as his right-wing and free-enterprise views, he became known as "Rudi the Nazi." A camera buff who knew how to talk the jargon of his CBC customers, he showed off some pretty sophisticated equipment of his own. It wasn't long before he had set up a special deal for the CBC to rent his hard-to-find Arriflex movie camera for $25 a day.

To all appearances Rudi's bonhomie was just the calculated strategy of a new and ambitious immigrant, making contacts, building social and professional networks, and earning extra money on the side. It paid off. After the birth of her second child, Inga decided she could no longer work behind the counter, and Rudi decided to sell the business while the going was good. Getting almost double the price he had paid for it only two years earlier, he took a job as a CBC sound man and began courses in film-making. Through an agency he soon found work on an advertising campaign for the Liberal party. By the middle 1960s he had established a reputation as an excellent and hardworking film-maker, and also ran a record distributorship for a West German company. He covered Lester Pearson's cross-country tour in 1965, toured the Halifax naval station for a program on the state of the navy, worked on a civil-rights documentary, and assisted news crews at the 1967 Liberal convention that chose Pierre Trudeau as leader of the party. The cameraman who worked with Herrmann later recalled that, at one point during the convention, Trudeau, as a joke, "leaned off the stage . . . and popped a few grapes into Rudi's mouth."

The fruits of Rudi's hard work soon showed. He and Inga bought their own house in Leaside, a solid middle-class area of Toronto, and in February 1967 they took out citizenship in a Toronto courtroom. The judge chose Rudi, now earning $50,000 a year, as the most outstanding member of the group in front of him to lead them all in taking the oath of allegiance to the Queen.

Then, only a year later, Rudi and Inga suddenly pulled up roots. Rudi applied for a U.S. visa, and by mid-1968 he and his family had left Canada for New York. Here Rudi set up business as Documatic Films, Inc., and soon he was landing lucrative contracts from IBM for sales and training films. It was a job that required a lot of travel. Frequently he would fly to Europe on business. Less often, he would get into his car and drive north, towards the Canadian border.

His destination, although no one knew it, was Quebec City. It was a place he knew well, especially the comfortable old bar of the Château Frontenac Hotel, overlooking the St. Lawrence River. There for years he had been meeting one of his agents. Rudi Herrmann was not just a shrewd and gregarious businessman who knew a lot about cameras: he was also the KGB's leading Illegal intelligence officer in North America. And the man who regularly met him over drinks at the Frontenac was Hugh Hambleton.

An Illegal is an intelligence officer or agent who operates in a foreign country without official status or cover such as that of diplomat or trade representative. He or she initially enters the target nation under a fictitious identity to live as a normal member of the surrounding

155

society. Illegals have many uses. They may be saboteurs or assassins who, in case of capture or failure, can never be linked officially with their country. They may be "sleepers," agents whose sole mission is to penetrate the highest reaches of the target nation regardless of how long it takes. In an emergency they may have to run their country's network of agents should the normal control centre, such as the embassy, be closed down or otherwise be put out of action. For that reason, Illegals need their own secure and independent communication links with home. This means at the very least a high-powered short-wave receiver for taking messages from their control centre.

Illegals are special and extraordinary, an élite among an élite so far as the KGB is concerned. They must enter into life in the target nation so thoroughly that they live in it like any normal citizen, finding and changing jobs; having a social life; mixing with friends and neighbours and colleagues; travelling in and outside the country; dealing with government officials, taxmen, and the police; going to the movies; shopping at the local superstore, or visiting the medical centre. Since their secret task can be a lifetime's mission, their external life has to be real. But at the same time it is an exercise in sustained deception. The true job is to remain loyal to the KGB, living a secret existence that is isolated and insecure. Unlike the society in which the Illegal lives, in which his efforts may be rewarded with a better-paid job, a new car, or a pleasant social life, Moscow Centre can hold out the promise of reward only when the mission succeeds, perhaps years down the line. Until then, the Illegal leads a double life that taxes his or her emotional and intellectual resources and demands extraordinary stamina and loyalty. Not surprisingly, Illegals are difficult to recruit. And once recruited, trained, and despatched on their missions, they become some of the most highly valued assets of the espionage business. Both sides put a high price on Illegals. To the West, a captured Soviet Illegal persuaded to talk can reveal precious information about Soviet methods and targets. To the Soviets, even a blown Illegal remains valuable because he can give them inside material about living in the target nation. That is, if they can get him back soon enough. For that, there's always the spy swap.

It was a spy trade that in 1962 returned the KGB's most important Illegal in North America back to the Soviet Union. It took place at the Glienicke Bridge, one of the few crossing points left between East and West during the years of the Berlin Wall. In a scene worthy of a John le Carré novel, Gary Powers, pilot of the American U-2 spy plane shot down over the Soviet Union in 1960, was exchanged in great secrecy early one dawn for KGB Colonel Rudolf Abel. Abel, whose real identity remains a mystery, has been described as the most resourceful secret agent the KGB ever managed to plant inside the United States. For nine years he successfully passed himself off as an artist and photographer with a studio apartment close by the Brooklyn Bridge in New York City. To his friends and neighbours he was Emil Goldfus, a modest and kindly man with conservative tastes who enjoyed sharing conversations about Bach and discussing the differing merits of artists such as Rembrandt or Van Gogh. *The Amateur*, a portrait of Goldfus/Abel in his studio with his paints and brushes, was even shown at a National Academy of Design exhibition in 1957 by an unsuspecting artist friend. But there was nothing amateur about the real Abel, and it was only the defection to the West by a disgruntled KGB agent that led the FBI to arrest him in 1957. In the trial that followed, Abel received a thirty-year sentence.

Canada, it was revealed, had played a small part in his career as an Illegal. It had been his point of entry into North America when he arrived at Quebec City in November 1948 as Andrew Kayotis, a penniless displaced person from the refugee camps of postwar Europe. At about the same time, the chief KGB officer in Canada was en route to Moscow after a tour of duty in Ottawa that had coincided with the unravelling of the GRU network during the Gouzenko affair. Vitali Pavlov had no sooner regained KGB headquarters than he was made number two in the North American division of the First Chief Directorate. From there he directed operations in Canada and the United States and became Abel's controller, providing him with detailed instructions about his espionage targets.

Abel's arrest left a gap in North America, which it took the KGB five years to fill. But eight days after Abel stepped back to the East over the white line painted across the surface of the Glienicke

Bridge, his successor arrived in the New World. On February 16, 1962, at Dorval airport in Montreal, Rudolf Herrmann, accompanied by his wife, Inga, and their four-year-old son, Peter, disembarked from the plane that had brought them from Germany. It was the coldest day Herrmann had ever experienced. And it was fifteen years as an active Illegal before his capture and confession finally allowed him to come in from the cold.

Rudi Herrmann's long years of success were the result of the expert training given him by the KGB. It was seven years before they were satisfied that he was ready, an apprenticeship of schooling and hard labour that guaranteed they had found a truly extraordinary man, a worthy member of the élite.

It all began in Prague in 1955, where, after seven years of Communist rule, the Czech intelligence service, the STB, was fully under KGB control. Moscow laid down its priorities and targets, KGB officers worked in its headquarters as advisers, and the entire Czech population was open to KGB recruiting. In the spring of that year Ludek Zemenek was a twenty-five-year-old private serving in a border-guards brigade on the German frontier. Born in a small Moravian peasant village, the son of an impoverished photographer, Zemenek became an ardent communist from the moment Soviet forces liberated his country from the Nazis in 1945. At school he founded and led the League of Communist Students. In summers he campaigned for the party and helped it to win 38 percent of the popular vote in the elections of 1946. After the communist takeover in 1948 he was admitted to the city's historic Charles University as a privileged student of international relations. Four years later he graduated with the Red Diploma, the highest of honours. But along the way Zemenek faced serious obstacles. These were the years of the great purges in Czechoslovakia, when even the first secretary of the party was stripped of his position and hanged as an agent of the bourgeois West. Despite his poverty, Zemenek was classified as "petty-bourgeois" because his father ran a small business. At every turn he found himself discriminated against in favour of working-class comrades. Although he was chosen as the student most qualified to study in the Soviet Union, for example, the party vetoed the award — as it did several others. Anyone less committed would have lost faith. But to Zemenek it simply reinforced Lenin's dictum on the need for sacrifice in the interests of the party, and adversity strengthened his loyalty to the communist cause. His posting as a lowly private to a border-guards brigade, when most of his friends were awarded reserve-officer commissions, was merely another necessary hardship along the chosen path. It was also the starting-point of his life as a KGB Illegal. A Soviet adviser in the Czech military took note of the politically articulate and dedicated soldier, and in March 1955 he was summoned to Prague. Before a panel of eight civilians he was thoroughly interviewed about his political views and personal life. Two months later he was told he had been selected for secret intelligence work that would take him abroad for many years. Asked if he needed time to choose, Zemenek immediately accepted his mission. Finally, the party had fully embraced him.

Within a matter of weeks Zemenek left Czechoslovakia and was installed in the East German city of Halle. Here, under the control of a KGB colonel, he mastered German by attending classes at the university. To learn the tradecraft of his new profession he was sent for individual instruction by the KGB at Soviet military headquarters at Karlshorst outside East Berlin. Already, he had assumed the first of many identities. To his fellow students he presented himself as a Soviet trade official from the eastern part of Czechoslovakia absorbed by the Soviet Union in 1945 — thus explaining both his Czech accent and the need to learn German.

Only when he could pass as a German did Ludek Zemenek become Rudi Herrmann. The identity was chosen for him by the Illegals section in the First Chief Directorate of KGB headquarters in Moscow. Like most legends, or false biographies, it was partly based on reality. There once had been a Rudi Herrmann, a Sudeten German from Czechoslovakia who, in the Second World War, had volunteered for a German labour battalion. After he was killed on the Eastern Front in 1943, the KGB had found personal papers on his body that established the main outlines of his life. More important, they discovered he had no living relatives. This was crucial, for it minimized the risk of exposure and made him the perfect candidate for use in the creation of a new, fictional identity. On the foundation of the dead Herrmann's life, the KGB constructed a detailed new biography for Ludek Zemenek. Up until 1943 it more or less followed that of the real Rudi Herrmann. Then it had him surviving the war and ending up in the eastern zone of divided Germany, working first in a Dresden canning factory, then in a bookstore at Magdeburg. Finally — when Zemenek put on the mask created for him — he moved in 1957 to Frankfurt an der Oder to be with his girlfriend. After that, the legend became what Zemenek actually made it.

To enter properly into the skin of Rudi Herrmann and to make the legend foolproof, the KGB had Zemenek visit the canning factory in Dresden and the bookstore in Magdeburg chosen for the story. Here he memorized everything he could, including photographs and names of co-workers, the ways in which trucks he would have loaded or driven in Dresden actually worked, and details of the cities themselves. The KGB arranged for the relevant employment records to be created and placed in the files.

There was one final step to be taken before Ludek Zemenek was ready to take on his identity as Rudi Herrmann. At Halle-Wittenberg University he had been quickly attracted to a female student of his own age who agreed to tutor him in German. Inga Jurgen was the daughter of Sudeten German communists. Along with several hundred thousand other Sudeten Germans, the family was expelled from Czechoslovakia after the war and ended up as refugees in East Germany. Here, Inga joined the party and diligently applied herself to a university education. Unknowingly, she was also preparing herself to become an Illegal. The KGB was keen to have Ludek married. That way he was less likely to compromise his mission by womanizing, and he would have a person to confide in and help with communications and other tasks. Once the KGB checked Inga out and she passed with flying colours, she too was given a new identity. Again, a dead person provided the basis of the legend. Inga became a German woman named Ingalore Moerke, killed in a bombing raid on Stettin in 1944. There was even an authentic birth certificate to prove her identity. To start the couple off as

Illegals, the KGB found Inga a job in a state design office at Frank-furt an der Oder. And it was here that Ludek, now the unemployed Rudi Herrmann, arrived looking for work in the winter of 1957. Out in the cold, he was now the sole guardian of his own legend.

Fortune and his own ambition carried Rudi on their backs for the next twenty years as an Illegal KGB agent in Germany, Canada, and the United States. Fate smiled on him immediately. In Frank-furt an der Oder he landed a job in a small auto-parts store run by an unrepentant old Nazi. When not learning the tricks of how to run a small business, Rudi absorbed more Nazi and anti-communist lore than even the KGB in its wildest dreams could have devised as effec-tive cover. This lasted for several months. Rudi and Inga married; Peter, their first child, was born; and a year later, following instruc-tions, Peter left East Germany to find a job in West Germany. In leaving the security of the East and taking his first mission in al-ien territory, Rudi had a secret lifeline. Hidden in the hollowed-out handle of his hairbrush was a cipher pad and a schedule of broad-casts from the East. With a standard small radio Rudi could tune into a commercial frequency at the right hour, note down the mes-sage transmitted in standard Morse code, decipher it with the help of his cipher pad, and then receive his regular instructions. One way or another, it was a pattern he followed for the next twenty years.

Once again, fortune followed him. In Freiburg, he was befriended by an elderly and wealthy German businessman who owned a large family textile factory. The businessman and his childless wife vir-tually adopted Rudi as a son, and were delighted when Inga and her child Peter arrived soon after to join him. The Herrmanns were given the third floor of the family's villa, and soon Rudi, from peas-ant Moravia, was learning the etiquette and lifestyle of a prosperous Western entrepreneur. He became a connoisseur of fine wines and learned how to dress as well as to run a large business. Ironically, he became almost too successful. After several months the factory owner offered to bequeath him the business. It was an offer Rudi had to reject because it would have wrecked his mobility. Instead, he set up in business on his own, first running a small mail-order operation and then acquiring the franchise to sell Japanese cameras and other optical equipment in Stuttgart. It took only two years of working in the postwar West German "miracle" economy for Rudi to become a prosperous businessman ready for the greater challenges of operating as a KGB Illegal in North America.

The order came from Moscow early in 1961. Marked "urgent," it instructed him to visit Canada and the United States as a tourist to see if he felt he could live and operate there. As soon as spring arrived, Rudi obeyed, sailing to Montreal from Bremerhaven on a tourist ship, *The Seven Seas*. He spent a few days in Montreal, then travelled, via Ottawa, Toronto, and London, into the United States, where he visited Detroit and New York. On his return, he dutifully reported that he could serve in either country. Canada and Canadians had struck him as particularly friendly. And although Toronto struck him as unsophisticated compared to Europe, it had a German immigrant community with shops and delicatessens that offered an easy entrée into the wider society. "Get an imimgration visa for Canada," Moscow replied, "and begin intensive course in English." While Rudi followed these instructions, Inga flew to KGB headquarters for a more detailed briefing. When she returned it was with the suggestion that they open a small business, perhaps a camera store, and work hard for Canadian citizenship. She also brought with her the equipment that would guarantee unbroken direct communication with Moscow Centre: cipher pads, a schedule of broadcasts, and a special oscillator that when fitted into a short-wave receiver would help reception of Moscow's coded messages. Once Rudi had sold his business, obtained the necessary visas, and arranged shipment of his BMW, they were ready to leave. The KGB had given Inga $5,000 (U.S.) in Moscow. Rudi had saved almost $10,000 of his own. Thus equipped, the Herrmanns arrived in Dorval as immigrants on that wintry February morning in 1962. They had no idea what specific mission the KGB had in mind for them. "Just settle in as good Canadians," Inga had been told in Moscow, "we'll tell you later what we expect you to do."

While the Herrmanns were busy living the legend that masked their secret life in Toronto, Hugh Hambleton was struggling to decide if

162

he wanted to continue the dangerous masquerade in which he was involved with the KGB. For if Rudi Herrmann was a convinced and dedicated communist driven by ideological faith, Hugh Hambleton was a middle-class fantasist who flirted with the excitement and danger of spying for the KGB. His ideological conviction was noticeable by its absence. When he got bored, or the game became a nuisance, he tried to drop out. But he quickly learned it wasn't quite as easy as that.

Seven years older than Rudi Herrmann, Hugh Hambleton celebrated his fortieth birthday in 1962. Born in Ottawa, he was an academic who spent a great deal of his life overseas. Schooled in Canada, Britain, France, and the United States, he served in the Second World War with the Free French forces in Algiers and Europe, lived in Paris for most of the 1950s, and was now dividing his time between Spain, where he owned a villa on the Costa Blanca, and London, where he had just enrolled for a doctorate at the London School of Economics and Political Science. If this seemed rather late in life, it was consistent with Hambleton's character. For behind the meticulous, introverted, and almost monastic exterior he presented to the outside world, there lurked a restless and romantic adolescent eager for travel and new experience. This had already caused trouble in his private life. His first marriage, to the daughter of a high ranking French-Canadian civil servant, had ended in divorce. The second, to the daughter of a wealthy Italian businessman, was by all accounts a stormy affair. It produced three children, but it too soon ended in failure. After that, there was a succession of girlfriends. None of them lasted very long.

The stability of Hambleton's second marriage was certainly not assisted by his decision to become a student again, especially as it meant giving up an important and well-paid NATO job in Paris. Before President Charles de Gaulle ordered NATO out of France, its headquarters were located on the outskirts of the French capital. Here, for five years, from 1956 to 1961, Hambleton, with a doctorate in economics from the Sorbonne already behind him, worked in the Economic Directorate as an expert analyst on the economies of the NATO and Warsaw Pact countries. Top-secret information provided much of the raw material for his reports, which in turn helped shape long-term planning for NATO's Council of Ministers. He enjoyed the job, relishing the influence he exerted and the secret knowledge he shared with his colleagues.

But Hambleton seemed quickly to forget it all as he applied himself at LSE to his research on the economic decline of Spain in the seventeenth century. His work went well, and soon he could add a second doctorate to his list of academic honours. In spring 1964, Laval University tempted him back to Canada with an offer of a professorship in the economics department. As he settled into his job in Quebec City, the prosaic routine of lunching with colleagues and teaching students basic economics seemed far removed from the glamour and prestige of his job at NATO. But if it belonged to the past, it was far from being history. After he met up with Rudi Herrmann it would return to haunt and eventually destroy him.

The reason was simple. During his five years at NATO, Hambleton had passed thousands of its secrets to the KGB. Cleared for top-secret work, he took hundreds of sensitive files home and photographed them with his 35mm camera in the second-floor study of his comfortable suburban villa. Then, at various points around the city, he handed the films over to his Soviet contacts. Instructions on what secrets to collect came direct from Moscow over Hambleton's short-wave radio receiver. Every Thursday at eight o'clock he would tune in to the correct frequency, note down the coded message, and unravel its instructions with the help of cipher pads provided by the KGB. It was dangerous work. Although security at NATO was lax, he could at any time be challenged by a guard as he left at night with his packed briefcase. In 1960 a French clerk working in the registry was arrested and sentenced to life imprisonment for working for the Russians. As the KGB stepped up its demands for an increasing number of documents, Hambleton backed away. In December of that year he told his KGB controller that he wanted to leave NATO to pursue his academic career at LSE. Surprisingly, his control did not resist. The next day Hambleton short-circuited his radio receiver and burned the set in the woods. Next he wrote a letter of resignation to his superior at NATO and enrolled for his doctorate in London. In summer 1961, as East–West relations reached a critical point with the building of the Berlin Wall, Hambleton spent a relaxed time in his villa at Torremolinos, relieved that he had escaped his mission without exposure.

But the KGB had invested too much time and effort in Hambleton to let him go as easily as that. Indeed, Hambleton himself was far more dependent on the link than he realized. In effect, he was an addict, captive of a fantasy world of spying that went back far beyond his years with NATO.

It all began in the Ottawa of the late 1940s. Fallout from the Gouzenko case was still intense, the Cold War was at its height, and the West was anxiously building NATO. Soviet officials felt uncomfortable in the Canadian capital, and there were few Canadians eager to be seen in their presence. A major exception was Hambleton's mother, Bessie Hambleton. The strong-willed wife of a prominent press correspondent, she was a formidable and emancipated woman with a strong and deep-seated interest in what she called "the Soviet experiment." She had an impressive knowledge of languages and indefatigable energy in acting as a society hostess. The Hambleton household on Ruskin Avenue became a gathering place for guests from around the world. Most were friends of liberal causes, and Bessie Hambleton always took care to see that ostracized East-bloc diplomats were included in her soirées.

She also took considerable care of the family's finances. Some shrewd real-estate investments had yielded a handsome profit, and this she reinvested in property in Spain — at that time extremely cheap; there was an apartment in Madrid, another in Torremolinos, and a villa — "Mariposa" (the butterfly) — in the hills of Mijas overlooking the Mediterranean at Marbella. It was all part of the life plan she had laid out for her son. He had returned in 1948 from a year's study in Mexico City with a master's degree in economics. He had also become fascinated by Spanish, which he spoke well, and had acquired an almost obsessive interest in the old Spanish monarchy. The properties his mother had acquired would provide him with a second home and financial security.

By early 1949, when he was twenty-six, Hugh Hambleton had packed in more experience and travel abroad than most Canadians enjoy in a lifetime. He had also acquired a thirst for excitement and involvement in the great events of history that explain much of his later life. Prewar France of the 1930s, torn by political conflict of the Popular Front era, had formed the backdrop for his early schooling when his father was posted there as a Canadian Press correspondent. He had then been sent to California to learn Spanish. The Second World War had broken out by the time he returned home, and France lay divided between the government of Vichy and German occupation. Hambleton answered an appeal for help from de Gaulle's Free French forces and was immediately recruited. With his ability in languages he was soon assigned to their headquarters at Algiers. A hotbed of intrigue between differing factions of the French in exile, the city was also a major intelligence centre from which to observe and infiltrate Nazi-occupied Europe. Here Hambleton worked in the intelligence directorate, translating reports. With the liberation of Paris in summer 1944, Hambleton and the Free French moved back to France. After a short while, the French made him a liaison officer with the U.S. Army's 103rd Division as it pursued the Germans across France and into Bavaria. Hambleton finally ended the war in the Canadian armed forces interrogating prisoners of war and analysing intelligence reports in occupied Germany.

The adrenalin flow of these years would never be staunched. From now on Hambleton felt he belonged to the centre-stage of history. "To be important, Leo, to have people pay attention to you," Hambleton confided in his old school friend, Leo Heaps, at this time, "that is what counts in life." In the inevitable dullness of the Ottawa to which he returned, only the contacts provided by his mother's vigorous social life kept boredom at bay. Increasingly he enjoyed playing with the short-wave radio set that kept him in direct touch with the dramas of Cold War Europe — the Berlin blockade, the purges in Eastern Europe, the division of Germany. Then, one day in 1949, there stepped into his life a man who once again made him feel that he was playing a part in world events.

Vladimir Borodin was an atypical member of the Soviet embassy, where he held the position of cultural attaché. Thirty-two years old, he had the easy-going manners of a polished and sophisticated diplomat of the old school. His French and English were fluent, and he was a lively conversationalist with a keen and genuine interest in what others had to say. He was a welcome guest at the party Bessie Hambleton held that year to celebrate the end of the winter. Hambleton, newly married and now working for the National Film Board, found him compatible and friendly. After that, there was a trip out to the Hambleton property in the Gatineau Hills and several more social encounters. At each of these meetings Borodin expressed the hope that the Soviet Union and Canada could understand each other and live in peace, and that Hambleton could help in the process. Hambleton remained non-committal, but was flattered by Borodin's attention and concern over his future career. By the time Borodin left Ottawa, there was a distinct bond between the two men. Hambleton had been made to feel that out of it could come something important in his life.

Borodin felt the same, but for a very different reason. As a KGB recruiter for the First Chief Directorate, responsible for foreign intelligence, he had spun the first strands of the web that would eventually entrap Hambleton into working for Moscow. Patience and persistence in cultivating the young academic would eventually be rewarded.

That time came four years later, in 1955. Now living in Paris and studying at the Sorbonne, Hambleton had almost forgotten his Soviet friend. Unannounced, Borodin turned up one evening with a friend, a fellow Russian whom he introduced as Paul. It was a friendly meeting, with much discussion about Hambleton's future career. What were his plans? enquired the Russians. Hambleton was flattered by their interest, as well as by their earnest solicitation of his views on world events. Shortly afterwards Paul contacted him with an invitation to dinner. Hambleton accepted, and over the next year the two men dined regularly together at expensive restaurants in obscure parts of the city. Paul became a confidant and adviser on Hugh's career, and early in 1956 suggested that he could best help their friendship by getting a job at NATO headquarters and postponing his plans to go on to LSE for his doctorate. Hambleton agreed. That November — just as Soviet forces were in the final stages of crushing the Hungarian revolution — NATO gave him a security clearance and he joined its staff as an economic analyst. Like Borodin, "Paul," variously identified as either Pavel Lukyanov or Alexis Trichinov, was from the KGB First Chief Directorate. For the next twenty years he would be Hambleton's principal Soviet controller.

At first, it was insignificant material that Hambleton gave to Paul — low-classification reports on such matters as coal production in France and Belgium or the state of political parties in Western Europe. Later Paul escalated his requests through the various NATO classifications until Hambleton was regularly providing him with the most secret grade of all — "cosmic" material. Much of this had to do with NATO military force objectives. At least one file was later alleged to have revealed the names of Western agents in the occupied Baltic states who were providing NATO with intelligence reports, although how Hambleton could have gained access to it remains unclear. In all, during the five years he worked in Paris, thousands of pages of secret NATO material found their way to the KGB.

For Hambleton, it was a game that made him feel wanted and important. In Algiers he had worked — or so he claimed — on the reports of underground agents. Now he was one himself, and the paraphernalia of the spy business lent his life an excitement that it otherwise lacked. "All this secret message stuff was a real kick," he confessed when his story first broke publicly in Canada many years later. "And it did feel good to make recommendations to a world power. You see, they put much more stock in anything they get surreptitiously."

To make regular contact with his KGB controller, Hambleton had precise instructions, a schedule to follow that if broken for any reason could be automatically resumed without further communication. Meetings were arranged two weeks apart at eight o'clock on Friday evenings at five different Métro stations in Paris, beginning at the Clichy station in Montmartre. Moving eastward — appropriately enough through the Stalingrad station — the last on the list was the

Danube stop. Then the sequence began again at Clichy. A missed rendezvous on one Friday meant that the next meeting would be two weeks later at the next station on the list. At the entrance of the Métro, Hambleton would wait until Paul arrived and then the two men would go off, either on foot or rejoining the underground system, to some discreet restaurant. At first Hambleton memorized documents and reported orally on their contents. Later, Paul gave him a Leica camera and several rolls of 35mm film. Hambleton now began to remove documents from the office at night and set up special lighting equipment at home. There was no danger there, because his wife had by now left him and there was only a house-keeper present during the day. Later still, he was given a powerful radio receiver built into a suitcase, a codebook, and a schedule of broadcasts. Instructions for NATO documents now came direct from Moscow. Clandestine encounters at Métro stations were no longer needed. All Hambleton had to do was deposit the films at agreed drop points. It only added to the thrill that he experienced. "The idea of being able to tune in to a given frequency in Moscow," he confessed later, "and knowing the message was beamed at me, was very exciting." He was never paid for his work.

The excitement became increasingly dangerous until Hambleton left NATO and moved to London. Here he was left alone by the KGB, and when he took up his job as a professor at Laval he thought he had shaken them off.

For the first two years he was in Canada, Rudi Herrmann was kept in ignorance of his specific mission. Occasionally he produced writ-ten analyses of political conditions in Canada that he deposited in "dead drops" (hiding places) in the Ottawa area for collection by So-viet intelligence officers operating out of the embassy. Regularly he listened to his powerful short-wave receiver according to a carefully plotted schedule prepared in Moscow. KGB experts had studied meterological conditions to determine the best days and times for the waves to reach Toronto. This meant that each month the sched-ule would be slightly different, and the time of day or night when Rudi would have to tune in could vary considerably. Sometimes it would be 8:00 p.m., others in the dead of night. For most of the time the messages were of thanks or encouragement. They helped his morale and made him feel secure, but had little operational significance. Then, early in 1964, he received instructions to travel to Moscow. Flying via Vienna, where a KGB contact gave him a new set of identity documents, he arrived in the Soviet capital for two weeks of extensive debriefing. Here he was finally told the purpose of his mission. It was twofold. First, he should prepare himself to take charge of agent networks in Canada in case the Soviet embassy there ever had to close down. For that, he should continue the excellent work he had been doing to establish himself professionally and financially. Second, he should search for Canadian "progressives," particularly journalists or politicians, who could be useful to the Soviet cause. Personality reports on their political or social views and their characters, especially any particular interests, vices, or weaknesses that could be exploited, would be particularly helpful.

Obediently, for the next three years Herrmann busied himself as instructed back to Toronto. But only ten days after his citizenship ceremony in 1967 Moscow told him to leave Canada and set up business in the United States. It was an order that upset and exasperated both Rudi and Inga, but they dutifully obeyed. Nonetheless, it took time to gain the necessary visas and to liquidate and relocate the business, and it was more than a year later that they moved south. And it was during this unsettling transition period that Herrmann received instructions that brought his career as an intelligence officer fatefully together with that of Hambleton.

To bring an Illegal together with an agent in the country where they were both residing is a departure from standard practice because it submits the Illegal to the risk of exposure. But the KGB was prepared to break the rules because Hambleton seemed to be slipping from their control. Since returning to Canada he had met with KGB officers on three separate occasions. Each meeting took place in front of the main post office in Ottawa following a schedule given to him at a special meeting with a KGB officer in Vienna. The KGB told him to try and get a job in the Department of External Affairs so that he could report back on important political matters. This, clearly, was the game-plan for which Moscow had invested so much time and money in Hambleton. In the meantime, they said, he should concentrate on pinpointing potential KGB recruits among students and faculty at Laval. But Hambleton was increasingly unco-operative. Since quitting the NATO job he had found himself an agreeable niche in life as a scholar, and he had no intention of either risking it or giving it up. So, after his initial meetings in Ottawa, he simply stopped turning up at the scheduled times. The silence lasted for eighteen months. It was then that the KGB decided to bring in Herrmann.

In autumn 1967, Moscow instructed Rudi by radio to confirm Hambleton's address in Quebec. Once that was done — by Inga, who travelled there personally to check it out — Moscow ordered Rudi to make contact with Hambleton. This he did, knocking one day at his university office door and introducing himself as a movie producer needing a consultant for a film about former Quebec premier Maurice Duplessis. Herrmann quickly thrust the cover aside when the two men met alone for dinner that night over a table at the Château Frontenac. Revealing that he spoke for their mutual friends in Moscow, Herrmann skilfully flattered Hambleton by stressing how much they needed his considered views about the Canadian political and economic scene and other issues that required his economist's trained mind. This time there was no mention of abandoning his job at Laval or of spying on his students or colleagues. Indeed, to Hambleton the meeting was reminiscent of old times, of pleasant meetings with people like Borodin or Paul, men with whom he could converse as an equal about trends in world affairs over good food and wine. Herrmann was obviously an intelligent and well-trained man, and Hambleton readily agreed to co-operate. It was the first of many meetings, in Quebec City and elsewhere, over the next five years.

The entry of Herrmann into Hambleton's life seemed to rejuvenate the middle-aged academic. For the next decade or so Hambleton's career resembled a travelogue as he roamed the world combining academic projects with missions for the KGB. Under the guise of doing historical research, he spent the summer of 1970 in Israel, preparing a report for the KGB on how to infiltrate agents under cover of the large exodus of Soviet Jews that the Kremlin was expecting in the 1970s. The report was accompanied by an analysis on the Israeli economy and an estimate of Israel's much-rumoured nuclear-weapons capacity. The next year found Hambleton in Peru under contract to the Canadian International Development Agency (CIDA) as an adviser to Peruvian strongman General Velasco Alvarado. By this time Hambleton had established a reputation in the university world as a specialist on Latin American and Caribbean affairs, and after his return from Peru, Laval granted him a two-year leave of absence in 1973 to work again for CIDA. This time the project was agrarian reform on the impoverished Caribbean island of Haiti. Here Hambleton lived in true grandeur in the capital, Port-au-Prince, working closely with officials of the notoriously corrupt and brutal government of its dictator, "Baby Doc" Jean-Claude Duvalier. His work in Haiti over, Hambleton again spent a summer in Israel before resuming his academic career at Laval. But the restless travels continued in the long academic vacations, and by 1978 Hambleton was free again, this time for a sabbatical year spent mostly in Europe. When it was over he returned to Laval in September 1979.

Throughout these travels, he supplied reports to the KGB. From Peru and Haiti he delivered assessments of the South American and Caribbean economies, and from Israel he produced a demographic study that stressed the likely political impact of changing immigration patterns. In addition, without visiting the country, he prepared a lengthy report on South Africa and its nuclear-weapons capacity. The KGB told him they appreciated these reports. Politburo members, they even said, had read the most important.

Flattered, as was the intent, Hambleton received an even larger boost to his ego while en route to Laval after his 1975 summer in Israel. Vienna was a regular stopover for him on these trips because here he met with his KGB contact for detailed briefings. Once again, the real world of spying seemed to be lifted from the pages of spy fiction. As a security precaution, the two men would exchange passwords after the meetings were arranged by signals chalked on a wall in a Vienna suburb close to the headquarters of the Austrian Communist party. "Do you have any etchings of Paris?" the KGB officer would ask. "Not in Paris but in London," Hambleton would reply. After one of these encounters in August of that year with his old controller from Paris days, Paul told him to get ready for a visit to Moscow. Two hours later, he was picked up by car, given a Russian passport, and driven across the border into Czechoslovakia. From Bratislava he was flown by a Soviet military aircraft to Moscow and given a luxury suite in an apartment block on Gorky Street. According to Hambleton, the KGB spent a week questioning him thoroughly about his analysis of Latin America and giving him advanced tradecraft training in secret communications. One instructor showed him the use of invisible ink; another taught him the secure use of drop sites; and another instructed him in the uses of a special device that he could attach to his Grundig short-wave radio to receive coded messages from Moscow. The device, which resembled a square grey box measuring about nine by six by two inches with ten dials on the top, was called a *luminaire*. It picked up signals in the form of numerals that could then be deciphered by means of a cipher pad — instead of the normal dots and dashes of a Morse code that had to be memorized and was more dangerous because it took longer to note down. The device had been specifically developed, Hambleton was told, for prized agents who could not master Morse code or who lived in a circumstance that made its reception dangerous. As soon as one was assembled, they said, he would receive a unit in Canada.

The source for details of this curious visit to Moscow is Hambleton himself, who gave a lengthy account to the American intelligence writer John Barron for his 1983 book, *The KGB Today*. Yet some, and possibly all, of it may have taken place only in Hambleton's imagination. Certainly, the alleged climax of his trip strains credulity. This, Hambleton claimed, involved a personal meeting over dinner with the head of the KGB itself, Yuri Andropov. Here the KGB chief questioned him closely about U.S. military spending, the position of Jews in American society, the views of young people on the Soviet Union, and the likely future of the European Common Market. Then, after listening to Hambleton's careful replies, he urged him to find work at some high-powered American think-tank such as the Hudson Institute. His final words before departing were, according to Hambleton, "You know, you are an unusual case."

That much was certain, whether said by Andropov or not. The Security Service case officer who later handled Hambleton in Canada apparently believed that the Andropov meeting was just another example of Hambleton's fantasy world. Nonetheless, delivery of the *luminaire* eighteen months later by a local KGB agent in a downtown Montreal underground parking lot only confirmed in Hambleton's own mind that he still had a major role to play in world affairs. He didn't seem to notice how banal was most of the information he supplied. His report on South African nuclear capacities was in response to one of the first messages he received by the new device, and it is probably typical of the material Hambleton provided. "I had received a report from a nuclear plant in South Africa," Hambleton later told a reporter from the *Ottawa Citizen*, "it was nothing special; just a lot of stuff meant to impress scientists and promote South Africa. I guess a lot of people got them in the mail. Anyway, I got a 35-millimetre camera and some film and took pictures of the whole report. It's just the sort of thing they'd have been interested in. Even the name of the place — Pelindaba — is Swahili for 'forbidden to speak of.' I don't suppose the film was any good — I don't know anything about lighting, and any pictures I take are always off centre. But I took the film down to a 'drop' I was instructed to use and left it."

In summer 1978, Hambleton was summoned to another meeting in Vienna. Here, over a three-hour meal at a fashionable restaurant on the banks of the Danube, Paul asked him for a general assessment of the Egyptian economy as well as an analysis of Israel's vulnerability to an oil embargo. For Hambleton this was a pleasure. It was his sabbatical year, and he had plenty of time. Besides, he liked travelling. It promised to be a good year. As it happened, it turned out to be his last job for the KGB.

Nemesis came through Rudi Herrmann. The two men had continued to meet at regular intervals following their first meeting in 1967 at the Frontenac. The meetings were usually fairly lengthy affairs over a bottle or two of wine, giving the two men the chance to grumble together about the stupidity of their Soviet controllers. When it came to business, Herrmann would often do no more than instruct Hambleton on when and where to make contact with some other KGB officer. But the KGB also used him to chase Hambleton down after he had failed to keep several scheduled rendezvous. During his stay in Haiti, for example, Hambleton had decided it was too dangerous to mail his reports to an address he had been given in East Berlin. The Haitian secret police, he told Herrmann, who arrived unexpectedly one day from New York to check up on him, would certainly trace the letters. Herrmann commended Hambleton for his security-mindedness.

Herrmann's life had become almost as busy as Hambleton's. His passport was covered with visas and entry stamps from constant travel to Europe and South America. But most of his work was in the United States, selecting drop sites for KGB agents at various strategic locations. Throughout, he maintained his cover as a film-maker on contract with IBM, and he felt secure. So, when a phone call came to his home one evening in May 1977 from a man who enquired about a photographic assignment, he readily agreed to meet his client a couple of days later. Once inside the door, he realized that the moment dreaded by every secret agent had finally arrived. Standing in front of him were two men who conspicuously failed to return his greetings. They were from the FBI.

It took a surprisingly short time for the FBI to persuade Herrmann to co-operate. It was clear that they already knew a great deal and had been on to him for at least a couple of years. Although he never learned how, Hermann was convinced that they had cracked communications from Moscow. The fate of his wife and children deeply concerned him. Co-operation and the promise of a new life in the United States with a new identity for all of them was infinitely preferable to a long spell in prison for himself, his wife, and his elder son, who had now been initiated by Herrmann himself into the mysteries of his parents' secret life. Herrmann began to talk. As he did so, he led the FBI to his many contacts. Only towards the end of his interrogation did he point the finger at Hambleton. It was, he claimed later, because he wanted to give Hambleton the opportunity to get away.

In May 1978, just as Hambleton was leaving Canada for his long sabbatical, three officers from the RCMP Security Service flew to Washington to interview Herrmann in a CIA safe house in Maryland. In front of a video camera the KGB officer told the full story of his contacts with Hambleton. His confession was then taken back to Ottawa, and during the next year, the Security Service built up a lengthy file on the professor from Laval. Finally, at 7:15 a.m. on November 4, 1979, Hambleton answered a knock at the door of his Quebec City apartment. Standing in front of him were three RCMP officers with a search warrant. For the next two and a half years Hambleton was under close surveillance. The Canadian press was rife with stories and speculations about Hambleton, who himself seemed eager to tell his story and clearly revelled in the publicity. There were endless questions in Parliament, and the Trudeau government came under bitter Conservative attack. But Hambleton remained free, and in the spring of 1980 it was announced that he would not be prosecuted. After the predictable outrage, the story slipped off the front page and seemed to die. Then Hambleton made the half-hearted attempt to escape that finally landed him in the dock at the Old Bailey.

It was at Heathrow, the busiest airport in the world, that the curtain went up on the final act.

Shortly after dawn every day the overnight transatlantic flights from North America begin to disgorge their hundreds of dishevelled travellers at Heathrow immigration control. Here, standing wearily in long lines, passengers shuffle slowly towards the officers who carefully ask them about the purpose of their visit, their length of stay, and their financial resources. Passports are closely scrutinized, and if all is in order they are stamped with the date of entry and permitted length of stay. It's all part of regular security. The occasional passengers awake or alert enough may lift their gaze from the immigration officer and note the eyes carefully scrutinizing them from the plain-clothed civilian standing casually just to one side. This is another layer of security, an officer of Special Branch, the police arm of MI5, specially trained to look for particular faces who may be travelling under a false name or passport.

But some of the most important security precautions take place before the passengers even land at Heathrow. Not infrequently the security authorities act before the traveller arrives at immigration control.

This was the case on the morning of June 23, 1982, when one of the overnight passengers from Canada turned out to be Hugh Hambleton. With his teenage son in tow, he was ostensibly arriving for a short sailing holiday on the south coast of Britain. Before they even reached the line-up, however, he heard his name being paged from the public-address system. On identifying himself, he was confronted by Superintendent Peter Westcott of Special Branch. Alerted in advance by the RCMP in Montreal to Hambleton's departure from Canada, Westcott was there to warn Hambleton that if he passed through immigration control and therefore officially entered the United Kingdom he could face prosecution for espionage. He could take that risk, or he could proceed to the transit lounge and return to Canada, in which case he would be left alone by the British authorities. Hambleton declined the offer. Instead, he agreed to give Westcott his address in London. He then proceeded through immigration control, took a taxi into central London, and spent the next two days with his son, behaving like any ordinary tourist enjoying the capital. But only forty-eight hours later he was officially picked up for questioning. At Rochester Row police station in Westminster he was interrogated several times over the next two days. Finally, on the morning of June 27, 1982, a police van took him to the Horseferry Road magistrate's court where he was officially charged under Britain's Official Secrets Act.

What explained Hambleton's years of freedom after Rudi Herrmann named him to the FBI and RCMP as a longtime and trusted Soviet agent? And why was he finally brought to trial in Britain and not in Canada? The answer lay in the needs of Western counter-intelligence, gaps in Canada's Official Secrets Act, and sharply contrasting political temperatures in Ottawa and London.

The capture and turning of Rudi Herrmann presented the Americans with a golden opportunity for a classic game of deception with the KGB. Once he had agreed to co-operate, Herrmann became a double agent working for the FBI to help counter and unravel other Moscow Centre operations. As long as Moscow continued to believe Herrmann was still theirs, he could be controlled by the FBI and used for information-gathering about other Soviet agents and operations in North America. He could also feed back to Moscow deliberately distorted and falsified information. The most important thing was that Moscow should have no hint of anything wrong. For Herrmann, it meant he continued to receive and act on his regular clandestine transmissions. It also meant giving Hambleton no reason to think anything was amiss, in case he alerted Moscow Centre, which in turn might guess what had happened to Herrmann. So, as long as the Herrmann double game lasted, Hambleton was untouchable.

Moreover, it allowed the RCMP to mount their own operation, codenamed "Red Pepper." Hambleton was placed under surveillance in the hope that he might lead the RCMP to other Soviet contacts in Canada. If nothing else, he might help them pinpoint KGB agents operating as "legals" under diplomatic cover from the Soviet embassy in Ottawa. In short, the Hambleton case, like that of Herrmann, was to be handled not as a criminal affair, but as a counter-intelligence operation in which one agent was set up to catch others.

This was the game played jointly by the FBI and RCMP for eighteen months after Herrmann's capture. Outside New York, Herrmann and his family operated as though nothing had happened. Moscow continued to express pleasure with Rudi, and early in 1978 promoted him to the rank of colonel in the KGB. In Mexico City a short while later, at a face-to-face meeting with a KGB officer in a downtown park, Rudi was told that his top priority should be the tradecraft training of his son, Peter — a clear sign that Moscow still considered him a secure long-term investment.

Then, in September, Rudi received an urgent order to select several likely places for drops close to Dahlgren, Virginia, site of the top-secret U.S. Naval Surface Weapons Research Center. This immediately suggested to his FBI controllers that the KGB had already infiltrated the Center or that they expected to, and that hiding places were needed for documents or reports that would be deposited by their inside agent. The FBI set up a massive surveillance operation involving several hundred people that lasted over several months. Then, abruptly, it was terminated in spring 1979 — apparently because of a threatened press leak that would have blown the operation as well as exposed the Herrmann double game.

It was a sign that time was running out in the FBI manipulation of Herrmann. Sooner or later, in one way or another, the KGB would realize he was operating under FBI control. Herrmann had already been forced to invent several excuses to explain why neither his wife nor his son could travel abroad to meet with KGB controllers in places such as Vienna or even Moscow — visits that the FBI considered far too dangerous for the security of their operation. By fall 1979, the FBI finally decided to call it quits. One night late that September, a van removed all the furniture and belongings from the Herrmann home and the family disappeared from circulation. Taken to a safe house, they were given new identities and relocated elsewhere in the United States. The deception game with Moscow was over.

This now freed the RCMP to take action against Hambleton, and the knock at his door came shortly afterwards. The search that followed, extended to the Ottawa house of the now elderly Bessie Hambleton, turned up the short-wave receiver, the incriminating *luminaire* given to Hambleton after his Moscow visits, and many other items of espionage tradecraft. In several interrogations over the next few weeks, especially after he was shown Herrmann's videotaped confession, Hambleton freely admitted everything.

Everything, that is, for the years covered by Herrmann's confession, which meant the period after Hambleton's return to Canada. On the NATO period and his spying against the Western alliance, he consistently stonewalled, refusing to answer questions from his Security Service interrogators. Hambleton, for all his oddities, was no fool. He had been officially cautioned that what he said could be used as evidence against him, and he knew that the only evidence ever likely to surface about his spying against NATO would be his own confession. So, to the frustration of his interrogators, he kept his silence on this crucial issue. It was this, more than anything else, that saved him from prosecution.

In January 1980 officials of the Security Service, the Department of Justice, and the Solicitor General's department met to review Hambleton's file and assess the case against him. It was a crucial meeting that determined much of what later happened.

As they carefully went through the files it became clear that while the information about his work for the KGB was voluminous, the evidence to guarantee a successful prosecution was missing. Under Section 3(1) of the 1970 Official Secrets Act — the so-called spying clause — information passed to a foreign power had to be *secret* information to qualify as espionage. Yet the reports that Hambleton had produced for the KGB since returning to Canada had been based on open, publicly accessible information. The KGB demanded it not because of the secrets it contained — there were none — but as a way of keeping their hooks in Hambleton on the chance that some day in the future he would turn out to be useful. Providing such information to the KGB was no offence. As Solicitor General Robert Kaplan was to put it later to the House of Commons, "Canada is a free country, and anyone can talk to whomsoever they want and cavort with whomsoever they want without necessarily breaking any Canadian laws." The case for a criminal prosecution was simply not there.

So what could be done? There was an obvious solution at hand. If Hambleton was told there could be no prosecution, perhaps he would then be willing to talk about his NATO years. If he had indeed spied on NATO for the KGB, as everyone suspected, his confession would provide useful evidence for other Western security services in their counter-espionage efforts against the KGB.

There was an obvious drawback to this solution. If Hambleton realized that the government could not prosecute because of lack of evidence and problems with the Official Secrets Act, what incentive would he have to talk? To work, the strategy had to be dressed up as a "deal," a bargain whereby the government *appeared* to make a concession in return for an agreement by Hambleton to talk. Politically, however, no one could talk publicly about a deal. The recent Blunt case in Britain was on everyone's mind. There had been a political outcry and international scandal in 1979 over revelations that Sir Anthony Blunt, Keeper of the Queen's Pictures, had been granted immunity from prosecution as a long-time KGB agent in a deal struck years before by the British government. There had to be no risk of that happening, or even seeming to happen, with Hambleton.

Over the next few weeks the package that would take care of these risks was carefully put together in Ottawa by the Security Service and officials in the Department of Justice. It was a time of political confusion. The Conservative government of Joe Clark was defeated in December on a vote of non-confidence, and an election campaign was in full swing. Before the issue could be decided, Pierre Trudeau's Liberals were back in power. The change of government and the arrival of new ministers meant delay. Finally, in April 1980, the recommendation on Hambleton landed on the desk of Justice minister Jean Chrétien. It had been prepared by Justice department lawyers Roger Leclaire and John Scollin, and was supported by deputy Justice minister Roger Tassé.

Chrétien was well aware that the last three prosecutions under the Official Secrets Act had been unsuccessful, and an unsuccessful prosecution of Hambleton would be political folly of the worst order. Chrétien was also quickly convinced of the merits of the case for extracting whatever could be got from Hambleton about NATO. On April 25, therefore, he ruled that there would be no prosecution. Shortly afterwards, the Security Service officer in charge of the case showed Hambleton an extract from a document written by the director of the Security Service, confirming the decision not to prosecute. Typed on a separate piece of paper, it seemed to Hambleton like a promise of immunity from prosecution, a "deal." Finally, he began to talk about his NATO years.

Over the next few months, as the full dimensions of his spying on NATO unfolded, the RCMP Security Service brought allied services into the case. MI5 was kept fully briefed, and to help identify possible KGB agents still at work in France the DST (Direction de la Surveillance du Territoire) sent a senior officer to interview Hambleton. What the Security Service later officially described as "a very successful counter-espionage operation which was very productive" was under way.

Still, not everyone was happy. Elements of the Security Service were deeply frustrated. To be seen to bring a Soviet spy to justice would provide much needed tonic for a demoralized service, and to have a prosecution ruled out was profoundly demoralizing.

Nor was the FBI happy at the decision not to prosecute. To Washington the Trudeau Liberals were "soft" on the Soviets. Many officials in the American intelligence community thought Canada generally lax on Soviet spying activities. Kept aware of the internal discussions going on in Ottawa about the difficulties of a prosecution, the FBI decided to bring public pressure to bear. On March 3, 1980, the first day of the new Trudeau administration, they stage-managed a dramatic appearance by Herrmann in Washington that for the first time publicly revealed his defection. Sitting silhouetted behind a screen at FBI headquarters, Herrmann told the assembled press about his KGB career in North America. He also named Hambleton as one of his agents in Canada.

This attempt to force Ottawa's hand failed when only seven weeks later Chrétien made his decision. After that, as Hambleton confessed his spying on NATO, the Security Service continued to hope that evidence that could be used in a criminal prosecution would emerge, while at the same time running him in their counter-espionage operation. The problem was that as part of the "deal" with Hambleton they had failed to give him an official caution about the possible use of the evidence against him, deliberately so, because when he had been cautioned in the past he had refused to co-operate. But without a caution, anything he said would be inadmissible in court. "A confession is a prosecutor's worst tool," Leclaire was quoted as saying. All the Security Service could hope for was that his continuing confessions would lead them to a third party who could then provide independent evidence of spying on NATO. But as Hambleton had probably calculated from the beginning, they never found such evidence. So the Security Service never had enough to go back to the Justice department to have the case reopened.

Hambleton, meanwhile, enjoyed the publicity. In between inerrogations he gave press interviews and embellished his role, spinning out fantasies that mesmerized his audience. At first he seemed not to realize the seriousness of his position. "I don't think of myself as a spy," he said. "A spy is someone who regularly gets secret material, passes it on, takes orders, and gets paid for it. I have never been paid." At other times he appeared to revel in providing details of his contact with Moscow through his short-wave radio. "The Russians love clandestine things like secret writing paper and codenames and all that hocus pocus," he told someone, and it was clear that he enjoyed the thrill of the game. To his students and colleagues at Laval he became something of a celebrity. Attendance at his lectures improved dramatically. Perhaps to prove that he felt untouchable, he travelled abroad. Only two months after Rudi Herrmann had publicly exposed him as a Soviet agent, he even flew to England to attend an academic conference at the University of Exeter. The Special Branch briefly questioned him, but then left him alone.

Gradually, public interest in Hambleton died down, and by 1982 his name had virtually disappeared from media coverage. But neither the RCMP nor the FBI had forgotten him, and to Hambleton himself the affair with its continuing interrogation by the Security Service was becoming intolerable. To escape the pressure, to do some normal scholarly work, and to resume his travelling life, he decided to spend the summer of 1982 in England with his teenage son. Such, at least, was what he told his Security Service watchers, men with whom he had built a relationship of some familiarity and even friendship over the past three years. To Leo Heaps, Hambleton later claimed he had been planning to defect to the Soviet Union and hoped to make final arrangements with KGB contacts in London. Whatever the truth — and the motives may have been confused and unclear to Hambleton himself — he was determined to get away. In the United States he knew the FBI would prosecute. In the United Kingdom, on the other hand, on the evidence of his previous trip, he might be safe. His Canadian minders told him not to count on it, but had no power to stop him from leaving the country. They may, indeed, have wished him to do so, knowing he would be prosecuted, and calculated that reverse psychology would do its work.

Thus, on June 22, 1982, accompanied by his son and carrying in his suitcase several copies of his latest academic research manuscript — on King Alfonso of Spain — Hambleton left Canada on the trip that led him to the prisoner's dock in the Old Bailey.

Hambleton's claim from the witness box that he had been a double agent for the French and Canadian intelligence services quickly disintegrated. Indeed, it was in trouble almost the moment he attempted it. Asked by the judge to identify "C," his Canadian handler, Hambleton at first refused on the grounds that his Security Service controller had ordered him not to identify Canadian intelligence officers. Told to do so, Hambleton finally scribbled a name and address on a piece of paper. It was tragedy turning to farce. The name he devised was "Jacques Laliberté" and the address turned out to be his own apartment in Quebec City. His French handler, whose role he claimed had been arranged by the Canadians, he named as "Jean Masson" — the name of a man, it later turned out, Hambleton worked with in Algiers in 1944.

It was Sir Michael Havers, Britain's attorney general personally leading the prosecution in court, who finally demolished Hambleton's defence. Havers was determined to succeed. The previous few weeks had produced espionage revelations that once again had shaken public confidence in British security. The Geoffrey Prime case had revealed a severe breakdown of security at GCHQ. A British lance corporal had been arrested for allegedly passing secrets to the Soviets during the Falklands War, and a junior British diplomat had received a suspended sentence for giving confidential information to the Egyptians. The reputation of Britain's MI5 and of the Thatcher government rested on putting Hambleton behind bars. Fortunately for Havers, the British Official Secrets Act could be more liberally interpreted than Canada's.

In a devastating presentation Havers destroyed Hambleton's credibility by revealing that he had consistently exaggerated the nature and significance of his war service. Then, with written denials from the RCMP and the French security service in hand, he demonstrated that Hambleton had concocted the fantasy of his double-agent life in a desperate last-minute attempt to justify his behaviour. The next day, Hambleton changed his plea to guilty, and the judge directed the jury to pass such a verdict. Shortly afterwards, describing Hambleton's offence as "very grave," he sentenced him to ten years' imprisonment. Taken below stairs, Hambleton exchanged his grey suit for prisoner's garb and was driven to Gartree prison, a high-security jail in Leicestershire. Here, a year later, it was reported that he was still to be found at his favourite pastime — listening to his radio. Only now, instead of high-speed bursts of code from Moscow, it was to hear orchestral concerts from the Royal Albert Hall.

This was not quite the end of the bizarre tale of Herrmann and Hambleton, KGB officer and agent, respectively. In June 1986, Hambleton was returned to Canada, transferred on humanitarian grounds under a prisoner-exchange convention that allowed him to be close to his ailing mother. He was released on mandatory supervision in March 1989, and he now lives just outside Ottawa.

Rudi Herrmann surfaced briefly in February 1988 to give a newspaper interview. Talking to a Toronto journalist in the safety of an FBI safe house outside Washington, D.C., he revealed that, unlike Hambleton, he could not go back home. He had once tried, he said, to return to Czechoslovakia, even going so far as to ship back several suitcases in advance. But the Czech embassy in Washington wanted nothing to do with him. As for Hambleton, he thought he had been valuable to the Soviets because he had given them reports that were devoid of the wishful thinking and ideological slant that distorted much Soviet reporting.

The Hambleton/Herrmann affair reveals a great deal about KGB strategy and tactics in Canada during the Cold War. Together, the two men represented a heavy investment of time, money, and effort. Herrmann was a well-trained professional whose life as an Illegal in Toronto was mainly the prelude to his major mission in the United States. Hambleton, however absurd a figure he may appear with his obvious kick in dabbling in espionage tradecraft and his vainglorious belief that he could be someone of importance on the world stage, was clearly regarded by Moscow as someone who, one day, some-how, might have access to, or gain useful influence in, Ottawa or Washington. Besides, he might be helpful in identifying oth-er "friends" of the Soviet Union. Canada and Canadians, like any other NATO country and its citizens, were fair game.

9.
FOREIGN EXCHANGES: SPYING AMONG FRIENDS AND ENEMIES

F or five years we bugged and burgled our way across London at the States' behest, while pompous bowler-hatted civil servants in Whitehall pretended to look the other way," wrote Peter Wright in *Spycatcher*, the 1987 international bestseller banned from publication in Britain by the Thatcher government. For more than twenty years Wright had worked in MI5, which he had joined as a technical expert in charge of inventing espionage gadgets such as concealed microphones. What guaranteed him notoriety, apart from his allegations that former MI5 chief Sir Roger Hollis had been a Soviet mole, were the detailed revelations about MI5 campaigns against a whole range of domestic targets, including former prime minister Harold Wilson. These attracted most of the international attention. But what was equally remarkable was how frequently Wright's activities had involved many of Britain's allies.

Canada was one of them. An early Wright operation was to help the RCMP plant hidden microphones in the Soviet embassy in Ottawa. It happened in 1956, after the old embassy on Charlotte Street had burned down in a fire on New Year's Day. Terry Guernsey, an RCMP veteran from British Columbia who had worked on industrial security in Toronto during the Second World War, was in charge of the RCMP's "B" Section, responsible for counter-espionage. Guernsey had been sent to Britain after the war for intelligence training by both MI5 and MI6. By the 1950s he was the driving force of Canada's counter-espionage efforts. In the rebuilding of the embassy Guernsey saw the perfect opportunity to plant hidden bugs to eavesdrop on KGB and GRU operations in Canada. But there was a problem. Their operation, codenamed "Dew Worm," needed the latest super-sensitive equipment, which Canada did not possess. To obtain it, and to supervise its installation, Guernsey turned to MI5 and its scientific expert, Peter Wright.

In July 1956, Wright flew to Ottawa. Over dinner the night he arrived Guernsey told him that the RCMP had successfully recruited the contractor responsible for the building, while the former Soviet cipher clerk and famous defector Igor Gouzenko had helped pinpoint the top-secret KGB and GRU areas within the building. "After studying the plans," Wright recalled, "I decided that a SATYR operation, using a cavity microphone activated from outside by microwaves, was not technically feasible. . . . It had to be a wired operation." Under Wright's supervision, microphones were installed inside the aluminum sash windows. The cable linking the microphones to head amplifiers in an RCMP safe house close to the embassy were then carefully installed in the two-inch air gap in the middle of the two-foot-thick walls. Developed by MI5, the cables were made of an especially thin wire that gave off fewer electromagnetic emissions than previous types and thus reduced the chance of detection by Soviet electronic-sweeper operations. Although Soviet countermeasures meant that nothing of intelligence value was actually learned, Operation Dew Worm, technically speaking, was a success.

Less than a year later Wright was back in Canada. This time the target was the newly authorized Polish consulate in Montreal, an old house that the Poles were thoroughly renovating. Wright decided that a wired operation was out of the question in this case, and recommended that a SATYR cavity microphone be used. Again the operation was a technical success, and Wright returned to Britain, where he found even bigger and more ambitious targets for his bugging skills.

These two episodes illustrate a major theme in the history of the Canadian security service, namely, its close relationship with allied services and its membership in a wider Western security and intelligence community. Not only did Canadian operations depend on British technical expertise, but Guernsey, the man in charge, had been sent to Britain for expert training (and later, indeed, returned there to take charge of intelligence liaison between London and Ottawa). Dependence on Britain has declined over the years. But the relationship remains extremely close, as was illustrated when the Canadian service alerted MI5 to Hambleton's flight to Britain in the summer of 1982.

The relationship with the Americans is no less close. In the 1970s it led to a widespread feeling that American outlooks and priorities were distorting or dominating the operations of the RCMP Security Service. A case in point was the affair of the Cuban trade commission. This was yet another incendiary matter that occurred sixteen years after the events involving Peter Wright and the Soviet embassy in Ottawa.

In the early hours of April 4, 1972, an explosion rocked the top floor of the twelve-storey office block in Montreal that housed the Cuban trade commission and consulate. The building also provided the cover for Cuba's spy headquarters in North America, located in Canada rather than the United States because of the latter's refusal to have any official dealings at all with Havana. A night watchman was killed, and the building was evacuated for several hours. Attempts by the occupants to destroy hundreds of secret documents before leaving were unsuccessful as they had been soaked by the all-too-efficient sprinkler system. Here was an irresistible opportunity. The Security Service recovered the documents, including for good measure the commission's codebook, and within hours the entire haul was at CIA headquarters in Langley, Virginia. "It was," writes one author, "one of the Security Service's biggest intelligence windfalls since Igor Gouzenko." The problem for the Security Service arose only later, when allegations surfaced that it had not only helped the CIA after the explosion, but had also been involved in planning it. Three years later, an aide to a member of the U.S. House Intelligence Committee claimed that the Montreal bombing might have been a deliberate diversion to allow the RCMP and CIA access to the building. The RCMP quickly issued a formal denial of complicity. Subsequently, however, two ex-Security Service operatives from Montreal told a Justice department official about their "participation and assistance to the CIA in offensive activities" — a reference taken by many observers to refer to the explosion at the Cuban trade mission. (After the 1972 experience, it is no wonder that when fire again broke out at the Cuban consulate in March 1988, employees obstructed Montreal firefighters for fifteen minutes while sensitive documents were destroyed — and while three consular employees died in the smoke and flames.)

The truth about RCMP and CIA involvement in the explosion has never surfaced. One reason is that the allegations immediately sparked calls from within the Security Service for a commission of enquiry that would examine Security Service practices in general rather than focus on particular incidents and the guilt of individual officers. And when the subsequent report of RCMP wrongdoing was published in 1981, the five chapters covering Security Service relations with allied agencies were withheld on national-security grounds. Nevertheless, the commission expressed a scarcely veiled warning about overly dependent or close relations with the Americans and referred darkly to "the danger of Canada's security intelligence agency adopting the outlook and opinions of a foreign agency, especially an agency which has come to be depended on heavily." Elsewhere, it remarked on the danger of the Security Service becoming a mere "appendage" of foreign agencies. This notion had a great deal to do with its central recommendation to establish a completely new and civilian security intelligence service — one free from old habits of thought and an unsophisticated acceptance of attitudes that could run counter to Canada's independent foreign policy. Even more determined in this objective was Prime Minister Pierre Trudeau. His close lieutenant, Michael Pitfield, had been in the key position of Clerk of the Privy Council and Secretary to the Cabinet throughout the deliberations of the McDonald Commission. Pitfield, who was deeply concerned about the uncontrolled operations of U.S. intelligence agencies in Canada, then chaired a special Senate committee to assess the legislation creating the Canadian Security Intelligence Service. Receiving final assent in July 1984, it was Trudeau's final legislative achievement.

Most threats to the security of Canada have an international dimension. The clandestine activities of agents of foreign powers have been, and remain, extensive in Canada. Terrorism is another threat, one that has grown significantly over the last twenty years. While some terrorism has been domestic, most is international.

Because so many threats to Canada's security lie outside Canada, the government must be able to obtain advance intelligence from abroad. Many of Canada's allies have their own foreign intelligence services to do this job. Canada does not. So, for what it cannot discover through open and public sources, it has to rely on its friends.

Relationships with foreign agencies are covered by a variety of agreements. Some are formal, others informal, and while some are of long duration, others are temporary and ad hoc. A certain number involve agreements to carry out joint operations, more relate to the exchange of information and liaison — about terrorism, or the security-vetting of travellers and immigrants, or espionage and counter-espionage cases. With Canada's most important allies, the relations between members of the various agencies are particularly close. Sometimes, as in the case with Britain, they are almost familial.

Commonwealth "family" links between security and intelligence agencies have been institutionalized since the Second World War under British lead. To bring together and expand the work of the various military intelligence directorates, Britain established its Joint Intelligence Bureau (JIB) in 1946. Its principal creator was the man who had served as chief of intelligence at Eisenhower's wartime Supreme Headquarters Allied Expeditionary Force (SHAEF), Major-General Sir Kenneth Strong. Strong, who later turned down an offer to become deputy-director of the CIA because he would have had to renounce his British citizenship, was obsessed with the need to maintain a strong Western intelligence community based on Commonwealth ties. As building blocks for such a structure, Strong persuaded Australia, New Zealand, and Canada to establish joint intelligence bureaus of their own, known respectively as JIB(M), JIB(W), and JIB(O) (Melbourne, Wellington, and Ottawa, respectively). Since then, the Commonwealth family has been kept together by regular

Commonwealth Security Conferences, usually held at the same time as the Commonwealth prime ministers' meetings. Officers of member countries also sit in on meetings of Britain's Joint Intelligence Committee and have permanent liaison officers in London. In extreme cases, such as those involving the unproven suspicion about former MI5 head Roger Hollis, an inner core of Commonwealth intelligence services — those of Britain, Canada, New Zealand, and Australia — have been confidentially briefed. Such was the case in early May 1974, when the heads of the British, American, Canadian, Australian, and New Zealand agencies met in London at a conference, codenamed CAZAB, to receive a full briefing on the Hollis case so that they could take appropriate countermeasures.

As we have seen, membership in the wider Western intelligence community carries risks as well as benefits. For Canada, the danger in the past has been that interagency agreements have sometimes been made without the knowledge of ministers in the Canadian government, and without any clear guidelines. In 1977, for example, Solicitor General Francis Fox asked the RCMP to provide him with a list of all existing foreign liaison arrangements. To his dismay, he found that no central record existed. Later, it took extensive research by the McDonald Commission enquiry to find out what these arrangements were. For years the RCMP Security Service had independently been making foreign-agency agreements in an area of clear national foreign-policy concern.

The RCMP, of course, had been doing other things, too, such as undercover spying operations in Quebec against legitimate separatist organizations such as the Parti Québécois. Mounties burgled PQ offices and stole its membership lists. A barn was burned. Agents were bribed into co-operation. It all smelled, it all played into the hands of those who denounced the *fédérastes* in Ottawa, and as the revelations mounted, the federal government found itself virtually forced, in July 1977, into creating the Commission of Inquiry Concerning Certain Activities of the Royal Canadian Mounted Police. Led by Mr. Justice D.C. McDonald, an Alberta judge, the commission reported in 1979 and 1981, and its recommendations led directly to the elimination of the RCMP's Security Service and to the creation of CSIS, a wholly civilian security organization, in the last days of the Trudeau government in 1984. Significantly, the Communications Security Establishment, Canada's most-secret intelligence-gathering organization, escaped untouched in the new legislative and organizational arrangement of powers.

Since the 1984 CSIS Act, all agreements reached by CSIS with foreign agencies must be approved by the solicitor general. Nonetheless, details of Canada's links with other Western intelligence organizations still remain a closely guarded secret. What co-operation do foreign agencies receive in Canada? How much do they tell us of what they do? Such questions remain largely unanswerable — and even if the Americans or French or Indians told CSIS of some of their actions on Canadian territory, would it be the whole truth?

"Do we spy on Canadians?" Paul Robinson asked when he received his initial intelligence briefing from the Central Intelligence Agency before coming to Canada. Ronald Reagan's ambassador in Ottawa recalled that the answer he received was "No." "Do Canadians spy on Americans?" Robinson then asked. "No," the briefing officer replied. "But they do spy on the people we would use if we did spy on them."

Those may have been honest answers, though Peter Russell, the University of Toronto professor who was research director of the McDonald Commission, has said publicly that "our friendly neighbour to the south" carries on intelligence activities in Canada. And, although there is a long tradition of exchanging and sharing intelligence information between the two neighbours, Russell added that "it is difficult to believe that their intelligence agencies keep us fully informed of their activities in Canada." Even Robinson's briefer suggested a certain wariness.

What this amounts to is that friendly nations, such as the United States and Canada or Canada and France, trust each other — but not too far and certainly not on every subject. Sensible nations, in other words, maintain a cautious attitude in all their international dealings. As former Liberal Defence minister Jean-Jacques Blais, currently a member of Ottawa's Security Intelligence Review Committee (SIRC) noted, there are always "conflicting interests between friendly countries." Those competing interests, of course, can be economic. As Peter Russell put it in a paper prepared for SIRC in December 1988: "To the extent that covert sources of intelligence and influence are an asset in gaining access to markets and technologies and in international bargaining," nations that have major intelligence assets around the world have an advantage. Canada, without spies abroad, "will be at a disadvantage with its major trading partners." Our friends and our enemies both, in other words, have to be watched.

Perhaps this caution is wise. Robert Bryce, a long-time senior bureaucrat and a former Clerk of the Privy Council, has said that Ottawa was one of the few places in which a CIA officer was openly listed on the complement of the U.S. embassy. That was a sign of trust and a recognition of the liaison role the officer filled with the RCMP and CSIS. But Bryce also remembered Ottawa's relief when an online cipher system between the Canadian embassy in Washington and Ottawa came into operation. Our telecommunications, he said, were always thought to be intercepted by the United States. Whether the online system is any more secure from the prying of the National Security Agency is unclear. And another senior bureaucrat has said that a (hypothetical) Canadian diplomat who happened to be a practising homosexual was likely to be just as vulnerable to American entrapment as to Soviet. A recent book by Jean-François Lisée, *Dans l'oeil de l'aigle*, moreover, states flatly that the NSA spied on the late Quebec Premier René Lévesque by electromagnetic means. Lisée strongly suggests that similar methods are still employed against other Canadian political figures.

The Canadian government, of course, would not use similar methods to gather information about the United States. Such activities do not fit the self-image we cherish; moreover, no Canadian agency, neither CSIS nor any other body, yet has a mandate to undertake intelligence operations outside Canada as does the American CIA or the British SIS, although one of Brian Mulroney's former solicitors general, Pierre Blais, has admitted that CSIS sends "agents" and "sources" — but not CSIS employees — abroad to gather information "from time to time", or to "investigate threats to the security of Canada." As of spring

1990, SIRC has precipitated public consideration of the establishment of a regularized Canadian system of foreign intelligence-gathering.

As things stand already, CSIS's occasional travellers are only a small part of Canada's sources of foreign intelligence. The Communications Security Establishment, as we have seen, scours the airwaves for Soviet radio transmissions. The Department of External Affairs has its inquisitive diplomats all around the world, and National Defence stations military attachés in many of Canada's embassies. These men and women collect information of all kinds — and not least in the United States. Apparently, however, they do not use covert means to acquire it, though we could scarcely expect Canadians to look the other way if something secret and American or British or Russian dropped into their outstretched hands. In 1948, for example, the counsellor at the Canadian embassy in Washington told a British embassy official (who in turn told a State Department officer) that "a diplomatic pouch outbound from the Soviet Embassy at Ottawa had recently come into the possession of the Canadian authorities." While the contents were not detailed in the State Department memorandum about the incident, there was obviously great interest in this unexplained intelligence windfall, which Ottawa, in violation of the sanctity of diplomatic mail, had read and analysed. If the same thing happened tomorrow, the eagerness with which Canadian and allied agencies pored over the pouch's contents would be just as great.

What is critical, however, is the extent to which the Canadian government gathers information about our neighbours. Ken Robertson, one student of Canadian intelligence policy, went so far as to argue that "the major concern of the Canadian government is timely and well-analysed information concerning the United States of America." The reason is obvious: "Friends, such as the United States, are capable of having a continuous and major effect on the economic, political, social and military environment so that knowledge of their thinking is vital in making decisions."

One example ought to be enough. In fall 1962, the USSR secretly installed missiles in Cuba. The United States discovered this, and President Kennedy duly went on television to announce a naval blockade of the Caribbean island until the missiles were removed.

The government of John Diefenbaker, its response to the crisis slow and hesitant, made much of the fact that the United States had not informed Canada in advance, as various treaties and engagements, including the two countries' participation in the North American Air Defence Command, required. In fact, two Canadian intelligence officers had been in Washington for a long-scheduled meeting where they heard what was coming two or perhaps three days before Kennedy's announcement. They called Norman Robertson, the under-secretary of state for External Affairs, and Bryce, the Clerk of the Privy Council, with the information, and they returned to Canada to brief the civil servants concerned. It is inconceivable that the prime minister was not informed what was about to occur.

Good intelligence, as this was, should have helped the Canadian government to formulate a response to its friend's actions. That it didn't — because the Diefenbaker government reacted foolishly and the prime minister publicly expressed doubt about Washington's good faith — doesn't alter the fact that information about allies can be just as important, if not more so, as that about enemies.

If Canadians are interested in their friends just as much as in their enemies, we should not be surprised that others may be interested in us or in the activities of their former nationals who now live here. In fact, Canada sometimes seems to be a hotbed of intelligence activities, and SIRC in its 1989 annual report admitted that more than two dozen countries conducted covert operations here. Even the United Nations, through its Office for Research and the Collection of Information, operates an "early warning system" that gathers intelligence and conducts analysis on behalf of the secretary general to identify potential trouble spots. At times in the past, and even more likely in the future, Canada may well have qualified as a "trouble spot."

But it's not the U.N. that worries Canada's counter-intelligence officials. To the end of 1989, at least, all of the Soviet-bloc countries ran intelligence operations from their embassies, the East Germans, the Poles, and the Hungarians being the most active. Whether this will change, or how it will change, after the stunning collapse of communist governments in Eastern Europe is still uncertain. Hitherto, the Soviet-bloc countries were especially interested in Canadian technology, but so are otherwise friendly countries. As SIRC noted in 1989, "Instances are known in which foreign intelligence officers have approached researchers at facilities where secret work was being done in Canada, and where pressure has been put on immigrants by the authorities in their countries of origin to obtain restricted technical manuals [and] to smuggle restricted goods out of the country." This technological espionage was, at least until the recent changes in Eastern Europe, a growth industry.

But most of the foreign intelligence-gathering in Canada is likely devoted to keeping watch on émigré groups or to attempts to turn "policy and events in Canada to their own purposes," or so SIRC described it in 1989. More often than not, such activities are not related to Canada at all, but to communities based here that might help or harm the causes of the government doing the spying. Some examples:

• The Israelis keep watch on Canadian Arab groups and on the PLO representatives here, and Israel's very effective spy agency, Mossad, and CSIS have close relationships in countering terrorists, as we shall see when we consider the case of Mahmoud Mohammad Issa Mohammad in Chapter 11.

• Cuba's intelligence service up until now has used Canada primarily as a staging area for operations against the United States. In December 1976, for example, Havana had fifteen confirmed and nineteen suspected officers in its embassy in Ottawa and its consulate in Montreal. After eight Cubans were expelled, the RCMP estimated that 40 percent of the Cuban mission's personnel worked on intelligence questions. If the Eastern European intelligence organizations try to put distance between themselves and the KGB, it is not unlikely that the Cubans, as Stalinist a group of communists as exist anywhere (other than in Albania), might become more important than ever as a Soviet surrogate. (Whether the KGB itself is changing as the USSR moves towards a more open society is another question.)

• The South African security service, BOSS, keeps watch on anti-apartheid activists in Canada, and the embassy in Ottawa finances pro-South Africa groups across the country and uses their members to collect and distribute information.

• The Republic of Korea follows the anti-government activities of its many immigrants in Canada, and intelligence officers attached to its diplomatic missions keep a wary eye, as does CSIS, on the efforts of North Korea to gain influence here.

• The Yugoslav intelligence service watches anti-government activists and activities based in Canada, something that almost certainly has intensified as ethnic pressures and separatist sentiments intensify in Slovenian and Albanian regions of Yugoslavia.

• The Indian government closely monitors Sikhs living in Canada. Reid Morden, CSIS director, admitted to the House of Commons Justice Committee in June 1989 that India had had spies operating here in the past, and deputy prime minister Don Mazankowski confirmed in Parliament in October 1989 that "the government" was investigating "these sorts of activities" by Indian intelligence against Sikhs living here.

• Taiwan's secret police worry about the activities of the People's Republic of China's (PRC) agents among the more than 300,000 Chinese in Canada.

• For their part, the Beijing government's men have kept close tabs on their country's students and professors studying in Canada and have done so ever since the possibility of Canada recognizing China became a live possibility soon after Pierre Trudeau became prime minister in 1968. RCMP commissioner W.L. Higgitt then warned the government that the establishment of a PRC embassy "will mean increased operations by agents from Beijing," and John Diefenbaker added that "I can just imagine the deluge of spies who will come in here." In fact, there were two cases of improper activities before 1989. One in 1975 involved the second secretary of the Chinese embassy who had smuggled money into Canada intended to support communist militants in the Philippines. The other, two years later, focused on the first secretary, Yuan Xianlung, who was caught trying to gather low-level classified information and to influence the policies of Chinese-Canadian groups. Both were expelled. That was only the tip of the iceberg, however. In its secret 1976 annual report that was distributed to Cabinet ministers, the RCMP Security Service pinpointed thirteen known and two suspected intelligence officers among the diplomats, support staff, and representatives with PRC missions. The Security Service added that these intelligence agents had penetrated more than eighteen Chinese-Canadian organizations, conducted operations to neutralize Nationalist efforts, and collected data on prominent members of the local Chinese community. "They have also approached highly qualified Chinese Canadians in universities, government, scientific research and industry in order to collect information," the report said, and were working to cultivate occidental "agents of influence."

More recently, during the Tiananmen Square protests in May and June 1989, some Chinese visitors in Canada apparently were harassed by the MSS, the PRC's security service, while students studying here claimed that agents based at the embassy had infiltrated their organizations, photographed those attending demonstrations, and prepared lists of pro-democracy advocates. Joe Clark, Secretary of state for External Affairs, took these claims seriously enough to protest to Beijing's ambassador, but CSIS director Reid Morden would say only that "we are monitoring the situation."

(In questioning in the House of Commons Justice Committee on June 15, 1989, the CSIS head was asked if he would not agree that Chinese intelligence-gathering about students in Canada constituted "a threat to their security." Reid Morden's reply: ". . . no, I guess I would not. Not within the mandate that we [CSIS] have, which is to look at threats to the security of Canada, which includes politically motivated violence, which includes . . . danger to an individual. . . . And to that extent, of course, we are concerned, and respond appropriately." There could not be much comfort in that reply for Chinese students in Canada.)

And then there are the French, friends and allies of long-standing. Close to 100,000 Canadians are buried in war cemeteries on French soil, killed in Canada's effort in two world wars to keep France free. But gratitude is often in short supply among nations, and the most serious attack on the Canadian nation since the end of the Second World War came from France. The story shows how closely linked diplomacy and espionage can be.

The issue, of course, was Quebec. After the death of Maurice Duplessis and the rise to power of Jean Lesage and the Liberal party in 1960, Quebec began to blossom under the liberating influences of the Quiet Revolution. Part of Lesage's intention was to restore close relations with France, the fount of French civilization, and visits of politicians, exchanges of students and artists, and cultural programs soon developed. There were bureaucrats, politicians, and academics in Quebec — and some in Ottawa, too — who hoped to increase the province's autonomy vis-à-vis Ottawa. For its part, the federal government could and did try to control separatists working in government departments in Ottawa. In 1963, the security panel heard its chair, Robert Bryce, the secretary to the Cabinet, say that "while an honest separatist could not be considered traitorous, he could not be considered reliable in the context of federal classified information."

Separatists in Quebec City's employ were out of reach of federal sanctions, however, and they found eager listeners in a small group of men in President de Gaulle's Paris that by the mid-1960s was already being called "the Quebec mafia." These men included senior diplomats such as Jean-Daniel Jurgenson, the head of the Quai d'Orsay's American (or Western hemisphere) desk and soon the political director in the Foreign ministry, and Bernard Dorin, attached to the office of the Minister of Education; Xavier Deniau, a Gaullist *deputé*; and Philippe Rossillon of the Haut Commissariat de la Langue française, which was attached to the Prime Minister's office. Jurgenson was a powerful figure, influential in any number of areas, and the de facto leader of the Quebec mafia. Dorin, like other Frenchmen who still resented the way the British and Americans had treated General de Gaulle's Free French movement during the war, was obsessed with visions of Anglo-Saxon conspiracies and, one senior Trudeau government minister remembered, would do anything to annoy Ottawa. Deniau was a troublemaker by inclination, and Rossillon, wealthy enough to do what he wanted whenever he wanted, had a crusader's fervour about the emancipation of Quebec.

The group in Paris was surprisingly small, though its influence was not. There were precisely twenty-seven in the Quebec mafia, Gérard Pelletier remembered. Pierre Trudeau's longtime friend and colleague, Pelletier had handled questions involving *francophonie* for the prime minister, served in three Cabinet posts and at the United Nations, and was ambassador in Paris from 1975 to 1981. Twenty-seven, and Canadian officials tried to keep watch on them all.

There was also representation in Quebec of the Service de Documentation Extérieure et de Contre-Espionnage (SDECE), one of the French secret services. Free of any parliamentary control or oversight, the SDECE was attached directly to the office of the president, and one of its "action branch" agents, a "Colonel Flamant," apparently offered "practical advice" to separatist groups and individuals in the late 1960s. Another Frenchman, René Vaillant, owned a small company in Canada, printed leaflets for and worked with the Front de Libération du Québec, and in 1968 was arrested in France for participating in Breton terrorist attacks there. According to Roger Faligot and Pascal Krop's authoritative history, *La Piscine: The French Secret Service Since 1944*, Vaillant's operations in Quebec, perhaps without his knowledge, "had been exploited by SDECE." What all this amounted to was unclear, though there could be no doubt that it was highly improper; certainly the SDECE reports reached de Gaulle.

The difficulty for the federal government was that the imperious French president was increasingly and openly sympathetic to the burgeoning *indépendantiste* movement in Quebec. Canada, to General de Gaulle, was both American and Anglo — neither word had pleasant connotations in his mind — and the French in Quebec had been treated badly for centuries. Now that they were at last coming alive, France had a duty to assist them. One demonstration of "assistance" was that soon after de Gaulle came to power in 1958, his intelligence services began operations in Quebec, initially directed by the consulate general in New York City. The General's major gesture to the separatists, of course, came during his visit to Quebec and Montreal in the centennial year of 1967. "Vive le Québec libre!" he had cried from the balcony of the Hotel de Ville in Montreal; the separatists had cheered him to the echo, but Ottawa's outraged protests led de Gaulle to return to Paris without paying his planned visit to Ottawa.

Relations between Ottawa and Paris seemed to have reached their nadir; but there was worse to come, especially after Pierre Trudeau became Liberal prime minister in April 1968. A tough-minded politician, a committed federalist, Trudeau had no patience with the idea of separatism and none at all with France's open interference in Canadian affairs.

And there was interference. Any suggestion that Paris and its embassy in Canada did not intervene in Canadian affairs was, one official close to Trudeau said, "bullshit. We're not naïve and they're not naïve." Trudeau himself agreed. "Whenever we found out that they were doing something improper," Trudeau said in a conversation about this subject, Ottawa went public with it. And Trudeau knew when such events occurred. The prime minister regularly chaired the Cabinet Committee on Security and Intelligence, and Paris's activities were central to its discussions in 1968 and after. Gordon Robertson, the Clerk of the Privy Council, chaired the parallel officials' committee, and he and Marcel Cadieux, the under-secretary of state for External Affairs, and Marc Lalonde, Trudeau's principal secretary, met frequently to consider the question whether it was best to intervene quietly to stop French meddling or to expose it publicly to try to embarrass Paris into desisting.

Certainly the activities of Philippe Rossillon in Canada amounted to deliberate attempts to stir the country's racial and linguistic pot. At the same time as the French government extended official recognition to a stream of visiting Quebec politicians (who could always get to see de Gaulle while Canada's ambassador, Jules Léger, was frozen out) and Canada and France were enmeshed in a series of public confrontations at francophone educational conferences in Africa, the millionaire Rossillon in 1967 was in New Brunswick, presenting himself to the province's Acadians as "the special and personal envoy of General de Gaulle." On his advice, Acadian leaders wrote to Paris, seeking financial and moral assistance in their struggle to keep *la race* alive. Early in 1968, Acadian delegates visited France where they were received by de Gaulle himself, and money (and medicine! — the French must have thought of New Brunswick as a primitive colony) was showered upon them and their newspaper *L'Évangeline*, up to four million francs in all, Rossillon recalled. There was nothing illegal in this, nothing overtly improper, except that Ottawa was informed only after the fact. Indeed, as François Leduc, the French ambassador at the time, recalled, Ottawa's reaction to this incident and others was so sharp that his telephone was tapped. So was Rossillon's room at the Château Frontenac in Quebec City on at least one of his visits. It was, Leduc said, all RCMP phobia.

Phobia or not, Trudeau had had enough. On September 11, 1968, the prime minister, quite deliberately trying to make France "pay" for its meddling in Canada, told the press that Paris had secretly sent Rossillon into Manitoba to stir up trouble among Franco-Manitobans. France had not troubled to inform Ottawa of Rossillon's visit, as would have been proper; in fact, the federal government had been informed only when Derek Bedson in the Manitoba premier's office reported on Rossillon's activities there. Long disturbed by Rossillon's activities in Paris, where he was friendly with FLQ representatives and in Canada, where he had some shadowy contacts with terrorist groups in Quebec and apparently provided financial aid to "certain members" of the Rassemblement pour l'indépendance nationale, Trudeau denounced "this underhanded and surreptitious way" of doing business by what he variously described as "more or less a secret agent," a "non-secret agent," and "an agent of a foreign state." The prime minister later said on television that France was trying "to demolish the unity of Canada."

Trudeau's crude tactic probably worked if its goal was to create embarrassment for and in France. The French embassy in Ottawa, now headed by Pierre Siraud, a former *chef de protocol* in Paris and a man who had been briefed personally by de Gaulle before taking up his post in Canada, predictably enough denied any impropriety. So did France's Foreign minister Michel Debré, who declaimed piously that Trudeau had been misled and was making "false statements." Pierre Carraud, counsellor at the embassy at the time, agreed, remembering that to call the activities of Rossillon and his coterie "a plot" would give the individuals involved too much credit. René Lévesque added his mite: "If Rossillon is a secret agent," the separatist leader said, "then I'm the Pope."

Perhaps the protests of innocence were sincere. But the simple truth is that the French ambassador in Ottawa was not ordinarily au courant with the activities of all Paris's men in Canada, let alone the SDECE. Even the consulate general in Quebec was not under the ambassador's control, as would have been normal, the diplomat in charge there reporting directly to Paris. And the Quebec government's *délégation général* in Paris also served as a channel to the Elysée Palace. Moreover, for a time pro-federalist diplomats were weeded out of the French embassy in Ottawa, their replacements carefully selected by the Quai d'Orsay to be sympathetic to separatist activities in Canada.

All this added up, as Gordon Robertson recalled, to the French being "pretty damn pretentious and obnoxious." Some might go further and accuse France of a deliberate attempt to connive at the destabilization of a friend and ally. So difficult did relations with Paris become before the end of the 1960s that the Trudeau Cabinet actually considered breaking relations with France or, as a lesser measure, an economic boycott. Cooler heads fortunately prevailed.

As it was, a number of French diplomats, including the consul in Quebec, Pierre de Menthon, the cultural attaché there, Philippe Bey, and at least four diplomats at the embassy in Ottawa, found themselves followed everywhere by the RCMP's Watcher Service. At the time of the October Crisis, Trudeau, according to Faligot and Krop, asked John Starnes, from January 1, 1970, the first civilian head of the RCMP's Security Service, if surveillance had been undertaken against the French Embassy. Starnes nodded, and Trudeau was said to have replied: "All right, but if you're caught out, I shall have to deny that I have been informed." A decade later, after he had testified before the McDonald Commission investigating RCMP wrongdoing, Prime Minister Trudeau refused to talk to the press "about the affair concerning the French Embassy, [or to make] judgments about embassies suspected of sheltering spies. In any case, no French diplomat has ever been declared persona non grata, or asked to leave the country," he said.

The prime minister was being uncommonly discreet. As far as he was concerned, the unpleasantness with France lasted without let-up and with only small variations in intensity through the de Gaulle, Pompidou, and Giscard d'Éstaing administrations in Paris. (An American State department paper on Quebec in August 1977 noted that "There have been reports of covert French activity in Quebec conducted by private French nationalists, but if true they are on such a limited scale as to be of no serious consequence. . . .") Not until the socialist François Mitterrand came to power, Trudeau said, did France finally ease up its disruptive activities and covert trouble-making in Canada. To Trudeau, the reason for Paris's activities was obvious: the French were keeping their hand in Canada in case the separatists won independence for Quebec; then they could say to the new Quebec government that they had been there to help. France, Trudeau told one of us bitterly, was always ready to advance the cause of French minorities everywhere in the world — except in France and its colonies. What made it all so galling to the prime minister was that Paris was simply ignorant of Canadian constitutional realities — being French, they didn't know the extent of decentralization in the federal system, for example, nor even that the provinces controlled education. And Trudeau had no doubt at all that money came from France — estimates from other sources indicate that Jean-Daniel Jurgenson of the Quebec mafia offered cash in 1970 to the tune of as much as $300,000 — to help the Parti Québécois. Whether it was official French government money he did not know; the RCMP couldn't find out when it sent an officer to Paris to talk to the SDECE. When the FLQ crisis struck in October 1970, the country would pay heavily for the Mounties' incapacity and lack of understanding of Quebec.

The FLQ was Canada's most notorious domestic terrorist organization. Loosely structured into cells, relatively tiny in its membership, the Front de Libération du Québec was an avowed separatist organization that sought to make Quebec an independent nation. Other less-developed nations had won their independence in the 1950s, some like Algeria out of a long revolutionary war. The ideology of liberation was in the air, and the youth of Quebec were not immune from its seductive lure. Frustrated by what they saw as French Canada's impotence in a federation that gave all power to English Canadians and enraged by the French Canadian élite's neglect of their own talents, the FLQ's members began to strike at federal government or anglophone institutions in Quebec in March 1963. Their aim was to rally the Québécois, to taunt the federal establishment, and to create the climate for revolutionary action by their compatriots.

The first targets were symbolic ones: the statue of General James Wolfe, the victor over Montcalm in the battle for Quebec in 1759, was destroyed in Quebec City, a bombing that met with not a few cheers and very little public condemnation outside the country's English-language newspapers. Then RCMP, Army, CNR, CBC, and Royal Canadian Legion premises were hit by firebombs or dynamited, and a caretaker at an Army recruiting office died in one attack. In May 1963, mailboxes were blown up, and one attempt to dismantle a bomb led to the death of an Army demolition expert, Sergeant Walter Leja. Police cracked the FLQ the next month, however, arresting sixteen members of one cell. The leader, Georges Schoeters, turned out to be a Belgian who had trained in terrorism in Algeria and Cuba. That Canada was home to international terrorists was almost as frightening as the idea that there were enough Québécois so dissatisfied with their situation to throw bombs.

But the FLQ had not been eliminated. In 1964, raids on armouries equipped the terrorists with machine guns, rifles, pistols, and ammunition. Again arrests followed, and this time the leader was one François Schirm, a Hungarian who had served in the French Foreign Legion and had established an FLQ training camp in the Laurentians. Two years later in 1966, yet another cell of the FLQ, led this time by an intellectual and writer named Pierre Vallières (who had, for a time, been an editor of *Cité Libre*, Pierre Trudeau's magazine), stole dynamite and rifles and, in bombing a factory, killed a sixty-four-year-old woman, Thérèse Morin. A later abortive attempt at an armed robbery led to the arrest of three members of the Vallières group, and police interrogation of those three put another fifteen in the bag. Vallières himself, by then living in the United States, decided to demonstrate for Quebec independence in front of the United Nations building in New York City, and he was soon under arrest. In jail, Vallières wrote a book, *White Niggers of America*, that set the rhetorical tone for the FLQ and Quebec separatists.

The elimination of Vallières, however, like that of Schoeters and Schirm, did not end the terror. In September 1969, Montreal Mayor Jean Drapeau's home was bombed and early the next year, the FLQ bombed a building at National Defence Headquarters in Ottawa. There was also suspected FLQ involvement in vicious strikes and riots involving taxi-drivers and the Montreal police, and revolutionary rhetoric was in the air. Not a few observers, including Prime Minister Trudeau, believed that the situation in Montreal was beginning to verge on anarchy. Most ominous, and suggestive of what was to come, in February 1970 two FLQ members were arrested for plotting to kidnap Israel's consul-general in Montreal; in June, police caught three more terrorists with plans in hand for the kidnapping of the American consul general there.

How was it that the FLQ, though repeatedly hit hard by arrests and obviously the object of infiltration attempts by the RCMP, military intelligence, and various Quebec police forces, still managed to survive? One answer was its classic cellular organization. The FLQ consisted of very small cells, some as tiny as two or three members. In all, an RCMP report leaked to the press in mid-October 1970 stated there were twenty-two FLQ cells with a total membership of 130 (along with sympathizers not directly engaged in the work of the cells, numbering some 2,000). Apparently none knew members outside his or her own cell, and they communicated, or so Liberal minister Jean Marchand suggested, through coded messages broadcast, knowingly or not, by radio stations. Some federal MPs also claimed that Radio Havana broadcast a half-hour program each day in French for FLQ members and the parliamentarians talked about Cubans, French Algerians, and East Europeans experienced in revolutionary war who had come to Canada to assist the FLQ. And Major-General Dan Loomis, a now retired officer who held senior posts in Quebec at the time of the FLQ crisis and who was privy to all the intelligence reports, put substantial weight on the presence in Quebec of 3,000 French conscripts, permitted by a benevolent Paris to work off their military obligation by serving in Quebec (and elsewhere in Canada) as language teachers and, Loomis implies, as "members of the insurgent organization." Loomis uses the word "deployment" to describe the presence of these conscripts; that comes very close to suggesting a direct role for the French government in the FLQ's activities.

Another factor in the survival of the FLQ was the weakness of the forces of order. The RCMP had never had much expertise on affairs in Quebec, one of the provinces where it did not provide the provincial police force. The RCMP also had relatively few francophone officers. Those it did have were on the policing side, not in intelligence. Most of its English-speaking officers were unilingual and, as had been true since the Great War, the Mounties remained obsessed with the threat of communism and interested only tangentially in other challenges to Canada's peace, order and good government. The RCMP, Pierre Trudeau remembered with genuine indignation, "was so damned ignorant about Quebec." Others, including E.A. Côté, deputy-solicitor general at the time of the crisis, take a more charitable view of RCMP capabilities.

The Quebec provincial police and the Montreal city police had close links with the RCMP, but jurisdictional disputes were nonetheless far from uncommon. The Montreal police had actually fought street battles against their provincial cousins during the police strike of 1969. In any case, all three forces' anti-terrorist expertise was limited although a combined anti-terrorist squad had been in existence since 1964. Still, the police had had some success in arresting FLQ bombers.

Unusually for Canada, where we tend to view the armed forces as hived off into their separate, underfinanced, and unimportant corner, there was another player on the board. Since the mid-1960s the

U.S. Army had been infiltrating radical groups to collect information for a series of secret contingency plans collectively known as "Garden Plot" and intended for use in the event that the army was called in to quell urban rioting.

(There may have been American agents of the Central Intelligence Agency operating in Quebec. The *Montreal Star* on September 24, 1971, published a photocopy of a CIA memorandum dated October 20, 1970: "Subject: Quebec. Sources advise that urgent action be taken to temporarily break contact with the FLQ militants since the Canadian government's measures may have undesirable consequences." This message, if authentic, is capable of differing interpretations, but it does suggest strongly that the CIA was operating in Quebec at the time of the October Crisis.)

Emulating the Americans, the Canadian Forces in Quebec, and especially Mobile Command headquarters at St. Hubert, had mounted active intelligence operations in the province for almost a decade. Mobile Command itself had spent some time in the middle of the 1960s developing a "concept of operations" for countering "protracted revolutionary war waged by national liberation fronts such as the FLQ," or so General Loomis described it. The military viewed the FLQ as an organization that aimed to seize power by revolutionary violence, and the bombings in the 1960s were "primarily examples of armed propaganda in the larger revolutionary struggle."

If this seemed to give the tiny claque of half-baked theorists and pseudo-revolutionaries of the FLQ substantially more importance than they merited, there seems no doubt that officers like Loomis took the threat seriously. According to Pierre Vallières' book, *The Assassination of Pierre Laporte*, and to a 1975 CBC-TV production on the October Crisis, military intelligence officers, operating under the mandate laid down by National Defence Headquarters's "Plan 210," set out to control agitation and agitators in Quebec. Military intelligence, as Vallières claimed, had "proceeded systematically to infiltrate the *indépendantiste* circles, the labour movement, the universities, and so on. They also infiltrated the political parties and even the executive council [cabinet] of Quebec." Although neither Vallières nor the CBC cites more than a few chapters and one or two verses, nonetheless, it is beyond doubt that military intelligence agents were active in Quebec in the late 1960s. More important, perhaps, when the October Crisis occurred in 1970, when two separate FLQ cells first kidnapped British trade official James Cross and then kidnapped and murdered Quebec Labour minister Pierre Laporte, the incapacity of the federal, provincial, and municipal police forces to analyse the data they had collected gave National Defence Headquarters and Mobile Command's intelligence specialists a critical role to play.

The irony of all this was clear. Canada was hooked into a variety of intelligence alliances with the Americans and the British and with NATO allies. France was similarly connected — in varying degrees — to those same information-sharing agencies. But if Trudeau and Loomis, among others, can be believed, and there is absolutely no reason to doubt them, France was actively working, both clandestinely and openly, to destabilize Canada both before and during the October Crisis. The Canadian Forces might be ready to share the defence of Western Europe with the Armée française, just as in the two world wars, but politics and geopolitics and mistaken concepts of Gaullist grandeur demanded that a vicious battle for high stakes be fought over Quebec's place in Canada. Happily, Canada won that battle. What, if anything, France and its secret service (after April 1982 known as the Direction Générale de la Securité Extérieure) are doing now as relations between the French- and English-speaking in Canada heat up again remains unknown.

10.
TECHNO-ESPIONAGE

S pying among "friends" may be unsettling or disruptive, but only rarely does it pose an actual threat to national security. In the area of technology, however, spying does threaten the security of Canada and its allies. Here, as usual, the Soviet Union has posed the most serious menace.

Despite their repeated protestations of world leadership in technical inventions and weaponry, the Soviet Union and its allies are backward nations in grievous economic shape. It is now evident to everyone — including the Politburo — that the Soviets have been unable to create an efficient food-distribution system that works or to supply the great bulk of their citizenry with most of the other necessities, let alone the luxuries, of twentieth-century life. And all this despite a system that is as labour-intensive as China's, so much so that one popular Moscow joke defines a job as five people not doing the work of one. The satellite nations, at last bursting the bonds that chained them to the corpse of the Soviet economic system, may be in as bad shape; Czechoslovakia and East Germany, traditionally manufacturing nations of great technical skill, now suffer from low productivity, demoralized work forces, and obsolete plants.

All this is serious enough. But just as important when nations consider their industrial and military strength, the Soviets have never been able to develop the computer technology that has pushed the West's industries ahead in the last quarter-century; they simply do not have the communications infrastructure that lets most of the free-market world talk and pass political, economic, and cultural information freely. The culture of secrecy, only now beginning to crumble under the impact of *glasnost* and the democratization of the Communist party and of the satellites, inhibited the easy interchange of ideas that might have solved the economic problems of Eastern Europe. Simply put, it is scarcely possible for a society to compete in the modern world without widespread access to Xerox machines and PCs.

What the USSR and its friends have had, and almost certainly still have, however, is a skilful system in place to steal — or buy — Western technology. This is despite the barriers erected by NATO and other U.S. allies to block the transfer of strategically important equipment and materiel eastward. The KGB and the GRU may well be the world's largest open and clandestine purchasers of Western technology, and their most successful spies likely know more about technical-equipment specifications than they do about NATO's missile deployment. Much of Soviet success in space technology, submarines and anti-submarine warfare, and missile development, for example, came directly from pirated, copied or stolen Western inventions.

Naturally enough, Western companies and businessmen often resented the rules that were put in place in Paris and in Washington by the U.S. government to inhibit the free flow of goods and technology to the Warsaw Pact nations and the People's Republic of China. Such rules, known as the COCOM lists, cut into their profits and, they complained to their governments, into the numbers of people they would otherwise employ. They compelled businesses to follow time-consuming bureaucratic procedures, they forced increasingly complicated security clearances on their staffs, and they generally wasted company time on endless form-filling. When detente is the rule, the business pressures to lower the barriers become almost irresistible. Until Gorbachev, until the startling events of the fall of 1989 and 1990, the West had little option but to continue to block uncontrolled technology transfer.

But in the pursuit of that desirable goal, situations on the interface between the corporate and government worlds could sometimes become almost Kafka-esque. Apparently innocent men have found themselves stripped of their security clearances by literally faceless bureaucrats, caught up in rules and regulations of which they knew nothing, and confronting unidentified accusers who denounced them for actions that were, until moments before, not only legal but officially sanctioned. An overstatement? Ask Peter Treu.

Alexander Peter Treu, who was born in Germany in 1912, had served in the *Luftwaffe* during the Second World War. Shot down and taken prisoner by British forces, he spent some time in a POW camp at Bracebridge, Ontario. Something about the country attracted him for, after securing a degree in engineering in Munich in 1953 and a doctorate in radio physics from Würzburg-Schweinfurt University in 1955, he emigrated to Canada in 1958 with his young family. By 1963, when he became a Canadian citizen, Treu was working for Northern Electric Co. on various projects. He specialized in communications electronics, and in 1964, his work on NATO's Air Defence Ground Environment System, or NADGE, led Ottawa to second him for two years to NATO headquarters in Paris. There he worked for NADGEMO (the NADGE Management Office), preparing specifications for the international consortium (or NADGECO) that eventually won the contract to build the air-defence communications network intended to weld the varying alliance members' systems into one. (In the blizzard of NATO abbreviations, NADGE, NADGECO, and NADGEMO were almost overly clear!)

Northern Electric was a principal sub-contractor, and after a year in London with NADGECO, Treu returned to its Montreal offices. There he helped design and build Northern Electric's portion of the NADGECO contract as project manager. Obviously, to do the sensitive work he did, Peter Treu required a security clearance to let him see documents up to top secret (cosmic), a very high classification indeed. Apparently, he had no difficulty in securing this clearance from the Canadian government which, as it always did, sent the RCMP out to talk to Treu's friends and neighbours and exchanged information about him with other NATO countries.

No problems so far for Treu. But by 1972, with NADGE ready to go into production, Northern Electric had changed management and made the decision to withdraw from defence contracting. So valuable was Treu that NADGECO asked him to set up his own company to help complete the project on which he had worked for a decade. With Northern Electric's support, and with Ottawa's blessing, Treu agreed, created a company that he named Canalatin Consultants Ltd., and he won contracts to supply engineering, logistical support, and equipment repair to NADGECO.

To do his work, Treu required access to vast quantities of classified documents, many of which he had previously signed out from Northern Electric. When he parted from the company completely in mid-1973, he took with him the documents he needed, and he continued to request more of them from NADGECO as the project went on. In June 1974, Treu learned completely by chance that, because he had changed his employment status, he had to reapply for security clearance, so "I hustled back to my office and made an application." He duly submitted the eighty-three-part form, heard nothing from Ottawa, and assumed that he still had his clearance.

While he awaited his NADGECO contracts, Treu sought other work. At the request of Nathan Ruvell, a New York lawyer in an international marketing agency, he put together what was known as a P-22, a ten- to fourteen-page prospectus, apparently on civilian air-traffic control systems, that was sent to the governments of India, Pakistan, and in 1973, through the agency of two Americans of Chinese origin, to the People's Republic of China. This "Chinese connection" was to be the root of Treu's troubles, although there is no evidence that the prospectus ever made its way to Beijing.

According to what the RCMP Security Service told the McDonald Commission, the Mounties had learned in August 1973 that Treu's prospectus contained much secret technical, scientific, and military information relating to NATO air-defence communication and surveillance systems. In November the RCMP asked the Department of Justice for a legal opinion on the likelihood of success of a prosecution under the Official Secrets Act. Justice considered the matter and contemplated charging Treu under one of the espionage sections of the act; but because key witnesses, never named, refused to testify, the department's opinion was that a successful prosecution was unlikely. Nonetheless, on March 29, 1974, as a result of Justice's consideration of the case, the RCMP called at Treu's home in the Montreal suburb of Beaconsfield and, armed with a search warrant, seized all his classified documents, variously estimated to weigh from 350 to 550 pounds. "They were lying all over the place," a federal prosecutor later claimed. Treu stoutly maintained that the documents, some "that I had written myself," were no more than a military application of a commercial air-traffic control system.

Most important, at the end of 1973, Treu's security clearance apparently had been revoked by Stanley Jenkyns, the director of industrial security in the Department of Supply and Services (DSS) in Ottawa, though Treu, in accordance with the usual government policy, was never advised of this. In other words, the RCMP had found that Peter Treu now held documents to which he was no longer entitled.

But if Treu was believed guilty of an offence under the Official Secrets Act, nothing in his business life seemed to change. After the Mounties' seizure of his papers, he heard not a word about any prosecution from Ottawa for two years. In the interim, he received governmental invitations to confidential conferences in Ottawa, meetings for which security clearance was required and to which access apparently was controlled by the same Stanley Jenkyns of DSS. Treu said later that "I was still actively working on a number of NATO contracts which were classified and I received classified information from the federal government, even though they were the ones who dropped my rating." Moreover, NADGECO continued to make use of his services, and Treu held eighty-five small NATO contracts for the repair of NADGE components from 1974 to 1977; he also designed new NADGE equipment, some of which NATO promptly classified as secret. The right hand of Ottawa — and NATO — knew not what the left was doing.

Not until March 1976 did the RCMP inform Treu that he was to be charged with violations of the Official Secrets Act: illegal retention of and failure to take reasonable care of classified information. Even then, incredibly, no one in Ottawa told NATO, for Treu continued to receive NADGECO work.

Treu steadfastly maintained that the documents in his possession had been properly signed out to him and were essential for his NADGECO work. Moreover, he had built alarm systems and secure cabinets in which to hold the "NATO-Confidential" documents. Information with that low-level rating was far from being highly secret. And even if his clearance had been revoked and even if he was no longer entitled to hold the documents, how could he know this if he had never been told?

As for the prospectus that might or might not have gone to China, Treu rebutted the government claim that it had "paraphrased a NATO document" and argued that it contained nothing of a confidential nature. The material was nothing more than any engineer could have obtained from a textbook, he said, and his role had only been to put it together in a single package. Most important, Treu maintained, the prospectus that went to India had "had the consent of the Canadian Government," the endorsement of the Department of Industry, Trade and Commerce and of Canada's High Commissioner in New Delhi. It is less clear if the submissions to Pakistan and China had Ottawa's endorsement, but George Bain of the *Toronto Star*, who conducted the fullest investigation of the Treu case, said that they "probably" did. Treu himself adamantly (and predictably) maintained that he had done nothing improper: "I'm not a spy. Do I look like one?"

Nonetheless, the government proceeded with its case against Peter Treu. On May 16, 1976, he appeared in court in Montreal and pleaded not guilty. Crown prosecutor Claude Belanger said that the delay between the seizure of the documents and the prosecution arose "because of the nature of the documents. . . . We had to call in different experts who examined them." RCMP superintendent Gerald Kennedy added his mite by telling the press that the documents related to anti-missile protection systems, a claim that was later repeated. Significantly, it was not one that was made in the first report of the McDonald Commission, published in October 1979.

When the case eventually went to trial, the Crown sought leave to hold it *in camera* under the terms of Section 14 (2) of Canada's draconian Official Secrets Act. The act, originally passed in 1890 and revised several times since, had been intended to protect information of an official nature from unauthorized use. When Treu's counsel made no objection to an *in camera* trial, the judge slapped a ban on publicity. Only Treu's sentencing, in the event that he was found guilty, would be public. Peter Treu had obviously believed in his innocence and had preferred to minimize the harmful effects of publicity on himself and his family. The "Star Chamber" proceedings in Montreal quickly created a major public furore and led to attacks on the Official Secrets Act by parliamentarians, notably Progressive Conservative MP Ged Baldwin, and jurists.

The trial was conducted in extraordinary circumstances. Everyone involved, including the judge, was subjected to a security check; the RCMP gathered up the evidence each day; and a special cabinet was installed in the judge's office for classified material. After seven days of testimony, on April 28, 1977, Sessions Court Judge Leo Trudel found Peter Treu guilty on the two counts under which he had been charged. The judge allowed the public to be present for his verdict, though the decision was not read in court. On May 4, Trudel sentenced Treu to two years in jail, and Treu, freed on a $10,000 bond, immediately launched an appeal. As his wife said, "We came to Canada because we believed in democracy, but I was innocent of the facts. . . . I never believed an entire trial could be held in secrecy here."

Crown prosecutor François Handfield said little about the prosecution case outside court. But in a statement he made before Treu's sentencing, he suggested that Treu had tried to exploit NATO secrets for commercial gain. He also drew the court's attention to the China connection, the prospectus: "I remind you to whom Treu's covering letter was addressed." Treu flatly denied that any covering letter was attached to his prospectus and reiterated that he had Ottawa's approval for it.

Peter Treu eventually won his appeal against his conviction under the Official Secrets Act. In February 1979, a three-judge panel of the Quebec Court of Appeal unanimously overturned the conviction. Mr. Justice Rodolphe Paré wrote that there was "no doubt" that Treu took serious precautions to protect the classified documents he held at his home. Another member of the panel agreed with Treu's lawyer that the Crown's use of the P-22 prospectus had helped to "poison the judge's mind" against his client: "It changed the atmosphere from what otherwise might have been a very ordinary case into a cause célèbre, with overtones of espionage and foreign intrigue."

Not everything that went on in this quite extraordinary affair is yet clear. Had the federal government agreed to Treu's prospectus going to the three Asian nations? And just what was the prospectus concerned with — ground-to-air communications, as Treu maintained, or missile defence, as the RCMP claimed? Why was Treu's security clearance removed and why was Stanley Jenkyns permitted to act as a czar, disposing of people's lives in a cavalier fashion? Why did Ottawa spend large sums on a prosecution that appeared so self-evidently flawed? Until those questions can be answered, nothing definitive can be said.

The last word belongs to Peter Treu. "I learned my lesson," he said after his ultimate victory. "As long as there are civil servants who can withdraw a person's security clearance without informing them, everyone working on classified projects will continue to have one foot in jail."

Treu was an apparently innocent victim caught up in the high-tech war between East and West. But there was plenty of evidence to suggest that as long as COCOM embargoes continued, Canada remained a major target of Soviet espionage in search of technology.

In 1988 expulsions of Soviet diplomats were a case in point. Although some of those expelled had been caught redhanded in attempts to penetrate CSIS ("to get inside the tribal knowledge," as one senior CSIS official put it), most had been trying to steal classified information on sensitive technology with commercial or military applications. The principal target was the Montreal-based company Paramax Electronics Inc.

Outside Ottawa, Montreal has traditionally been the main centre of Soviet espionage activity. Of the seventeen Soviets making up the original lists of expellees, twelve were Montreal-based, spread between the consulate general, the Aeroflot office, and the headquarters of the International Civil Aviation Organization (ICAO). The Soviet delegation at ICAO had long been identified as a centre of

Soviet espionage. A top-secret RCMP security service report of 1976 identified five of the forty Soviet staff members as known or suspected intelligence officers, one of them being the KGB officer who ran Illegal networks.

At the time of the 1988 expulsions, CSIS had been enjoying an inside view into the operations of the Soviet ICAO delegation for at least a couple of years. Their source was Yuri Smurov, an interpreter with the delegation. A fifty-one-year-old Russian from Leningrad, Smurov in reality was an intelligence officer and had enjoyed a previous posting at ICAO in the 1970s. Shortly after returning to Montreal in 1985 with his wife and daughter, he began providing information to CSIS. In spring 1988, he learned that he was soon to be posted back to Moscow. Deciding to defect and remain in Canada with his family, he alerted CSIS. On June 13 — the day before Kelleher's phone call to the prime minister that precipitated the spy wars — he pulled his daughter out of school in Westmount and the family disappeared to a CSIS safe house. Joe Clark confirmed the defection in the Commons, thus making Smurov the first publicly admitted Soviet defector in Canada since Gouzenko.

Smurov had played a key role in helping CSIS track the operation against Paramax. The company, a subsidiary of Unisys Corporation of Detroit, manufactures naval-combat and electronic systems. Highly classified and heavily protected against electronic snooping, the main Paramax facility includes a 16,000-square-foot building specifically designed for testing its naval products. Inside is a full-scale replica of the operations room and bridge of a patrol frigate. In summer 1988 Paramax was fulfilling a $1.25-billion contract with Ottawa to design, test, and install electronic and combat systems for Canada's new patrol frigates under construction at the Saint John shipbuilding yard in New Brunswick. More important, it hoped to win orders for the (then) planned ten or twelve nuclear-powered submarines that the government had announced in its 1987 white paper on defence. Intense negotiations about the possible transfer of U.S. naval and nuclear technology embedded in the British Trafalgar-class submarines being considered as an option for Canadian purchase formed a backdrop to the drama. The

Americans — especially after the Walker spy case — needed re-assuring that their naval technology would be safe in Canadian hands. Once again, alliance needs had spoken. And another thing that Canada's allies were certain about was that Moscow was desperate to gain sophisticated Western technology.

When Ronald Reagan arrived in the White House in January 1981, he immediately ordered the CIA to investigate the strategic effect of legal and illegal technology transfers to the Soviet Union. In Reagan's view the theft of top Western technology did much to explain the shift in the balance of power that he was determined to reverse. The next May, the U.S. Congress considered a report that identified a massive and global Soviet program to acquire militarily significant technology. Its success, the report noted in alarmist tones, eroded "the technological superiority on which U.S. and allied security depends." The CIA claimed that European manufacturing equipment was being used to build Red Army trucks; that American radar systems were being used by the Soviet Air Force to shoot down cruise missiles at Soviet test-flight facilities; that large Western mainframe computers helped co-ordinate Soviet troop movements in East Germany; and that Western micro-computers were guiding Soviet missiles in Syria. The list went on, echoed in a score of other estimates that surfaced over the next few years throughout the West. Up to 70 percent of all new Warsaw Pact weapons systems, one West German expert said, were based on pirated Western technology, while a U.S. consultant calculated that the value of Western technology "borrowed" by the USSR over a twenty-year period amounted to $100 billion. In 1985, the CIA produced an update of its 1981 study. Entitled *Soviet Acquisition of Militarily Significant Technology*, the report was even more alarmist about the Soviet campaign to get its hands on Western know-how. "Western products and technology secrets," it concluded, "are being systematically acquired by intricately organized, highly effective collection programs specifically targeted to improve Soviet military weapons systems. The Soviet intelligence services — the KGB, the GRU, and their surrogates among the East European services — and the Soviet trade and scientific organizations are actively involved in obtaining this technology. Targets include defense contractors, manufacturers, foreign trading firms, academic institutions, and electronic data bases. Only recently has the full extent of illegal Soviet technology collection efforts become known." While sceptical of some of this, a British specialist writing in the *Bulletin of the Atomic Scientists* in 1987 agreed with the basic thesis about an increased Soviet espionage drive. Noting the strengthening of Western embargoes on strategic materiel in the mid-1980s, and a weakened Soviet access to convertible currencies through lower oil prices, he concluded that "the Soviets will probably be more tempted than in the past to seek Western technology by clandestine channels for purposes that are not directly and immediately related to military production. The Soviet industrial espionage effort is therefore likely to intensify."

Most of the data supporting these conclusions came to the West as the result of the "Farewell" affair. This was the Western codename for a high-ranking KGB officer specializing in technology, who, in 1981, turned over substantial evidence about Soviet spying to the DST (Direction de la Surveillance du Territoire, the French security service). The dossier was shown by President Mitterrand to Ronald Reagan when he attended the 1981 Ottawa summit — an initiative that also reassured the U.S. president about the socialist Mitterrand's credentials as a reliable member of the Western alliance. Farewell's documents also played a key part in the dramatic expulsion by France, on April 8, 1983, of some forty-seven intelligence officers, most of them engaged in industrial espionage. Farewell himself was eventually caught by the KGB and executed for treason.

Why did the Soviet Union need to spy to acquire Western technology? Surely this was available on the open market? Much of it was, and could be acquired by Moscow through the legal exploitation of open sources or through the purchase of "dual-use" technology (technology that can be used for civilian or military purposes). But key portions were and are not. They are either highly classified in themselves, and thus not even on the open market within the West, or have been subject to export controls that ban their transfer to the Soviet Union and its allies.

COCOM — the Co-ordinating Committee for Multilateral Export Controls — was established in 1949 at the height of the Cold War. All NATO countries except Iceland are members, as are Japan and Australia. Housed in an ugly office block just off the Champs Elysée, in an annex of the American embassy in Paris, it exists to define, expose, and combat technical and scientific espionage. Its embargo lists provide a guideline for all members to follow, although individual NATO countries impose and police their own controls. COCOM deliberations are carried out in secret, and all COCOM documents are classified.

In the 1980s many countries instituted special measures to ensure that the revised and updated COCOM lists, by then containing more than 100,000 items, were effectively applied. Project "Exodus" was begun in the United States, Project "Arrow" in Britain. Even before Ronald Reagan had arrived in the White House, Jimmy Carter, prompted by the Soviet invasion of Afghanistan, had pushed for more stringent COCOM lists. As a result, Congress passed the Export Administration Act (EAA) that restricted not just technology useful to the Soviet military, but also technology that strengthened the entire Soviet industrial and energy base. Reagan's victory saw the U.S. administration pushing even harder for more stringent controls and the updating of COCOM lists to keep abreast of new technological advances. Many European allies resisted the Reagan drive, as did a number of U.S. companies, frequently supported by voices within the Department of Commerce. Still, by the end of the decade, Western controls were tighter and more determined. So was the Soviet drive to overcome them.

At the apex of the Soviet system for acquiring military technology lay the VPK, or Military Industrial Commission of the Council of Ministers. Comprising ministers of the major defence manufacturing industries (machine-building, aviation, radio, communications equipment, shipbuilding, and electronics) and working with an annual budget of well over $1 billion, the VPK co-ordinates the development of all Soviet weapons as well as the Soviet program to acquire Western technology. Once needs have been identified and listed in order of priority, the VPK tasks and finances various collection agencies responsible for acquiring the technology, legally or illegally. Annually, the list runs to about 3,000 items published in a volume the size of a large telephone directory.

The KGB and the GRU are the most important agencies responsible for illegal acquisitions. Until recently they were sometimes assisted very substantially by other intelligence services of the Soviet bloc.

Inside the KGB, Directorate T of the First Chief Directorate is responsible for science-and-technology operations. The CIA estimates that the directorate has some 1,000 officers, of whom 300 or so are on foreign assignment. According to Czech defector Ladislav Bittman, it has also, since the 1960s, "been the fastest growing operative sector of Soviet foreign intelligence." Most Directorate T officers work under cover in such positions as science or commercial attachés in Soviet missions or international organizations (such as ICAO). Others work as officials in trade missions or as members of scientific exchanges. More aggressive and successful than the KGB in the field of military-technology espionage is the GRU, the Chief Intelligence Directorate of the Soviet General Staff. Collection of this sort of data has been a priority since the GRU's birth in the 1920s — as indicated by its targeting of Allied nuclear and scientific secrets in Canada and the United States during the Second World War, clearly revealed by the Gouzenko case.

Most GRU officers working outside the USSR have cover that gives them better access to scientific secrets than that enjoyed by KGB officers. Many of them operate in the scientific or commercial divisions of Soviet embassies or consulates, or in international organizations and foreign trade offices. In addition, they are frequently to be found working for Aeroflot or Mosflot (the Soviet merchant marine). Until 1989 and the revolution that swept Eastern Europe, East European intelligence services such as the Czech STB, Polish SB, or East German MFS were often more effective than either of the Soviet services. "East European services have had considerable success not only in the United States but elsewhere," stated the 1985 CIA report on Soviet acquisition of military technology, "because they are generally perceived as a lesser threat than the Soviets; they may often not be perceived as operating in a surrogate role; in some countries, including the United States, they operate under less severe travel restrictions; and some, especially the Czechoslovaks and East Germans, probably find it easier to operate in the West European cultural and commercial climate." New governments in Eastern Europe have made it clear that this state of affairs is now history.

Principal targets of the Soviet drive for high-tech secrets identified in 1985 by the CIA were the United States, Britain, West Germany, and Japan. Canada, nonetheless, was also a target, being one of the world's most technologically advanced (if smaller) nations deploying high-tech techniques across a spectrum of activity. Moreover, because of its closeness to the United States, Canada has also provided a convenient avenue to American technology secrets. As the Paramax case shows, the patrol frigate program, a high-cost defence project using American technology, clearly made Canada a target for Soviet attempts to acquire U.S. secrets.

That Canada's scientific and technological assets are vulnerable to espionage attack is apparent from a special report delivered to the solicitor general by the Security Intelligence Review Committee in April 1989. Although the report is classified, outlines of the conclusions were made public by the SIRC in its annual report that September. From this it emerged that Canada enjoys no central apparatus charged with all aspects of safeguarding its scientific and technological assets, including both the enforcement and the intelligence-production functions. Instead, different departments and agencies set their own boundaries, assisted by COCOM guidelines. Enforcement of security in science and technology is largely the task of Revenue Canada (Customs), DEA and the RCMP; intelligence production — estimating the threat — is the job of many government departments, as well as CSIS (which is a member of the Canadian delegation to COCOM).

SIRC was clearly critical. "We betray no secrets," its 1989 report says, "when we say that the present system can be improved."

One recommendation SIRC made was greater co-ordination within CSIS of all science and technology (S&T)-related investigations. Another was for CSIS to seek from the government a mandate to assign a higher priority to protection of S&T assets. "We need," stated SIRC, "to protect key scientific and technological secrets from the agents of foreign countries and from 'technobandits' — free-booters, some of them Canadian, who are prepared to smuggle restricted goods out of the country for a quick buck." The government listened. Five months later, to a major conference of the country's intelligence experts meeting in Ottawa, Solicitor General Pierre Blais announced that the protection of science and technology was one of the five priorities he had just given to CSIS.

It scarcely required insiders' knowledge, however, to appreciate that Canada, like other Western countries, had long been a target of the Soviet drive for illegal high-tech resources.

The high-tech struggle has been waged on two fronts: the conventional war of espionage, and the guerrilla campaigns of "technobandits." Canada has seen both in action in recent years. Several East-bloc diplomats have been publicly expelled for high-tech spying. Others have quietly been asked to leave. One of those publicly expelled was Mikhail Abramov, the Soviet assistant trade commissioner in Ottawa, in April 1982.

The Abramov affair began not long after he arrived in Ottawa in 1979. On the lookout for any technology of interest to the Soviet Union, Abramov was grateful to receive an approach about a legitimate sale from a New Brunswick businessman, Elton Killam, the president of Northumberland Cable Co. Ltd. of Petitcodiac, N.B. His company had recently negotiated a deal with AT&T (the American Telephone and Telegraph Company) for the salvage of 2,400 kilometres of undersea cable dating from the 1950s that linked Washington state and Alaska. Would the Soviet Union be interested in purchasing this? Killam enquired. Abramov, immediately seeing a chance to acquire more than just some old undersea cable, told Killam that he was. More meetings followed, at which, according to Killam, Abramov offered to "do interesting and good business, other than this cable." Killam immediately reported the Abramov approach to the RCMP Security Service. The Mounties then kept a watch on Abramov, probably eavesdropping on at least one of the meetings he held with Killam at the Dorval Hilton Hotel in Montreal. At one such encounter Abramov offered Killam $9 million for the old cable, plus embargoed fibre-optic cable of military application, as well as some other high-tech items. In the meantime, following U.S. sanctions slapped on exports to the Soviet Union in 1981 after the imposition of martial law in Poland, Killam withdrew his original offer to sell the cable to Abramov. But Abramov continued to meet with him, and the RCMP continued their investigation, until the operation came to an end when External Affairs minister Mark MacGuigan announced Abramov's expulsion at a specifically summoned news conference in Ottawa on April 2, 1982. "This does indicate," MacGuigan later told the House of Commons, "the high technology sanctions, which were tightened as a result of the Soviet invasion of Afghanistan, really do have considerable bite. The Soviet Union is . . . obviously prepared to go to extreme lengths to obtain the kind of technology which is denied." Shortly afterwards, another Soviet, also implicated in the affair, prematurely returned home.

Eighteen months later, two more Soviets were expelled. Anatoly Solousov had worked since 1979 at ICAO headquarters in Montreal; Victor Tsekovisky, a senior KGB officer, worked under cover as a trade official in the Soviet consulate. Together, they had targeted an employee at a Montreal-based aeronautical company in an attempt to acquire highly classified information about aircraft jet fuel and the use of ceramics in the combustion chambers of jet engines. Alerted by the employee and his company to these Soviet approaches, the RCMP Security Service tracked the case for some three years before deciding to blow the whistle.

Early in September 1983, the two men were quietly asked to leave Canada. Then Korean Air Lines (KAL) flight 007 was shot down, killing 269 people, including 10 Canadians. The tragedy inflamed anti-Soviet feeling, and External Affairs minister Allan MacEachen decided to keep the expulsions secret. Once the KAL affair died down, however, the news leaked out. Confirming it, Solicitor General Robert Kaplan explicitly aligned Canada's actions with the general Western campaign against the illegal Soviet acquisition of high technology. Canada, along with its allies, he said, was studying ways in which to protect high-technology secrets in the face of what he termed "a very significant" increase in espionage.

Less than two years after that, in July 1985, there was another highly publicized spy case. This involved Raikov Delibaltov, assistant trade commissioner at the Bulgarian consulate general in Toronto. Holidaying in Bulgaria, Delibaltov was declared persona non grata and denied permission to return. This was the first such case in which CSIS had been involved — and the first for the Mulroney government, too. While no details were released, it seemed clear that this case also dealt with attempts to steal industrial secrets. The Bulgarian secret service was long noted for being trained, monitored, and guided by the KGB and was frequently involved in the high-tech espionage game. At the time of the Delibaltov affair, a Bulgarian trade official in the United States was facing charges of attempting to purchase nuclear-weapons secrets; and only the year before, a Bulgarian diplomat in Japan had fled after security officials started probing his unusual interest in high-tech secrets and genetic engineering.

So the Paramax affair was merely one more case in a long sequence of Soviet-bloc attempts to acquire high-tech secrets in Canada. Of equal concern to the government, however, was the activity of "technobandits," a continuing problem.

Technobandits are Western businessmen and companies who knowingly attempt to export embargoed technology to the Soviet Union — or any other country for that matter — that is covered by export controls. Several dramatic and highly publicized cases surfaced in the West in the 1980s. One of the more notorious was the Bruckhausen affair. This involved a network of companies in California operated by Werner Bruckhausen, a flamboyant German businessman who at the height of his success commissioned a hand-painted wristwatch face for $1 million from Spanish painter Salvador Dali. Through a network of companies in Europe, Bruckhausen, who had been recruited by the GRU, for years shipped some of Silicon Valley's most sensitive computer secrets to the Soviet Union. Moscow thus acquired basic manufacturing equipment on which they could then reproduce Western technology. "Using Bruckhausen," one computer expert claimed, "the Soviets were able to acquire all the hardware to build a complete modern integrated-circuit plant with 100 percent spares. They got the best they could get — all state-of-the-art equipment. And they showed very good taste in getting it." For this, the Soviets had paid at least $30 million in hard currency for equipment that cost Bruckhausen only $8 million. Indicted in 1981, Bruckhausen fled the United States but was returned for trial in 1987 after being arrested and deported from Britain. In 1987, he was sentenced in California to fifteen years' imprisonment on multiple counts of fraud in connection with the violation of U.S. export laws. "The Werner Bruckhausen case," writes one expert, "is a paradigm of how the Soviets illegally acquire U.S. high technology." Through sophisticated buying on the basis of needs and priorities determined by the VPK, the Soviet Union had profited from a Western smuggling scheme that used multiple-format companies and falsified export-control forms, and consistently lied to electronics companies about their activities.

Canada has seen nothing on the scale of Bruckhausen. But some Canadian businessmen have been implicated in similar schemes. Canada has also been the scene of events surrounding one of the most notorious of the more recent U.S. technobandits.

An example of the former is the case of Peter Virag. Virag left Hungary after the 1956 uprising and settled in Montreal, where he became a lawyer. In 1972 he incorporated a company called DeVimy Test Lab Ltd., whose ostensible interest was in manufacturing and testing integrated circuits. Over the next few years he bought a considerable amount of computer and electronics equipment from U.S. manufacturers for his Montreal plant. Most of the material was COCOM-embargoed, but because Canada was the stated destination the U.S. authorities permitted its export.

In reality, DeVimy Test Lab Ltd. existed only on paper, and Virag's operations were part of a complex scheme established deliberately to sell embargoed high technology to the Soviet bloc.

The story began some two years before Virag incorporated DeVimy Test Lab Ltd., with an Israeli called Jacob Kelmer. Kelmer had acquired a degree in electrical engineering from Rensselaer Polytechnic Institute in Troy, New York, and in about 1970 he established a company called DEK Electronics in Halifax to represent U.S. electronic firms in Israel. Some of the most important items he sold for them over the next couple of years included oscilloscopes essential in the testing and repairing of nuclear weaponry, lasers, and military-telecommunications equipment. The customer, Kelmer seems to have told his U.S. suppliers, was the Israeli army. This, too, was a fiction. The oscilloscopes were shipped on from Israel to Vienna, from where they disappeared into Eastern Europe. (Evidence later gathered by Israeli police investigators suggested that Kelmer had been recruited by a man in London who passed on to him purchase orders for Soviet high-tech needs that had been communicated by Soviet intelligence officers.)

U.S. Commerce officials soon became suspicious of Kelmer's business and in 1972 banned him from receiving U.S. exports. To get around the ban, Kelmer turned to Virag in Montreal.

Through a mutual acquaintance living in the United States, Virag was recruited for a scheme that he apparently believed was being set up to benefit Israel. The contact told Virag that he had a cousin in the Israeli army who needed to buy U.S. electronics materiel secretly. Would Virag help the State of Israel? The Montreal lawyer, who was Jewish, agreed. To carry out the scheme, he established DeVimy Lab. Virag was now caught in a scheme that eventually brought him to court.

On behalf of Kelmer, whom he apparently believed — or pretended to believe — was an Israeli Army major, Virag ordered large quantities of sensitive high-tech equipment supposedly for use in his Montreal laboratories. Kelmer's initial orders were for items of relatively small strategic interest, but they soon escalated into more important items such as a photorepeater machine that etched integrated circuits onto semiconductor chips. The two top U.S. manufacturers, Electromask Inc. and GCA Corporation, produced machines far more sophisticated than anything produced by the Soviets.

Virag plumped for the GCA machine, and in 1976 it was shipped to Montreal from the GCA plant in Bedford, Massachusetts, supposedly for installation in a DeVimy factory. It stayed in Montreal only a day. Virag and Kelmer immediately had it shipped to Amsterdam, whence it was promptly reshipped to Prague. GCA was paid by Virag with money from two accounts in Zurich, Switzerland, that investigators were unable to trace back any farther.

The Soviets were apparently pleased with the Virag–Kelmer operation, and in 1976 ordered another photorepeater. This proved to be Virag's downfall. On attempting to purchase a second photorepeater from GCA in Massachusetts, Virag was asked about the first, which should have been in operation in Montreal but of which there was no trace. GCA were not convinced by Virag's responses. Suspicious, they contacted the U.S. Commerce Department. There then began an investigation that lasted for several months and involved the RCMP as well as U.S. investigators. At the end of it, in 1978, Virag pleaded guilty in a U.S. federal court in Albany, New York, to a count of exporting restricted items without a valid U.S. licence. Kelmer, also found guilty, was denied U.S. export privileges for fifteen years.

Virag's case was a classic "false flag" operation that through dummy companies and several "cut-outs" (go-betweens) saw Western high-tech secrets find their way to the Soviet Union. Virag himself was complicit, although he may genuinely have thought the items were bound for Israel. As one U.S. Commerce Department officer concluded, "the issue of high dollar profits . . . encouraged Virag to become a willing dupe in an illegal plot. Once involved, Virag was unable or unwilling to extract himself."

Many other Western entrepreneurs have taken similar routes. In summer 1989, at least one Canadian found his name in the news in connection with alleged high-tech illegal exports to the Soviet bloc.

In July 1989, Warren Wetstein, of the Toronto-based Asset Conversion Specialists Inc., was named in a U.S. indictment along with four Texans associated with a Houston company called Technology International Consultants Inc. Wetstein, U.S. Customs alleged, had been involved with the others in a $1.8-million deal to smuggle U.S. computer equipment via Canada to the Soviet Union. The route was to be carefully concealed, passing through Belgium and then on to Bulgaria. The U.S. government's case rested on information provided by a Dutch member of the Belgian operation who had turned informer after being arrested in the United States. The equipment to be smuggled to the Soviet Union was two Vax-8820 computers manufactured by the Digital Equipment Corporation. Digital had been exporting computers to the USSR since 1972, and its Vax line is the favourite of many Soviet scientists. The Vax-8820s, embargoed for export to the Soviet bloc, were wanted to help improve the Soviet air-defence system. U.S. officials alleged that ever since May 1988, when a young West German dramatically landed his plane in Red Square, the Soviet military had been desperately trying to obtain U.S. computer equipment to strengthen their air-defence systems.

The Texans allegedly involved were taken into custody in June 1989. Warren Wetstein, however, disappeared, and was still being sought in Canada early in 1990.

Meanwhile, the Canadian legal system was struggling with one of the biggest and most notorious cases of all, that of Charles McVey.

McVey, a sixty-three-year-old American weighing three hundred pounds, had been on the U.S. Customs Service's most-wanted list for years in connection with illegal high-tech exports to the Soviet Union. Like Werner Bruckhausen, he lived in style, shifting residences and travelling on various passports, including a Guatemalan one describing him as Carlos Julio Williams. Like Bruckhausen, he owned several front companies based in California that exported computer equipment overseas. Indicted first in 1983, then again in 1987, McVey had allegedly directed several million dollars' worth of computer equipment to the Soviet Union through West Germany and Switzerland between 1972 and 1981. Satellite-image processing systems, as well as oscilloscopes, were also involved. McVey, it was charged, had also employed two Britons to work for him in the Soviet Union. One, who visited the Soviet Union twenty-five times on McVey's behalf, had not only helped repair and install equipment, but had also consulted with the Soviets to determine what orders they should place with McVey. The other, a software consultant, taught courses in Minsk to Soviet technicians and later admitted that "millions of dollars[' worth] of sophisticated U.S. computer equipment" was bought by McVey on behalf of the Soviet Union. It was McVey's habit, his California secretary said, to burn most business telexes. And when he sent his computer shipments to his accomplice in Zurich, a man named Rolf Leinhard, he would send a telex message that said simply "Baby on the way."

McVey fled the United States on the eve of his 1983 twenty-three-count indictment, and for the next four years escaped capture by flitting between his residences in Switzerland and Malta. Then, on August 18, 1987, his escapades came to an abrupt end in an unlikely spot, the small Yukon village of Teslin. By this time, he was top of the ten most-wanted technobandits on the U.S. "Project Exodus" list.

McVey had continued his exploits while on the run, and some time in 1987 he managed to enter Canada. Here he became involved in yet another smuggling scheme involving a supercomputer called the Matrix I. Manufactured by the Silicon Valley Saxpy Computer Corporation, the Matrix I is a high-speed machine of considerable value in anti-submarine warfare where it can calculate potential missile trajectories. In mid-1987, the software and documentation for the system was stolen from Saxpy by Ivan Batinic, one of its engineers, who passed it on to a man called Kevin Anderson. He, in turn, contacted McVey in Canada, and shortly afterwards, Anderson, Batinic, and Batinic's brother Stevan visited British Columbia. Here they met with McVey, who was using his Carlos Julio Williams alias. Money changed hands, and on their way back to the United States the three were briefly detained by Customs officials at Vancouver airport. Here they admitted that $16,200 in large-denomination bills in their possession had been given to them in a taxi by "Williams."

For the next few weeks, Anderson's activities were closely monitored by U.S. Customs officials through an informer. First he travelled to McVey's home in Malta, then on to the Soviet Union where, it was alleged, he arranged to sell the Saxpy software for some $4 million. The route to be taken for its smuggling would be via Mexico. After his return from the Soviet Union, Anderson was arrested, along with the two Batinic brothers, and in August 1988 he was sentenced to six years in jail after pleading guilty to conspiracy to violate U.S. export laws.

By this time the moving spirit behind all these schemes was himself in jail. McVey's presence in Canada had become known, and over the summer of 1987 the RCMP received a tip from the Americans that he enjoyed fishing in the Yukon. Photographs were distributed and a widespread search began. On August 18, a sharp-eyed corporal spotted the tall, oversized American in a local Teslin restaurant. Shortly afterwards, he was flown to Vancouver to face extradition charges.

Since then McVey and his lawyers have fought the case in the B.C. courts. Three times he has been freed, and three times he has been re-arrested. On the first occasion he was let go on the technicality that his arrest warrant had been issued in Vancouver but served in Yukon where the signing judge had no jurisdiction. Immediately re-arrested on a new warrant seeking his extradition to the United States, he was ordered released on the grounds that making false statements to the U.S. Customs was not an extraditable offence. Once again he was re-arrested, in December 1987, on charges of illegally transporting and possessing a stolen computer manual that had significant military implications. The extradition case eventually reached the B.C. Court of Appeal. After almost two years, on November 8, 1989, it quashed the U.S. effort to get him back on the grounds that he had committed no extraditable offence. Immediately he disappeared, only to have yet another charge thrown at him, this time an immigration one issued by Canada.

Fortune had again come the Mounties' way. Two days after his release by the Court of Appeal, he was picked up during a routine traffic check at Osoyoos, near the U.S. border. His large girth appears once more to have proved his downfall, when he was pulled over for not wearing his seatbelt. Back in Canadian hands, McVey in the spring of 1990 was facing yet another round of immigration hearings that would help determine whether he will be remembered as one of the most notorious of the contemporary technobandits.

The fight against Soviet high-tech espionage provides another example of how Canada's security and counter-intelligence efforts are shaped by its membership in the Western alliance. There is a story that when COCOM was established at the very height of

the Cold War some forty years ago, Washington considered for-
bidding the export of buttons, zippers, and belt buckles to the
Soviet bloc. The reason, a defence expert claimed, was that "if
Russian soldiers' pants are unbuckled and have their flies open,
they won't be able to fight." Apocryphal or not, the point of this
story is clear. COCOM was established to deny the Soviet Union the
ability to carry out aggressive military expansion.

With the Cold War over, the Berlin Wall being dismantled and
sold for souvenirs, and the Soviet Union facing possible disintegration, where does this leave COCOM and Canada's commitment to
denying the export of high-tech goods to the Soviet bloc? Do not
continued embargoes simply force the Soviet Union to spy and to
steal, thus reinforcing old patterns and stereotypes of Soviet behaviour that prevent Canada's security intelligence apparatus from
focusing on more important and newer threats?

The answer, once again, comes back to politics — as nearly all
espionage does in one way or another. The Reagan administration's
concentrated focus on the Soviet high-tech threat was politically driv-
en by the concept of "the evil empire." Tightened COCOM embargoes
in the 1980s then set in motion a dynamic that reinforced the stereo-
type of the Soviet threat as Moscow turned to espionage to acquire
what was forbidden. Even with the collapse of communism in Eastern
Europe and multiparty democracy edging into the Soviet Union, some
voices in Washington have continued to sing old tunes when it comes
to denying the Soviets high-tech goods. One of the most prominent
has been that of the so-called Zorro of COCOM, Stephen D. Bryen. Director of the Defense Technology Security Administration in the U.S.
Department of Defense, Bryen played a key role in the 1980s drive
against Soviet high-tech acquisition. Confronted with Gorbachev's
perestroika, Bryen was more convinced than ever, it seemed, that
the Soviet Union should be seen as an adversary and that U.S. national security required tighter technology security through continued
COCOM embargoes and other Western measures. "Our objective," he
is reported to have told the conservative Heritage Foundation on July
29, 1989, "is to impede the re-industrialization of the USSR, because
we know . . . their objective always remains only military."

Will cocom, will Canada, accept these views? The European members of cocom have long resisted more extreme pressures emanating from Washington, and there remain disagreements about the sale of sensitive technology to the Soviet bloc. Nonetheless, by the spring of 1990, the tide of history appeared to have washed ashore at cocom headquarters. Already, at the June 1989 NATO summit, U.S. President Bush had announced the removal of some U.S. restrictions on technology exports to the Soviet bloc and External Affairs minister Joe Clark had said that the meeting had underlined the need to extend Western experience and know-how to Eastern countries "in a manner which responds to and promotes positive change."

What this meant in practice involved intense negotiations at cocom, discussions that accelerated considerably after the Berlin Wall had opened and the communist house of cards collapsed so dramatically throughout Eastern Europe. The prospect of a new market in the East of nearly 400 million people placed renewed pressure on Washington, traditionally the hardliner, to drop its insistence on curbs of exports of computers and telecommunications equipment to the countries of the former Soviet bloc.

Speaking to a *New York Times* reporter in December 1989, U.S. Commerce secretary Robert Mosbacher confessed that in the face of the East European revolution, "We're going to have to sit down and look at the whole picture. I'm not sure that any of us until recently thought about the possibilities that have opened up." This time, crucially, the Commerce Department found support from Bush's powerful secretary of state James Baker. Baker gave the go-ahead for the milestone visit in December to NATO headquarters by Soviet foreign minister Eduard Shevardnadze, and simultaneously was pushing for change in cocom. "We still want to protect strategic technology," he confessed, "but we should rationalize the system to the extent that things that are to some extent available off the shelf should not be locked up."

This was far, of course, from saying that cocom controls should be abolished, and as cocom prepared for a crucial meeting in Paris in February 1990 some observers thought it might confront one of the most serious crises it had faced in its forty-year history. On the one hand stood the United States, with a three-point strategy that emphasized (1) placing higher "fences" around a core of fewer but really significant technologies in the military and nuclear fields; (2) giving preferential treatment to countries such as Poland, Czechoslovakia, and Hungary in order to assist reform in Eastern Europe; and (3) lifting controls on "off the shelf" items available in the West. Against this stood several European countries, who sensed in Washington a continued adversarial attitude that lay rooted in the Cold War — and possibly also a desire to maintain COCOM embargoes in an effort to protect some U.S. industries from competition. Canada joined them in pushing for rules that would also differentiate between the various countries of Eastern Europe according to the pace of reform. The United States, on the other hand, still insisted that all Warsaw Pact countries should be treated equally.

By spring 1990 some form of compromise had been patched up, and ad hoc liberalization was under way; it was expected that by the end of the year restrictions on the export of personal computers operating on 80386 microprocessors would be lifted, and at the February Paris meeting it had been agreed to lift embargoes on certain telecommunications equipment and machine tools. Major changes in the rules governing the export of aircraft and aerospace components were also edging on to the agenda.

Still, it was clear that changes in COCOM would lag behind reform in Eastern Europe. "Once you have opened the door to technological exports," said David Ryan, the director of DEA's Export Controls Division, "the horse has left the barn." The process cannot be undone, in other words, if reform comes to a halt in Eastern Europe.

This means that high-tech spying is likely to persist. COCOM embargoes still remain on a core of Western technology products, and even traditional items recently taken off the lists require amounts of hard currency that the Soviet Union — and others — may find difficult to raise. Illicit means will continue to remain an option. Indeed, CIA chief William Webster told a Baltimore audience in February 1990 that American counter-intelligence experts had concluded that the KGB had stepped up its work, "particularly in the United States, where recruiting of people with technical knowledge or access to technical knowledge has increased." The explanation, Webster said, lay with the Soviet Union's continuing economic problems and the fear that it might lag even further behind the West. As history has shown, Canada provides a back door to U.S. technology, and if Webster is right then we will continue to be a target for the KGB and GRU high-tech espionage drive. Other countries, too, will seek to evade high-tech export controls. China is subject to certain COCOM embargoes, and certain Middle East countries are anxious to develop high-tech capabilities.

Still, there is little doubt that some of the incentives to resort to espionage for Canada's high-tech secrets have been removed by the extraordinary events of 1989. It remains to be seen whether those that remain will be as important in the 1990s as they have been in the recent past.

11.
THE TERRORIST THREAT

For many Canadians, terrorism in Canada truly began with the kidnappings of James Cross, the British trade attaché in Montreal, and Pierre Laporte, Quebec's Labour minister, in October 1970. The Trudeau government's imposition of the Draconian provisions of the War Measures Act and Laporte's garroting at the hands of the Front de Liberation du Québec brought home the nature of the threat.

But terrorism in "the peaceable kingdom" did not begin with the October Crisis. The Fenian-inspired assassination of D'Arcy McGee, a major proponent of Confederation and an MP, in April 1868 was an early demonstration that Canada could not be immune from the effects of foreign entanglements. On the domestic front, British Columbia's Sons of Freedom Doukhobors after 1923 had used terror to battle Canadian governments and their efforts to compel sect members to send their children to school; as late as 1961 and 1962 they had claimed responsibility for seventy-three separate incidents of bombing and arson. The Sons of Freedom had attracted widespread attention, not least because its women members stripped and paraded nude at acts of arson perpetrated by the group. (This habit led to one of the rare flashes of wit by long-time prime minister Mackenzie King. When he was asked in Parliament by an Opposition MP what he would do if he was confronted by a nude Doukhobor woman, the prime minister quick as a flash shot back that he "would send for the Leader of the Opposition," R.B. Bennett, who was, like himself, a bachelor. This was the true spirit of bipartisanship at work.)

By the end of the 1960s, however, international terrorism had stopped being funny. Forced out of their homeland by the creation of the State of Israel in 1948 and a succession of Arab–Israeli wars, Palestinians all across the Middle East launched guerrilla attacks on Israeli military and civilian targets. When the effectiveness of Israeli defences began to impose unacceptable losses on the Palestinian groups, other, softer targets were picked — airliners, cruise ships, individuals from countries friendly to Israel and especially the United States. Aid for the terrorist organizations was easy to come by. The Soviet Union provided training and weapons, and Colonel Qaddafi's Libya was always ready to stir up trouble. Iraq, Syria, and later Iran regularly provided arms and money.

This soon began to worry Canadians. As late as 1969, the Mackenzie Commission had not even mentioned terrorism as a threat to the security of Canada and Canadians. But by the beginning of the next decade Canadians travelling in the Middle East were in jeopardy, and there was danger that the violence there might spread to Arab and Jewish groups here. There were other organized groups, including Armenians seeking revenge on Turkey for the slaughter of their people almost three-quarters of a century ago, and Sikhs trying to create a separate state of their own in India, who were using Canada as a base for their operations.

Canadian security officials particularly feared that the Montreal Olympics of 1976 might become a focus for terrorist activity, as had the Munich Olympics four years earlier. To counter the threat, the RCMP developed what it called COILS — the Computerized Olympic Integrated Lookout System — which was, in effect, a terrorist alert system. At the same time, the Mounties' Security Service was extending its efforts to identify terrorist activities within the Arab, Japanese, Latin American, and European communities in Canada. The Japanese Red Army, the author of brutal attacks against Israeli targets, was especially feared, and the RCMP found two members, Yoshimasa Gyoja and Toshi Omura, in Canada on false passports; they were expelled. The Popular Front for the Liberation of Palestine, the terrorist group that had slaughtered Israeli Olympic athletes in 1972 in Munich, was also dangerous, and the Security Service monitored PLO activities in Canada in an effort to determine if any organized "terrorist infrastructure" existed here. The Olympic

Games also provided the opportunity for the Security Service to crack down on Toronto's Western Guard, a neo-Fascist group, and the militant Jewish Defence League. The complete absence of any disruptions of the Montreal Olympics suggested that the RCMP's measures were effective.

By 1986, after terrorist atrocities of various kinds had been planned and committed on Canadian soil, the Senate took the extraordinary step of creating a special committee to take evidence on "matters relating to terrorism as a real or potential threat to Canada and to Canadians." The committee's report, published in 1987, made a variety of recommendations.

- Closer co-operation between CSIS, the RCMP, and local police forces was essential.
- The lines of communication to the Cabinet had to be simplified.
- Investigations of potential immigrants to Canada had to be thorough enough to screen out potential or past terrorists.
- The media, whose activities sometimes seemed almost to encourage terrorist activities, should consider adopting guidelines to govern the conduct of journalists during terrorist or hostage-taking incidents.

Canada had always been immune from the horrors perpetrated abroad, or so Canadians had liked to believe. Terrorism in the late twentieth century, however, had guaranteed that there were no safe havens.

Here we cannot discuss the acts of Canadians dissatisfied with their governments' policies; such domestic terrorism in any case has markedly declined in recent years. The Senate Special Committee on Terrorism and the Public Safety declared that the "major threat" to Canada comes from abroad, and a Department of National Defence study prepared by Anthony Kellett for the Operational Research and Analysis Establishment similarly noted that the major danger comes from "émigré attackers striking at diplomatic targets." In keeping with those assessments, our focus is limited to the ways in which international terrorism impinges on Canada.

Three major movements merit consideration: the struggle by Sikhs for a separate state on the Indian subcontinent; the Palestinian fight for a homeland to be carved from Israel; and Armenian efforts to secure revenge for Turkey's genocidal attacks on their people in the post-Great War period.

That Canada provides no fireproof house in the contemporary world of international terrorism became hideously apparent on June 23, 1985.

The "Emperor Kanishka," an Air India Boeing 747 aircraft, had taken off slightly behind schedule the previous evening from Montreal's Mirabel airport bound for New Delhi and Bombay, via London. Aboard were 329 passengers and crew, the majority from Toronto where the flight had originated. Most were Canadians, and almost a third were children accompanying their parents to visit relations in India now that the North American school year was over. Flight 182 followed a normal transatlantic flight path, and at 8:06 local time the next morning, a Sunday, the crew made contact with the Shannon Air Traffic Control Centre in Ireland, the first European landfall. All was normal. Breakfast had been served, and passengers were beginning to stretch their legs and move around the cabin. Heathrow airport was no more than about an hour ahead.

Only eight minutes later, and just 110 miles off the southwest coast of Ireland, the plane, without warning, disappeared from the radar screens. Even before the Shannon traffic controllers realized that anything was wrong, the Boeing 747 had plunged to the sea from a height of nearly six miles, hitting the water at something approaching nine hundred miles an hour. There were no survivors. Of the 131 bodies recovered, none had had time to put on a life-jacket, and many were grotesquely dislocated by severe decompression. The end of Flight 182 had taken a mere forty-five seconds.

Suspicions of a terrorist bomb began as soon as the bodies began to arrive at Cork Regional Hospital and were placed under the custody of the Irish Garda. The black box, or flight recorder, recovered seventeen days later from the seabed, confirmed that nothing had been wrong with the aircraft or its crew before the plane abruptly disappeared from view. This, combined with other evidence salvaged from the wreckage, led an official Indian government enquiry to conclude that the "Emperor Kanishka" had been destroyed by an explosive device. Although not proven beyond doubt, and with no one yet indicted or convicted for the attack, this conclusion seems inescapable, thus making the killing of more than 300 Canadians the bloodiest terrorist act of the 1980s. It was also, as described by the chairman of the Security Intelligence Review Committee, Ron Atkey, "the most heinous act of violence in Canadian history." Certainly it was the moment at which international terrorism really hit home to Canadians. "We will not allow this country," declared Deputy Prime Minister Erik Nielsen shortly afterwards, "to become a killing ground for international terrorism." Since then the fight against terrorism has been the top priority of the government and the security service.

The downing of Flight 182 took place a year to the month after "Operation Bluestar," the storming by Indian troops of the Golden Temple at Amritsar. This marked the climax of the bitter conflict between the Indian government and militant Sikhs fighting for an independent state of Khalistan. Only four months after that, Prime Minister Indira Gandhi was assassinated at her official residence in New Delhi by two of her Sikh bodyguards. There followed a massacre of thousands of Sikhs by enraged Hindus in the Indian capital.

Following Operation Bluestar, threats were made against Air India flights around the world. Suspicions of a connection between the destruction of Flight 182 and the Khalistani movement in Canada were strengthened by an almost simultaneous bomb explosion at Tokyo's Narita airport. Exactly fifty-five minutes before the destruction of Air India's Flight 182, a bomb exploded in a suitcase being transferred at Narita from a Canadian Pacific flight that had arrived from Vancouver, B.C., to an Air India flight from Tokyo to Bangkok, instantly killing two Japanese baggage handlers. Investigations revealed that the suitcase had been checked in at Vancouver by a passenger calling himself Mr. M. Singh. A Mr. L. Singh at the same check-in counter had simultaneously checked in a suitcase on a Canadian Pacific flight to

Toronto for onward transmission to New Delhi. The flight to which it was transferred was Air India Flight 182. The explosion at Narita, moreover, was revealed by forensic security to have been caused by a bomb concealed within a radio cassette player — which had been purchased in British Columbia by a Khalistani activist.

This and other evidence launched the biggest and most expensive criminal investigation in Canadian history. In 1990 it is still under way and has cost some $80 million. Four years after the "Emperor Kanishka" plunged to the ocean floor, wreckage salvaged from 2,000 metres of water was still being shipped to Vancouver for investigation. The Sikh responsible for purchasing the cassette player, who moved to England following the disaster, has been deported to Canada to face charges in connection with the Narita explosion and for questioning about the Air India disaster. Others are still being sought for questioning by the RCMP. Critics have complained that the investigation was botched, and there have been calls for a royal commission of enquiry. Most controversial of all was the claim, made by two Toronto journalists in a 1989 book, *Soft Target*, that agents of the Indian government were responsible for the disaster. Certainly, there was plenty of evidence to suggest that the Indian intelligence service had been active in Canada, stirring up trouble in the Sikh community. Some were expelled from Canada as a result of CSIS investigations. That they had knowingly allowed the destruction of Flight 182, however, seemed highly implausible, and the evidence was unconvincing. Still, in October 1989 the Sikh community formally asked the Canadian government for an enquiry into the allegations.

Even prior to the events of June 23, 1985, Khalistani militancy had left its mark in Canada. Sikhs are no newcomers to Canada. They began arriving from the Punjab before the First World War, mostly to become labourers in British Columbia. Ironically, some were also militants supporting the Indian nationalist cause against the British Empire. As we have seen, British imperial and local Canadian authorities kept a close eye on them, often co-operating with the Americans. The creation of a Punjabi state within independent India satisfied most Sikhs, but by the late 1970s a Khalistani separatist movement had become active, and political violence had broken out in the Punjab. A new wave of immigrants to Canada increased the size of the Sikh community to 250,000 (some 100,000 in Vancouver alone) and brought the new credo with it — along with a small minority prepared to use violence. Much of this was caused by disagreements and rivalries within the Sikh community itself. Intra-Sikh disputes over the Khalistani cause led to a courtroom murder in Toronto in 1982 and a violent demonstration later that same year when three people were shot. Violence continued after the Air India attack, and several Khalistanis were convicted for various offences, some involving conspiracy in Canada for acts committed or planned elsewhere. But it was Flight 182 that dominated people's minds when the issue of terrorism and how to fight it was discussed in government and public circles.

The destruction of Flight 182 affected the fate of more than its 329 passengers and crew. The affair had a major impact on Canada's security-service and law-enforcement agencies, claiming another set of victims as well as calling into question Canadians' tolerance for new immigrants and long-standing visible minorities. The tragedy came when CSIS was less than a year old and passing through the most difficult phase of transition in its divorce from the RCMP. Pressure to identify sources of Khalistani terrorism became intense. Eventually, the urgent need to uncover intelligence about Sikh activity exposed weaknesses in the service that led to the departure of many of its veterans and precipitated a major enquiry into its management. Most dramatic of all, it forced the resignation of its first director, Ted Finn, in September 1987.

Within days of the attack CSIS agents began preparing affidavits in British Columbia to carry out wiretaps on suspected members of the extensive Sikh community. Making a case of urgently imperilled national security, the service was granted, on July 26, 1985, extensive wiretap facilities or a "basket clause," by a judge of the Federal Court. One of the targets of surveillance was a Surrey, B.C., construction contractor, Harjit Singh Atwal. As one expert later noted, "basically, everywhere he went in Vancouver you could bug." Several months later, on May 25, 1986, a Punjabi government minister privately visiting Vancouver Island to attend a wedding was attacked by gunmen at Gold River and seriously wounded. Atwal was one of several men, all Sikhs, arrested and charged with conspiracy to murder. Much of the evidence used in the case was provided from the CSIS wiretaps. The defence forced an intensive justification of the wiretaps, and in August 1987 it was finally revealed that information contained in the affidavits required to obtain the warrants was faulty. Working under intense pressure, local CSIS officers had relied on information about Atwal from an informant who had already been declared unreliable by the service. This invalidated the warrants and led to the conspiracy charge being stayed. Two weeks later, on September 11, amid intense publicity about bungling in CSIS, Finn resigned, effectively fired by a government that had become embarrassed by a succession of CSIS controversies. Most of these, such as allegations or revelations that CSIS had infiltrated trade unions or investigated left-wing magazines, stirred up unwelcome ghosts from the scandal-ridden RCMP days of the old Security Service. "The service needs this like a hole in the head," said Archie Barr, a security-service veteran who, as head of the CSIS counter-terrorism division, had signed the affidavit prepared by officers in British Columbia, and who retired from the service at about the time he learned of the affidavit's error.

Barr was understating the case. The Atwal warrant affair and Finn's resignation led to a crisis that sent CSIS morale plunging and threatened the future of the service. For the Air India disaster and Khalistani violence were not the only affairs that CSIS seemed to have bungled.

Another controversial case involving terrorism that spanned Finn's directorship and troubled his successor, Reid Morden, was that of the Palestinian, "Triple M." Here, too, CSIS came under fire.

The aircraft from Spain landed at Toronto's Pearson airport in the afternoon of February 25, 1987. The passengers, tired from their flight, made the usual long trek through the dreary concrete-block corridors of Terminal 1, then queued up at the Immigration desks to show their Canadian birth certificates or foreign passports. Mahmoud Mohammad Issa Mohammad, accompanied by his wife and three children, was one of those passengers, and he carried papers, issued at the Canadian embassy in Madrid, certifying him and his family as landed immigrants. But CSIS had been tipped off by still-unnamed foreign intelligence services about Mohammad, and the Immigration officers at Pearson had been warned to watch out for him. Unfortunately, the airliner had arrived just as shifts changed, and one of the new desk officers looked at the papers that Mohammad pushed under his nose and mistakenly punched up the wrong list of Mohammads, a common-enough name, on his computer screen. The warnings had gone for naught, and the Immigration officer stamped the visa and welcomed the Mohammads to Canada. Triple M, as he was soon to become known to the Canadian press and public, was now a landed immigrant, entitled to all the rights and protections afforded by the law.

A pudgy man with soft brown eyes, Mohammad scarcely looks like the popular conception of a terrorist. This is no hot-eyed firebrand. Instead, he is a Palestinian Arab, one of those ten of thousands displaced from their homes and lives by the creation of the State of Israel in 1948 and the subsequent wars that have tormented the Middle East for more than forty years. Born in a small Arab village near the Lebanese border in 1943, he and his parents had fled into Lebanon in 1948, eventually ending up in a squalid refugee camp in Tyre. Mohammad was a bright student who studied history in Cairo and eventually taught school in Beirut. But teaching was secondary to his involvement with Palestinian resistance movements, notably the Popular Front for the Liberation of Palestine (PFLP). And, after the 1967 Arab–Israeli War with its decisive victory for Israel, Mohammad, like thousands of others in similar circumstances, turned to terrorism.

After commando training in Syria and the Soviet Union, he and a PFLP comrade flew on December 26, 1968, from Beruit to Athens, an airport renowned then and since for having the weakest security systems in the Western world. Armed with a tourist visa and the sub-machine guns and hand grenades that they had apparently carried in their luggage, Mohammad and his friend ran onto the tarmac and threw their grenades at a loaded Boeing 707 jet from Israel's El Al airline. They then raked the windows of the aircraft with machine-gun fire, sending the passengers and crew fleeing in terror. One passenger, an Israeli, died in the attack, and the two Palestinians were captured by the Greek police. "We wanted to destroy an Israeli plane," they said, "and kill Jews." The Greek courts duly sentenced Mohammad to seventeen years' imprisonment. Only three months later, however, he was freed from jail and deported to Lebanon when PFLP terrorists boarded a Greek airliner and held its passengers hostage until Mohammad and several other convicted terrorists were released.

For the next ten years, Mohammad was deeply involved in the activities of the Popular Front for the Liberation of Palestine. According to a ghost-written book, *Je suis un fedayin*, published by Editions Stock in Paris in February 1976 and subsequently acknowledged by Mohammad to be a dramatized story of his life, he then led the PFLP operation that forced three airliners to land with their passengers in Jordan in 1970 and ended in the destruction of all of the planes. Mohammad then singled out the Israeli and American passengers from those airliners and held them hostage at secret bases in Jordan while negotiations for their freedom in exchange for imprisoned Palestinians in Israel were conducted. In 1973, back in Beirut, Mohammad played an active role in the Palestinian struggle against the Falangist Christians. Then, according to the book, which ends its story in 1975, Mohammad went into business and married, but he kept up his PFLP membership and continued to travel under a false Iraqi passport.

The remaining years before Triple M came to Canada are less than clear. According to Interpol information made public by the Israeli Airline Pilots Association (information that could only have found its way to them via Israeli police or security channels), Mohammad quit the PFLP to join the Palestine Liberation Organization's Abou el-Hol group in Lebanon in 1982, at precisely the same time that he began to seek entry to Canada as an immigrant. When Israel invaded Lebanon in 1982, Mohammad and his family fled to Cyprus where they lived for two years and to which he was subsequently forbidden re-entry. In April 1984, as a result, he moved with his family to Spain, from where, the Israeli Pilots Association claimed, he had participated in an abortive attack against Jewish groups in Morocco in August 1986. Whether Mohammad in fact had taken part in that raid, however, is uncertain at best. Michel Vastel of Montreal's *Le Devoir*, the journalist who covered this story most extensively, argued that the Interpol documents in fact referred to another terrorist's role in the Moroccan affair.

Whether Mohammad was involved in that action or not, his record was already bloody enough. The Canadian Air Line Pilots Association, naturally concerned to see those who had attacked airliners in the past kept out of Canada, urged Mohammad's deportation: "to us, he is a murderer."

No one, except Mohammad and his lawyers, seemed prepared to argue against that charge. Mohammad himself had been routinely interviewed by Canadian officials in Spain and had denied membership in any terrorist or subversive organizations as well as any convictions. The CSIS officer at the embassy duly spoke with the Spanish police and probably tried to contact such Lebanese security forces as remained after that country's internal struggles and foreign invasions and occupations. Mohammad's evasions, however, withstood the cursory screening of his application in Madrid. And his later claim that he had told the truth about prior convictions because he believed that he had been pardoned when Greece exchanged him for imprisoned Palestinians is, to say the least, a straight-out lie.

Once he had landed in Toronto in February 1987, officials from CSIS, who were later absolved by SIRC from responsibility for Mohammad's entry into the country, began scrambling to repair the damage. The day after his admission, agents interviewed Mohammad, only to be met yet again with denials that he had ever been a terrorist. But fingerprints, sent to Interpol in Paris, eventually demonstrated the falsity of that claim too.

The Triple M story thus far was one of bungling and lies. "We have learned how easy it is for a convicted terrorist to get into Canada," NDP MP Iain Angus said, "even when CSIS and Immigration know which flight he's arriving on." CSIS, though free of blame, looked foolish:

its security screening of Mohammad in Spain was demonstrably slip-shod. Moreover, there were suspicions that Mohammad had been allowed to come to Canada so that CSIS could get its hands on a real terrorist who might have information that could be "traded" to other intelligence agencies. The Immigration department, already suffering from widespread public contempt, looked incompetent. And the fact that the government had to wait until May to receive Interpol's report on Mohammad's fingerprints, then until June to convene a senior officials' meeting to discuss the case, until July to tell the minister of Employment and Immigration, until October to begin deportation proceedings, and then until December 9, 1987, to inform Mohammad of the proceedings against him, suggested lethargy at every level of the bureaucracy and the political executive.

There was more to come. On February 22, 1988, just after the deportation hearing against Mohammad had opened, the RCMP spirited the Palestinian out of Canada. A deal had been reached between the Mounties and Mohammad's lawyers to let the terrorist go, apparently to Algeria first and subsequently to Tunis where the PLO has its headquarters. In Parliament, the minister of Employment and Immigration, Benoît Bouchard, told MPs that Mohammad's lawyers had "approached departmental officials last week and said that their client wished to leave the country on his own accord, and . . . he is entitled to do so." But the arrangements had fallen apart, the minister said, and Triple M was on his way back to Canada: as a landed immigrant, Bouchard went on, "he has every right to return to Canada."

There are widely differing explanations for this extraordinary event. One suggestion, widely publicized in the media, was that news of Triple M's departure from Canada had apparently been leaked to the press by a Canadian Jewish businessman who had been told by a ground hostess that Mohammad was at the airport. Another explanation, quietly whispered by CSIS agents, was that telephone calls between Mohammad's entourage in Canada and Algiers were intercepted by an unnamed intelligence agency that did not want to see Mohammad leave Canada. The story, in this explanation, was deliberately leaked to block his departure, and the tale of the Jewish businessman was deliberately created as a plausible cover story.

In any case, when Mohammad's Air Canada flight had landed in London, he was met by a panoply of TV cameras and pressmen. Then Air Algérie refused to allow him to board its aircraft to Algiers on the ostensible grounds that he lacked a visa. Given the secret arrangements made by the lawyers and the RCMP, this explanation seemed almost inconceivable. In fact, the publicity obviously had forced the Algerians to back off from the plan to issue Triple M a visa in Algiers, the airline's officials in London deciding that they did not want their country to acquire the reputation of being a terrorist haven.

Then new wrinkles were added. Very quickly, reports appeared that CSIS had deliberately aborted the arrangements made by the RCMP to spirit Mohammad away, presumably as yet another shot in its ongoing turf war with the Mounties. Certainly this was the view of Rashad Saleh, the director of Toronto's Arab Community Centre and one of Triple M's entourage. Saleh said that Mohammad had been interviewed in January "in a hotel somewhere in southwestern Ontario" by CSIS agents who "told him explicitly" they were gathering information for the CIA and Mossad, the Israeli security agency. As CSIS co-operates with the CIA and Mossad in countering terrorism, that was probably true, if indiscreet. "The information they tried to squeeze out of him, they made it very clear it was for Mossad and the CIA." Saleh also added that CSIS agents — at least two — had been on the scene in both Toronto and London airports, and their presence had caused Mohammad to believe that he was being set up to be killed by Israeli agents in league with CSIS. That concern, while perhaps understandable, was unlikely to be valid, if only because CSIS would have feared a media backlash in Canada if Mohammad had been killed.

For their part, CSIS and the then-responsible minister, Solicitor General James Kelleher, denied the charges that the organization had leaked the story to the media; press reports even suggested that CSIS officials were looking for an Israeli agent who might have done so. And Ron Atkey, chair of the Security Intelligence Review Committee, told the House of Commons Justice Committee that CSIS had never been advised of the plan to get Mohammad out of the country. "I would have thought, in an operation of this delicacy," Atkey said with evident surprise, "that CSIS would have been consulted. . . . They were not."

With a reluctant and unhappy Mohammad back in Canada, the deportation hearings now got under way in earnest; they were destined to last eleven months more. In December 1988, finally, the decision was handed down: Mohammad should be deported because of his attack on the El Al aircraft and because of his lies to get into Canada. But, as the Immigration adjudicator noted, he could not order that deportation be carried out: Triple M had made a refugee claim, and under Canadian law that had to be heard first. Mohammad's lawyers added that appeals could conceivably stretch out the process for a further eight years.

Whatever the denouement of this messy tale, several things stand out starkly. Mohammad was a terrorist whose actions made him precisely the kind of immigrant Canada and Canadians did and do not want. The immigration system has to be impermeable enough to bar those who resort to terrorism from entry into Canada. If those defences fail, then the appeal process has to be tough enough to result in an order for the deportation of terrorists. As it is now, hearings, appeals, and counter-appeals go on endlessly and bring Canadian law into public and international disrepute.

That having been said, however, it is also clear that terrorism arouses strong emotions that can lead to major abuses of civil liberties and injustice. Governments come under intense public pressure to deal firmly with real or suspected terrorists. In turn, they put the squeeze on their security services to deliver hard intelligence and real or imagined villains. In the process, due process of law can be easily violated. The public often does not care — or even approves. Such a case was dramatically revealed in Britain in October 1989. Four Irish "terrorists" ("the Guildford Four"), convicted fifteen years earlier to life imprisonment for murder, were found to be innocent, the victims of a police frame-up, a legal system weighted against the defence, and a public indifferent or actively hostile.

The Atwal affair, where CSIS short-cuts taken under intense political pressure produced a fiasco in the courts, illustrated the problem in Canada. Another case that touched civil liberties surfaced in 1989.

This one arose from terrorism within yet another immigrant community, that of the Armenians.

Shortly before 7:00 a.m. on March 12, 1985, a U-Haul truck, rented the day before in the Montreal suburb of Laval, arrived at the gate of the Turkish embassy in Ottawa. It backed quietly up to the entrance, and three heavily armed men jumped out. The lone Canadian Pinkerton guard on duty was immediately shot and killed as he tried to stop them. They then blasted their way through the front door with explosives. The ambassador, awakened in his second-floor bedroom by the noise, escaped by jumping out the window, but he broke his pelvis and two limbs in the process and thereafter lay helpless on the ground while shooting went on around him. Inside, after rounding up several hostages, the gunmen contacted the media by telephone. "We are the Armenian Revolutionary Army," one of them announced to the Canadian Press within five minutes of the attack. "We want our land back and we want the Turkish government to recognize the Armenian genocide of 1915. We have hostages, we have demands, and we plan to stay."

Quickly the embassy was surrounded by armed RCMP officers. Despite the early bravado, the siege lasted for only four hours. Before noon, the hostages had been released, and the three terrorists emerged from the embassy to surrender to the police. Despite the quick end to the crisis, voices were quickly raised attacking the lack of effective security in Ottawa and demanding the creation of a special anti-terrorist unit. "Canada dithers as terror burns," editorialized the *Ottawa Citizen*. Solicitor General Elmer MacKay, summoned to a special Cabinet meeting later that day along with the commissioner of the RCMP, Robert Simmons, emerged to tell the press that terrorism was an international phenomenon. "It appears that in this country now," he said, "we are less of a sanctuary than we used to be."

This had been obvious for some time. Foreign conflicts had already been imported violently into Canada, and the Armenian issue in particular had made its terrorist mark several times within the previous three years. This reflected the emergence in the early 1970s of a radical wing within the worldwide Armenian diaspora that sought violent redress of their grievances against the Turks over the genocide of 1915. Emerging from Syria and Beirut in particular, where contacts with the PLO were close, a new generation of younger Armenians adopted revolutionary methods to achieve their ends. Turkish diplomats became targets of attack, and by the early 1980s extremist Armenians were committing terrorist attacks throughout the West, aimed against Turks and symbols of Turkish authority. In Canada, where there was an Armenian population of some 50,000, the arrival of refugees from war-torn Beirut injected an unaccustomed militancy into the community. Soon, it made its effects dramatically felt.

The first incident took place in January 1982, when a bomb exploded near the Turkish consulate in Toronto. No one was hurt but it meant that Canada had now joined Europe and the Middle East as a venue for Armenian terrorism. The previous year there had been several bombings and an assassination in Los Angeles, and early in April the FBI sent a warning to Ottawa that the Turkish embassy was threatened. Until then, the embassy had been the target of Armenian demonstrations, but all had been peaceful. The FBI warning proved too late for one of its staff. On April 8, 1982, Kani Gungor, the commercial counsellor, was shot and badly injured in the garage of his Ottawa apartment as he got into his car to drive to work. The attack left him a paraplegic. Only four months later his embassy colleague, the military attaché, Colonel Atilla Altikat, was ambushed and killed while his car was stopped at a red light during the Ottawa morning rush hour. He was shot ten times at close range by a gunman who was never captured, despite a massive road block immediately thrown round the capital.

Both these brutal attacks shocked Canadians, and the government offered an unprecedented $100,000 reward for information about them — the first ever for an act of terrorism. Responsibility for each was openly proclaimed by groups seeking vengeance and redress for the 1915 massacre. Calls from Beirut and Athens said the attack on Gungor had been carried out by the Armenian Secret Army for the Liberation of Armenia (ASALA), a Marxist group that had claimed several terrorist attacks over the previous few years. The Beirut office of Agence France Press received a call saying that the military attaché had been shot by the Justice Commandos of the Armenian Genocide.

The 1985 embassy hostage incident marked the climax of militant Armenian action in Canada. Threats shortly afterwards that a bomb would be detonated in the Toronto and Montreal subways caused headlines and public anxiety, but nothing happened. Armenian-related violence subsided almost as abruptly as it had begun. But the after-effect lingered on. Like the Air India attack that came only four months after the Turkish embassy hostage-taking, violence in some of Canada's immigrant communities placed heavy pressure both on CSIS and on the legal process. Neither came out unscathed. Seven years after the attack in Ottawa on Gungor, controversy surrounded the attempt to deport a member of the Armenian community as a threat to the security of Canada. The case threw into sharp relief the problem of finding clear-cut intelligence in the shadowy world of terrorism and establishing the right balance between civil liberties and national security.

Following the Gungor attack, three Toronto men, all of Armenian origin (two of whom were Canadian citizens), were convicted of conspiracy to murder (the actual killer has never been found). Shortly after their trial in June 1986 a fourth man, Nicholas Moumdjian, a landed immigrant, was ordered provisionally deported, subject to an investigation by the Security Intelligence Review Committee. He was, declared the federal government, one of those persons described in the Immigration Act "who there are reasonable grounds to believe will engage in acts of violence that would or might endanger the lives or safety of persons in Canada or are members of or are likely to participate in the unlawful activities of an organization that is likely to engage in such acts of violence."

Moumdjian had not been involved in the Gungor shooting. But he had been closely involved with the convicted conspirators in other activities within the Toronto Armenian community, and had helped raise money for their defence. An immigrant to Canada in 1979, he had grown up in Beirut. As a teenager during the civil war he had worked for the Armenian self-defence militia and had been caught up in the tribal feuds that plagued the Christian forces in the city. All this, along with his sympathy for the ASALA cause, was used in evidence when he appeared before a SIRC tribunal in 1987. The result was to confirm the CSIS view that he was a security threat. "I believe," wrote Saul Cherniak, the SIRC member who heard the case (and a former member of Ed Drake's wartime Discrimination Unit), "that Mr. Moumdjian was involved in acts of violence in the past. However, he has made no such admission, nor has he shown any indication of regret or any sign of a change of heart. . . . I have reasonable grounds to believe that Mr. Moumdjian will engage in activity that constitutes a threat to the security of Canada."

There is no evidence to show that Moumdjian had been involved in criminal activity in Canada. The judgment about his likely future involvement as a security threat rested essentially on an assessment of his character in the present and an extrapolation from the past. This in turn was based heavily on assessments and evidence produced by CSIS. For some critics, it confirmed their view that the security service was incapable of finding real terrorists hidden in Canada's ethnic communities and therefore inevitably resorted to picking on scapegoats. Others questioned the assumption that past activity — especially in a city like Beirut — was a reliable indicator of likely behaviour in Toronto. Yet others, when news about the Moumdjian appeal became public in 1989, thought that Canada was being too soft on an obvious undesirable — despite the SIRC verdict. As of early 1990 the matter still rested with the federal government and Moumdjian was still living in Toronto. How many others like him are in Canada it is impossible to say, but what is clear is that good intelligence about terrorists and terrorism will continue to be important into the twenty-first century.

Only a cockeyed optimist would believe that Canada will be immune from terrorism in the future; on the basis of our past record, only a wishful thinker could believe that our defences are strong enough to meet the threat. Anthony Kellett, whose paper on terrorism written for the Department of National Defence has already been referred to, is no wishful thinker. Nonetheless, his thorough study makes the point that the émigré attacks of the early 1980s have diminished and, he adds, Canada is one of the least threatened of Western nations. Still, the threat is there and must be countered.

Some weapons are already in place. A few examples:

• the federal government has made public what Fred Gibson, a former deputy solicitor general, called a "no concessions" policy. The fundamental demands of terrorists will never be met, period;
• the Solicitor General's department in Ottawa has been preparing contingency plans against aircraft hijackings, kidnappings, and hostage incidents since 1973;
• in 1975, a Special Threat Assessment Group of scientific and technical experts was formed to advise the government on the threat posed by terrorists using nuclear, chemical, and biological agents;
• in 1984, the RCMP created a National Security Enforcement Unit to exchange and co-ordinate information on terrorists with CSIS;
• CSIS itself from 1985 onwards has had the countering of terrorism as its top priority;
• in January 1986, the RCMP established a Special Emergency Response Team (SERT) "to act as a dedicated hostage rescue force and crisis intervention team that could resolve situations beyond the normal capabilities of the RCMP and other police forces."

How effective all these measures would be in a crisis still remained to be demonstrated.

Certainly, there was no evident enthusiasm for the SERT role. In 1985, likely as a response to the Armenian attack on the Turkish embassy, the Mulroney Cabinet directed the Security Service and the armed forces to prepare proposals for the organization, location, and operation of an anti-terrorist emergency response team. The RCMP's proposal, to the Security Service's obvious alarm, was selected. The armed forces have agreed to carry SERT's fifty men to any point in Canada in the event of a crisis.

What would happen, however, if terrorists took Canadians hostage outside Canada is more difficult to foresee. The Senate's Special Committee on Terrorism and the Public Safety zeroed in on this problem in its 1987 report. The RCMP Act limits the Mounties' police powers to Canadian soil, and in foreign countries SERT would have no special status and no police powers. The senators urged the government to give SERT the ability to respond to extra-territorial crises; whether the government has accepted this recommendation remains unknown. The committee also recommended that the government hand the emergency-response function to the military. Its reasoning was based on the "plethora of SERT teams" already to be found in many locations and on SERT's perceived inability to respond to two or more coincidental terrorist incidents. Unless an incident was protracted, the senators noted, "A SERTeam located in Ottawa would often be unable to arrive in time to have an impact." The government to date has not acted on the committee's recommendation.

Meanwhile, SERT continues to prepare. Based at Dwyer Hill, just east of Ottawa, team members go through constant physical and mental drills. Members, always experienced RCMP officers with ten or more years' service, stay with SERT for three years. The SERT "Leader" — his name is not released — told the press that "in other parts of the world there are centres just like this where men are training — maybe just as hard as we are — to do the things we've got to stop them doing." SERT was nearby during the 1988 Calgary Winter Olympics, the Economic Summit in Toronto the same year, and the meeting of foreign ministers in Ottawa in February 1990; happily no incidents requiring its intervention occurred.

No one can foresee how well SERT would do in a hostage crisis; certainly the team will have a higher chance of success than would ordinary policemen or servicemen. But a counter-terrorism force is likely to be only as effective as its intelligence permits it to be. That means that the turf fights between the RCMP and CSIS have to end, and happily there are at last some signs that peace has been declared between the two agencies. That at least holds out the prospect of good intelligence about any new terrorist threats and a measured response should attacks occur.

What now ought to be considered in Ottawa is whether or not the preparations to meet the terrorist threat have been overblown. Incidents have declined in Canada and that led the 1989 SIRC report to say that "we believe that the Government and senior CSIS management, after focussing strongly on the counter-terrorism program for the past few years, should give more attention to the policy and resource requirements of the C[ounter]I[ntelligence] program." In other words, SIRC appears to have concluded that the terrorist threat had once again been exceeded by the danger of "conventional" espionage.

In mid-1989 that judgment seemed precisely correct. But after the swirl of events in Eastern Europe and the accelerating process of change in the Soviet Union, SIRC's suggestion may no longer be as sound. The shape of the strange new world of espionage and terrorism in the 1990s is difficult to predict.

12.
FUTURE SPY WARS

Where do we go from here? Is espionage finished in Canada? Has the need for counter-espionage ended? The answer is yes . . . and no.

When a Pan American jumbo jet blew up in the sky over Lockerbie, Scotland, just before Christmas 1988, Iranian or Iranian-sponsored terrorists immediately became the leading suspects. Painstaking investigation over the next year by British, American, and European security services turned up some potential leads, but one of the few pieces of hard evidence made public was that the Boeing 747 and its passengers had been destroyed by Semtex explosive packed tightly inside a large radio. Semtex is a powerful brand of a new generation of explosives made in Czechoslovakia, and it has been a favoured weapon of choice for terrorists for years. The Czech security services, in co-operation with the KGB and other East European security services, have long provided assistance to anti-Western terrorist groups, assistance that included the provision of money, arms, and vast quantities of explosives and the training of up to 6,000 "guerrillas" from the Palestine Liberation Organization and other affiliated groups.

But Czechoslovakia today is almost completely transformed from the hardest of hard-line communist states it was until the end of 1989. The Interior minister, a non-communist, has already announced the disbanding of the country's secret police. It will take time to turn Czechoslovakia's foreign policy around completely, to be sure, but can anyone believe that this new and democratic Czech government in the future will provide Arab or Iranian terrorists with explosives intended to destroy civil aircraft or for anti-Western terrorism? (President

Vaclav Havel said in March 1990 that the previous Czech Communist government had provided 1,000 tonnes of Semtex to Libya, itself
one of the major suppliers of arms and assistance to terrorist groups.
"We have ceased exporting this explosive some time ago," Havel said.
"Two hundred grams are enough to blow up an aircraft, so world terrorism has supplies of Semtex to last 150 years." Closing the barn door
opened by others, Havel promised a unilateral halt in the production
of undetectable Semtex.) To ask the question is to answer it.

What happened in Czechoslovakia in a few dramatic weeks has
occurred in varying degrees throughout the Soviet bloc. In the German Democratic Republic, a country on the verge of economic
disintegration and of being swallowed whole by the Federal Republic of Germany, rampaging crowds in East Berlin sacked the
headquarters of the *Ministerium für Staats-Sicherheit*, the hated
Staasi or secret police, leading to official concern that documents
about East German espionage activities in Canada and the United
States may have been stolen. The new government promptly created
a commission to disband the Staasi, to wipe out its computer data,
and to decide what to do with its files on six million East German
citizens. The government even permitted the publication of a book,
Orders and Reports of the Ministry of State Security, detailing the
workings, targets, and findings of the secret police. Those decisions were signs of the new mood, but there was more. Gunter
Guillaume, a remarkably successful spy in the Chancery of West
Germany's Willy Brandt until his arrest in 1974, was subsequently swapped to East Berlin for some imprisoned *Bundesrepublik*
agents. Guillaume, recently retired as a senior spymaster in the
Hauptverwaltung Aufklaerung (HVA), East Germany's foreign intelligence agency, told West German reporters in February 1990
that there were at least 3,000 of his agents operating in West Germany, men and women who had now been left out in the cold. "I'm
sure they feel very nervous and insecure," Guillaume said almost
wistfully. Peace, in other words, was certain to destroy many but,
unless they are picked up by the KGB, which has been scrambling
to secure the HVA files and a line on its agents in West Germany,
the East Germans' main area of responsibility, the only punishment

such spies now seem likely to receive is unemployment and the loss of their GDR pensions.

In Romania, the revolution against President Ceaucescu left the secret-police organization in ruins and its control in non-communist hands. The Hungarians, desperately seeking economic links with the West and warned that thefts of sensitive technology will hamper plans to ease the curbs on the legal export of high-tech products, have made noises about wanting to co-operate with the United States to put an end to the leakage of sensitive technologies to hostile nations. And the Poles, now led by Solidarity and with the new deputy minister in the Interior Ministry having been appointed directly from the leading Catholic opposition weekly newspaper, can scarcely be expected to pursue the secret war with the same vigour that was followed under a Party government. For one thing, espionage costs money, and hard currency is desperately needed to get the battered Polish economy back on its feet. Moreover, many of the former satellites are negotiating the withdrawal of Red Army troops stationed on their territory; their foreign ministers are talking openly about the demise of the Warsaw Pact, a tendency that is certain to speed up as soon as a reunited Germany guarantees its neighbours' borders.

Even in the Soviet Union itself, its centralized and controlled economy slowly running down like a worn-out grandfather clock, the iron hand of the KGB (and virtually every other agency of the state) is beginning to be challenged. The leadership of the security agency has already moved to reduce the secrecy of its operations, and in 1989 General Vladimir Kryuchkov, the KGB director, appeared before the Congress of Deputies and a national television audience, obliged to defend his agency's actions and policies before the questions and complaints of sometimes hostile legislators. Kryuchkov went so far as to send some of his senior officials to answer questions on a television phone-in show. ("Tell me, Comrade Colonel," the questions might have gone, "when you tortured prisoners in the Lubyanka, did you prefer electric shock or drugs?") In May of the same year, the KGB actually committed itself to "the creation of a flawless mechanism of accountability to the people and supreme bodies of state authority and the active participation in the elaboration of legislative

acts concerning protection of the state's constitutional foundations."
While that pledge was offered in the old-style, mind-numbing Soviet
doublespeak, the message sounded very different. Nothing like it
could have been uttered in 1964 or 1974 or 1984, for example.

That the Soviet security apparatus's firm control on dissent has
broken down is now beyond doubt. New newspapers and magazines and new political parties with a reformist (or sometimes with
a reactionary and nationalist) bent spring up almost at will. And
in Lithuania, Latvia, Estonia, Azerbaijan, Armenia, and Moldavia,
not to say the Ukraine, there are independence movements with
massive public support behind them. Moreover, the KGB has begun tentatively to co-operate with Western intelligence agencies to
counter terrorism. Will co-operation in other areas follow?

In the light of these stunning events and the simultaneous onrush
of arms-control agreements between East and West, it is almost impossible to believe that the Soviet Union and its Warsaw Pact allies
any longer have the economic capabilities, military capacity, and political cohesion and will to mount a ground attack on NATO forces in
Western Europe or an ICBM attack against the United States and
Canada. Even the Department of National Defence, in 1987 the
source of a militantly anti-USSR and hardline white paper, has
responded to the new mood. At a conference in Edmonton in
March 1989, months before Eastern Europe threw off its chains,
General David Huddleston, the associate assistant deputy minister (Policy) at National Defence Headquarters, offered the new
line. "My understanding," the general said, "is that Canada does
not currently designate the Soviet Union as the enemy. . . . Mr.
Gorbachev has renounced those assertions of his predecessors, that
the object of his system is to dominate systems such as ours." And
the director of the CIA, William Webster, spoke similarly when he
told a congressional committee in March 1990 that "There is little
chance that Soviet hegemony could be restored in Eastern Europe."
A White House official put the new state of affairs even more clearly in a comment to the *New York Times* on March 18: "the Soviets
aren't going to plow through countries that are unfriendly to them
in order to get at Europe. Where we had enemies, we now have

a big fat buffer in Poland and Czechoslovakia." The military threat from the Warsaw Pact is now a tissue-paper tiger.

The same kind of reasoning also suggests that it is now or soon will be difficult to believe that the KGB and GRU, their hands full at home, will much longer have the capacity to mount extensive operations against the West. Or will they?

First, there is an understandable tendency in the West to worry about the permanence of the new state of affairs in the Soviet Union. What if Gorbachev is overthrown or assassinated by some disgruntled Russian nationalist colonel? What if hard-liners come to power, crush dissent in the Baltic and Muslim republics and elsewhere in the USSR, and use the Red Army, still enormously powerful and still present on the ground in large numbers in the Eastern European nations, to drive out the new democratic regimes and reinstall the Stalinists in power? Every day that passes, every triumph of Gorbachev over the conservatives in the Politburo, makes those eventualities seem less likely, but Western governments would be remiss not to consider them. It may well be that good sense and prudence demand that a dismantling of Western defence capacities proceed very cautiously.

There are other reasons for making haste slowly. According to American officials and to the retiring chair of SIRC, despite the new mood in East–West relations there has as yet been no slackening in East-bloc efforts to steal Western technology and military secrets. "We don't see very much indication that any of these countries are diminishing their overseas intelligence activities," a State Department official told the New York Times at the end of 1989, "with the possible exception of a somewhat greater emphasis on their own interests as opposed to the broader interests of the East bloc." SIRC's Ron Atkey added his mite: "The loosening of tensions with Eastern European countries and the approach to capitalism in those countries is going to increase the incentive of the sworn agents of those countries to steal Canada's assets."

(How long that technology-oriented espionage effort will have to go on as COCOM controls begin to be revised and as the desire of Western companies to sell their products to the East increases is, of course, likely to be measured in months. On the other hand,

Eastern Europe and the USSR's desperate shortage of hard currency may make stealing technology preferable to paying for it for some time yet. Industrial espionage, one Polish government official said, "is much cheaper than research and development." The Soviets have also lent support to those who feared a new Russian effort to steal Western technology. KGB chief Vladimir Kryuchkov in May 1990 told an extraordinary briefing session for ambassadors in Moscow that his agency would now use its resources to increase the competitiveness of Soviet companies. "Our companies," Kryuchkov said, lack experience in commercial operations, and "they are vulnerable. I believe the KGB must help them acquire appropriate experience," most especially through the efforts of its "powerful analytical branch specializing in economics.")

CIA Director Webster shares Ron Atkey's outlook: "Let us not assume that because we are getting friendly and seeing freedom come up from the streets, that freedom has been endorsed by some of those aggressive intelligence services." There is one final reason for caution. CSIS's Reid Morden told a Parliamentary committee on November 2, 1989 that East European intelligence agencies "will be taking a look at controlling restive minorities at home and populations that are anxious for real improvement, greater independence." There should be no doubt of that.

But if those comments all in all sound like nothing so much as hawkish short-term assessments — already in need of revision as events continue to unfold — from those with a keen concern to protect their budgets and roles against legislators searching for an elusive "peace dividend," others in the intelligence establishment have taken a longer view. The continuing KGB and satellite operations (and no one doubts that operations are continuing at present) may well be like the twitching of a chicken's limbs after its head has been lopped off — a reflex action that eventually ceases. "In general," one American official said of the co-operation between the KGB and the spy agencies of the former satellites, "what liaison there was is going to break down further; no question about it. If I were [KGB chief] Kryuchkov, I wouldn't be a happy man right now."

Whether CSIS and the CIA are any happier at the turn of events is unclear. It is a normal human emotion to prefer the familiar to the novel, and as Professor Reginald Whitaker, a clear-eyed commentator on Canadian intelligence questions, has noted, "new, and dangerous, threats may be given short shrift by agencies, like CSIS, reluctant to shift their long-term investments, give up assets painstakingly developed over many years, and start again at zero." But change must come. For example, the American and British spying and electronic eavesdropping operations working from West Berlin and West Germany against the Warsaw Pact nations now seem anachronistic, and the Bonn government, contemplating its new powers and soon-to-be-expanded territories, may well ask for their removal. In other words, old established patterns of activity and analysis in, and co-operation between, Western intelligence agencies are sure to be altered by the stunning events of 1989 and 1990.

In its baldest form, the question for Canadians can be put like this: If the Soviet threat to Canada and the West is rapidly diminishing and soon will no longer exist in a credible form, is there any need for CSIS, CSE, and the other intelligence agencies of the Canadian government to continue to exist?

To begin to answer that question, one might pose another: What has been the most serious threat to Canada's national security, broadly defined, in the post-1945 era? The answer, without doubt, was the October Crisis of 1970, the separatist bombings that preceded it, and the sub rosa manoeuvrings that followed it. Those difficulties were largely political and internal but, as we have seen, there was significant meddling by French government agents in Canadian affairs. The RCMP Security Service did not handle this crisis well at all, to be sure, but the need for a security service to deal with similar crises in the future can scarcely be denied.

Consider terrorism. The Air India disaster and the simultaneous bombing of a Canadian Pacific jet at Narita airport in Tokyo demonstrate irrefutably that Canada has been an important area of operation for Sikhs interested in seeing the creation of a separate state for their co-religionists in India. The attacks on Turkish diplomats in Ottawa by Armenians similarly indicate that terrorists here have mounted a threat of some significance in the past, one that weighs on Canada's international standing. Such threats may have diminished recently, though we are not convinced of that; even if they have, tomorrow there might be a new terrorist threat from the Basques, for example, or the Koreans, or the rightwing South Africans who use Canadian soil for attacks on diplomats or as a base to attack targets in, say, the United States. Without a security agency, the country would be incapable of responding properly — or at all. In other words, there are still potential threats to Canada and Canadian interests that have to be met.

This does not mean that substantial adaptation to the new realities is unnecessary. The security service's counter-subversion role, its effort to keep track of individuals or domestic groups that advocate radical political change, has long outlived its usefulness. The fact that this role is apparently being wound down at SIRC's insistence (and over CSIS's protests) attests both to the government's reading of the situation and to CSIS's continuing to be frozen in time, much like a fly in aspic. The demands of domestic politics, in other words, have forced reality on CSIS, in this area at least. (There is no unanimity on this position. Jewish and Sikh groups have argued for a continuation of the counter-subversion role, urging the House of Commons committee studying CSIS to give the security agency a new mandate. Instead of focusing on threats to undermine the government, representatives of the Canadian Jewish Congress argued in March 1990, CSIS legislation should cover any threat to a "constitutionally entrenched democratic and pluralist society." Such a wording would allow CSIS to monitor threats by neo-fascist or racist groups against vulnerable minorities such as Jews or Sikhs or Muslims.)

There are other areas where change might be considered. The Communications Security Establishment, its sensitive receptors pulling Soviet military transmissions and diplomatic communications to and from embassies in Ottawa from the air every hour of the day, may no longer be as necessary as it once was; at the very least, CSE's expensive activities (an estimated $150 million a year) could be scaled down. The Watcher Service, that bane of East-bloc (and French) diplomats, also may soon be a relic of the Cold War. Moreover, as readers will have noticed long before they reached this point in the book, the inexperience and incompetence of the RCMP Security Service led so frequently to the bungling of Canada's counter-espionage efforts that suggestions for radical cutbacks in the 1990s are, frankly, hard to counter effectively, even though CSIS has been much less accident-prone.

But if the political and economic logic of the day suggests cutbacks, CSIS and SIRC are looking to expansion. Ron Atkey has argued that Canada may need an offensive security service, one able to operate abroad in the Canadian national interest. In its 1989 report, SIRC suggested that "since we have no capacity to collect foreign intelligence by covert human means, we are dependent upon other countries for some types of information about foreign countries, which may pose a threat to Canadian independence in some circumstances. To the extent that covert sources of intelligence are an asset in gaining access to markets and technologies and in international bargaining, Canada will be at a disadvantage with its major trading partners." On the face of it, this seems simply ludicrous in the light of the developing world order. In a curious way, SIRC seemed to be suggesting that for Canada to have its own CIA or MI6 operating abroad, its very own agents in domestically made trenchcoats would be a badge of nationhood, a symbol of Canadian maturity. What is behind this? In the absence of hard evidence about the reasons behind these suggestions, it is difficult to know. The decline in the need for counter-espionage, the traditional Canadian security-service role, may well have provoked the desire for a new role for CSIS. Still, it seems unlikely that the government will pay heed to those who are preaching for a call: the potential for political and international embarrassment from despatching our Keystone Kops abroad appears to be much greater than any potential benefits.

Finally, as we have shown throughout this book, Canada has never been an independent actor in the intelligence arena. If we are to scale down our counter-intelligence or communications-interception efforts or end them altogether, it is almost certain that we will act only with the concurrence and support of our friends. The Americans and the British would look very harshly on a country that unilaterally dismantled its intelligence apparatus, and indeed, if the CSE packed up shop simply to satisfy the budget-cutters in the Department of Finance, the effect on our allies could be serious. History and simple practicality suggest very strongly that no major changes, no sudden shifts in focus, will come unless our friends move in similar directions.

Changes can be made and must be made to meet the new situation. But the world has never been a peaceable kingdom, nor is it ever likely to become one. The spy wars will continue, as they always have. The antagonists may be different, the motives more idealistic, the stakes temporarily smaller. But so long as conflict continues between nations, countries such as Canada will have to play the great game, even if only at the margins.

SELECTED BIBLIOGRAPHY

We have drawn extensively on royal commission reports, parliamentary debates and proceedings, annual reports of the Security Intelligence Review Committee (SIRC), press reports, private papers, many articles published in scholarly journals, and, where possible, documents released under the Access to Information Act. We are particularly grateful to the federal government and Canadian taxpayers, for example, for the large file of press clippings so meticulously copied and sent to us in response to our Access request in connection with the Hambleton affair. In addition, we have found the following selected list of sources particularly useful:

Adams, Ian. *S: Portrait of a Spy*. Toronto: Virgo Press, 1981.

Allen, Thomas B., and Norman Polmar. *Merchants of Treason*. New York: Dell, 1988.

Bamford, James. *The Puzzle Palace*. New York: Penguin, 1983.

Barron, John. *KGB Today: The Hidden Hand*. London: Hodder and Stoughton, 1983.

_____ . *The KGB: The Secret Work of Soviet Secret Agents*. London: Hodder and Stoughton, 1974.

Barros, James. *No Sense of Evil: Espionage, the Case of Herbert Norman*. Toronto: Deneau, 1986.

Beeby, Dean, and William Kaplan, eds. *Moscow Despatches: Inside Cold War Russia*. Toronto: Lorimer, 1987.

Blaise, Clark, and Bharati Mukherjee. *The Sorrow and the Terror:*

The Haunting Legacy of the Air India Tragedy. Markham, Ont.: Penguin, 1988.

Bothwell, Robert, and J.L. Granatstein. *The Gouzenko Transcripts*. Toronto: Deneau, 1982.

Bowen, Roger. *Innocence Is Not Enough: The Life and Death of Herbert Norman*. Vancouver and Toronto: Douglas and McIntyre, 1986.

Brook-Shepherd, Gordon. *The Storm Birds: Soviet Post-War Defectors*. London: Weidenfeld and Nicolson, 1988.

Canada. Senate. *Report of the Senate Special Committee on Terrorism and the Public Safety*. Ottawa: Supply and Services Canada, June 1987.

Dziak, John. *Chekisty: A History of the KGB*. New York: Ivy, 1988.

English, John. *Shadow of Heaven: The Life of Lester Pearson. Vol. I: 1897–1948*. Toronto: Lester & Orpen Dennys, 1989.

Ford, Robert A.D. *Our Man in Moscow*. Toronto: University of Toronto Press, 1989.

Franks, C.S.E., ed. *Dissent and the State*. Toronto: Oxford University Press, 1989.

Granatstein, J.L. *A Man of Influence: Norman Robertson and Canadian Statecraft, 1929–68*. Toronto: Deneau, 1981.

_____ . *Canada, 1957–67*. Toronto: McClelland and Stewart, 1986.

Hanks, Peter, and John D. McCamus. *National Security Surveillance and Accountability in a Democratic Society*. Cowansville, PQ: Yvon Blais, 1989.

Harvison, C.W. *The Horseman*. Toronto: McClelland and Stewart, 1967.

Heaps, Leo. *Hugh Hambleton: Spy*. Toronto: Methuen, 1983.

Hersh, Seymour. *"The Target Is Destroyed": What Really Happened to Flight 007 and What America Knew About It*. New York: Random House, 1986.

Hilliker, John. *Canada's Department of External Affairs, Vol. I: 1909–1946*. Montreal and Kingston: McGill-Queen's University Press, 1990.

Hyde, H. Montgomery. *The Quiet Canadian*. London: Constable, 1989.

Kashmeri, Zuhair, and Brian McAndrew. *Soft Target: How the Indian Intelligence Service Penetrated Canada.* Toronto: Lorimer, 1989.

Kellett, Anthony. *Contemporary International Terrorism and Its Impact on Canada.* OREA R100. Ottawa: Department of National Defence, 1988.

Littleton, James. *Target Nation: Canada and the Western Intelligence Network.* Toronto: Lester & Orpen Dennys, 1986.

Lyon, Peyton V. *The Loyalties of E. Herbert Norman.* Ottawa: Department of External Affairs, 1990.

Martin, David. *Wilderness of Mirrors.* New York: Ballantine, 1980.

Metcalfe, Robyn Shotwell. *The New Wizard War: How the Soviets Steal U.S. High Technology—And How We Give It Away.* Washington, D.C.: Tempus, 1988.

Pincher, Chapman. *Their Trade Is Treachery.* Toronto: Bantam, 1982.

Richelsen, Jeffrey T. *Sword and Shield: The Soviet Intelligence Security Apparatus.* Cambridge, MA: Ballinger, 1986.

Richelsen, Jeffrey T., and Desmond Ball. *The Ties That Bind.* Boston: Allen and Unwin, 1985.

Robinson, Gilbert de B. *Recollections, 1906–1987.* Toronto: University of Toronto Press, 1987.

Sawatsky, John. *For Services Rendered.* Toronto: Doubleday, 1982.

———. *Gouzenko: The Untold Story.* Toronto: Macmillan, 1984.

———. *Men in the Shadows: The RCMP Security Service.* Toronto: Doubleday, 1980.

Soviet Acquisition of Militarily Significant Western Technology: An Update. Washington, D.C.: Central Intelligence Agency, 1985.

Stafford, David. *Camp X: Canada's School for Secret Agents, 1941–1945.* Toronto: Lester & Orpen Dennys, 1986.

Suvorov, Victor. *Inside Soviet Military Intelligence.* New York: Macmillan, 1984.

Tuck, Jay. *The T Directorate: How the KGB Smuggles NATO's Secrets to Moscow.* New York: St. Martin's, 1986.

West, Nigel. *Molehunt: The Full Story of the Soviet Spy in MI5.* London: Weidenfeld and Nicolson, 1987.

Wright, Peter. *Spycatcher.* Toronto: Stoddart, 1987.

INDEX

Abel, Rudolf 157
Abramov, Mikhail 225-6
Abwehr 32ff, 39-40
Adams, Ian 112, 144ff
Air India #182 17, 241ff
Andropov, Yuri 173-4
Angleton, James Jesus 132, 134
Argentia 2, 5
Armenians 252ff
Atkey, Ron 18, 250-1, 263, 267
Atkinson, Don 137
atomic research 57, 63-4, 65-6
Attlee, Clement 59
Atwal, Harjit Singh 244-5

Barron, John 8, 173
Barros, James 91, 100
Bennett, Leslie James 106, 112, 130ff
Benning, Scott 60
Bentley, Elizabeth 64, 100, 123
Blais, Jean-Jacques 193-4
Blais, Pierre 18-19, 194
Bletchley Park: See Government
   Communications Headquarters
Blunt, Anthony 91
Bowen, Roger 102
Boyer, Raymond 60
Brandes, Harry 112
British Security Coordination 41-2,
   56, 76ff
BRUSA 44, 46
Bryce, Robert 91, 104-5, 194, 196
Burgess, Guy 68, 96

Cadieux, Marcel 202
Camp X 58, 80-1, 86
Canadian Forces 115ff, 208-10
Canadian Forces Supplementary
   Radio System 23
Canadian Security Intelligence
   Service (CSIS) and Ratkai case,
   5ff; end of cold war, 13ff; and

terrorism, 17ff; creation of, 190,
   192-3; and Chinese spying, 199-
   200; and terrorism, 244ff; and
   Triple M case, 248ff; future role,
   267
CANUSA 46
Cardin, Lucien 121, 124
Carr, Sam 48-9, 52, 62
Central Intelligence Agency (CIA) 13,
   17, 193, 209, 220
Chrétien, Jean 181
Clark, Joe 9-10, 199, 219, 235
Coates, Robert 115ff
COCOM 212, 218, 222, 233-6, 263
codes, Soviet 65
Commonwealth Security Conferences
   192
Communications Branch, National
   Research Council 132
Communications Security
   Establishment 20ff, 266
communists 48ff, 88ff; and public
   service 71ff, 88ff
"Corby" case: See Gouzenko case
Crean, G.G. 70-1
Cuban missile crisis 195-6

Dare, Michael 145-6
Deniau, Xavier 200
Department of External Affairs 30,
   58,. 89ff
Department of National Defence 30
Diefenbaker, John 101, 112, 118,
   198; and Spencer case, 121; and
   Munsinger case, 124ff; and Cuban
   crisis, 196
Direction Générale de la Securité
   Extérieure 210
Direction de la Surveillance du
   Territoire 181, 221
Discrimination Unit 44
Donovan, William 79

272